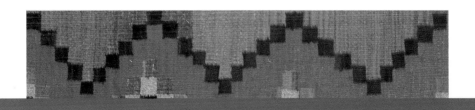

PACKING
▼IRON▼

GUNLEATHER
OF THE
FRONTIER WEST

In Memory of

LAWRENCE A. RATTENBURY
and
MARTI J. McCARTNEY

They made life all the richer.

Copyright ©1993.
Zon International
Publishing Company.

All rights reserved.
No part of this book may be
reproduced or transmitted in
any form or by any means,
electronic or mechanical,
including photocopying,
recording, or by any information storage and retrieval system, without permission in
writing from the publisher.

Fourth Edition
Printed in China

Published by
ZON INTERNATIONAL
PUBLISHING COMPANY
P.O. Box 6459
Santa Fe, NM 87502

Phone   505/995-0102
Fax   505/995-0103

Library of Congress Catalogue-
in Publication Data

Rattenbury, Richard C.
    Packing Iron: Gunleather
of the Frontier West/ by
Richard C. Rattenbury; with
a foreword by Norm
Flayderman.
        p.   cm.

Includes bibliographical
references and index.

    1. Holsters — West (U.S.) —
History. I. Title.

TS535.2.H64R38   1993
685—dc20   93-17019
                              CIP

ISBN 0-939549-08-5

PACKING
IRON

GUNLEATHER OF THE FRONTIER WEST

By Richard C. Rattenbury

FOREWORD BY NORM FLAYDERMAN

ZON INTERNATIONAL PUBLISHING COMPANY

WILLIAM MANNS PUBLISHER

ACKNOWLEDGMENTS

The completion of this work would have been impossible without the generous assistance of many individuals and institutions around the country. To all of these, the author is indebted.

For access to historical collections: Joe and Murlene Grandee, Bill Mackin, Lacey and Virginia Gaddis, Phil Spangenberger, Rick Bachman, John E. Fox, Joe Gish, Brian Lebel, Jim Holley, Ron Soodalter, S. P. Stevens, Norm Flayderman, Scott Meadows, A. P. Hays, Bill Cleaver, George T. Jackson, Robert W. Smith, Dr. Georg Priestel, Donald Yena, Douglas Deihl, Herb Lyman, William R. Williamson, Donald Bates, Danny Neill, Hayes Otoupalik, Jim Naramore, George Pitman, Al Luevand, Bill Bentham, Paul Hoffman, Don Spaulding, Dominick Cervone, Arizona West Galleries, and the staffs of the Arizona Historical Society, the Gene Autry Western Heritage Museum, the Buffalo Bill Historical Center, the Colorado State Historical Society, the Museum of the Horse, the Museum of New Mexico, and the Smithsonian Institution. And for the provision of contemporary western gunleather: Bob McNellis of El Paso Saddlery, Phil Spangenberger of Red River Frontier Outfitters, Rick Bachman of Old West Reproductions, J. C. Stewart of Stewart Saddlery, and Bill Cleaver of Wild Bill's Originals.

For the provision of historical images: Rick Bachman, Jean King, Lawrence Jones, Guy Logsdon, John McWilliams, Scott Meadows, Herb Peck, Jr., William Schultz, Lee Silva and the Greg Silva Memorial Old West Archives, Charles Worman, and the staffs of the Arizona Historical Society Library, the Buffalo Bill Historical Center, the Amon Carter Museum, the Western History Department of the Denver Public Library, the J. Paul Getty Museum, the Houston Museum of Fine Arts, the Kansas State Historical Society, the Library of Congress, the Montana Historical Society, the State Historical Society of North Dakota, the Oklahoma Historical Society, the Western History Collections at the University of Oklahoma, the Panhandle-Plains Historical Museum, the Southwest Museum, the Western Reserve Historical Society, the Wyoming State Archives and Museum, the American Heritage Center at the University of Wyoming, and Brigham Young University Photo Archives.

For the provision of trade literature and other research material: John Bianchi, Bill Cleaver, Clay Dahlberg, Jim Dunham, Bill Mackin, J. S. Palen, George Pitman, Phil Spangenberger, and the staffs of the Western History Department of the Denver Public Library, the Nita Stewart Haley Memorial Library, the Montana Historical Society, the Panhandle-Plains Historical Museum, the Princeton Collection of Western Americana at Princeton University, the Pueblo Public Library, the Barker Texas History Center at the University of Texas, and the American Heritage Center at the University of Wyoming.

At the National Cowboy Hall of Fame and Western Heritage Center, special thanks to Executive Director B. Byron Price for encouraging the project and allowing the time to complete it; to Curator of Art Ed Muno and Archivist Chuck Rand for their excellent photographic rendering of the majority of the artifacts; and to Donna Dolf, Judith Dearing, M. J. Van Deventer and Edwina Johnston for their patient production and editing of the manuscript.

For their constructive critiques of the manuscript, particular appreciation is extended to Rick Bachman, Bill Cleaver, Jim Dunham, Norm Flayderman, J. Edward Green, Bill Mackin, Scott Meadows, B. Byron Price, and Phil Spangenberger.

Finally, it remains to thank my wife, Suzette, for her abiding support and sense of proportion during the course of this project.

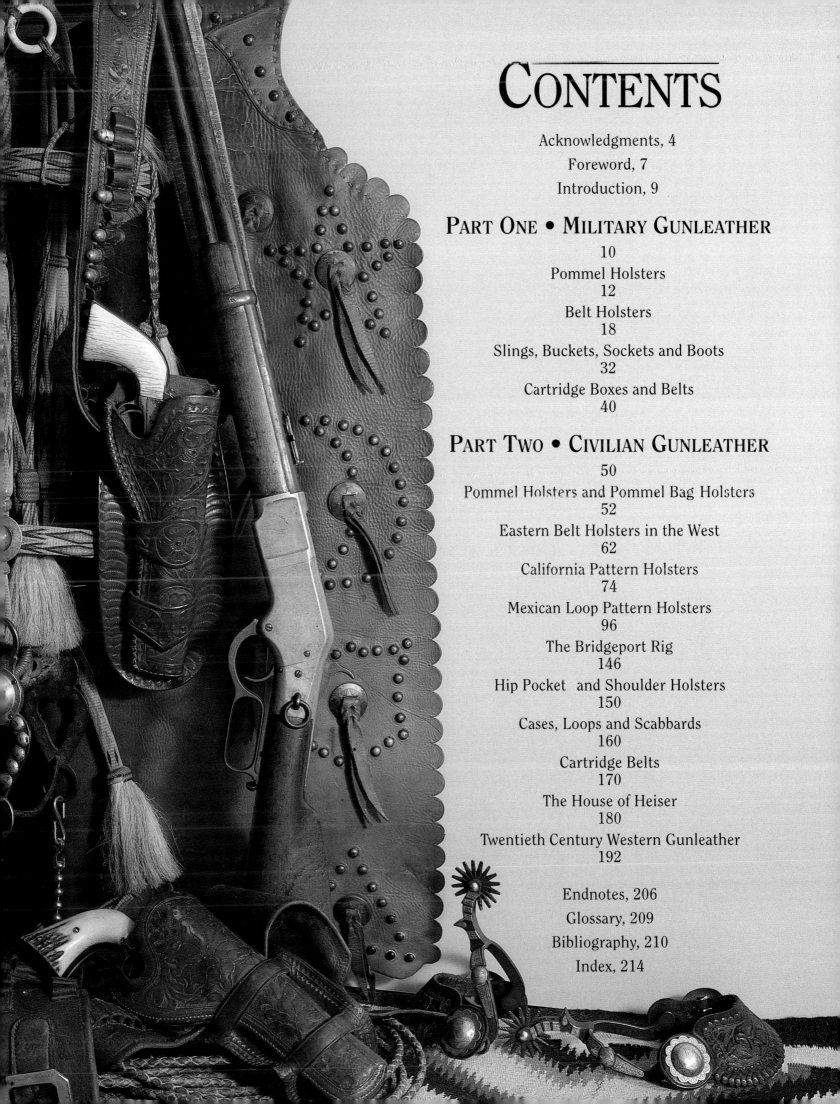

CONTENTS

Acknowledgments, 4

Foreword, 7

Introduction, 9

PART ONE • MILITARY GUNLEATHER
10

Pommel Holsters
12

Belt Holsters
18

Slings, Buckets, Sockets and Boots
32

Cartridge Boxes and Belts
40

PART TWO • CIVILIAN GUNLEATHER
50

Pommel Holsters and Pommel Bag Holsters
52

Eastern Belt Holsters in the West
62

California Pattern Holsters
74

Mexican Loop Pattern Holsters
96

The Bridgeport Rig
146

Hip Pocket and Shoulder Holsters
150

Cases, Loops and Scabbards
160

Cartridge Belts
170

The House of Heiser
180

Twentieth Century Western Gunleather
192

Endnotes, 206

Glossary, 209

Bibliography, 210

Index, 214

FOREWORD

It is ironic that "gunleather," a term literally part and parcel of American western lore, has received so little authoritative research and publication over the years. Although always recognized as collectable artifacts (and in recent years having greatly appreciated in interest, desirability and value), the history and development of western gunleather, especially in the civilian sector, has remained among the least examined fields of nineteenth century material culture. *Packing Iron: Gunleather of the Frontier West* will do much to fill this void.

The first work to competently and acccurately describe the holsters, gunbelts, saddle scabbards and various other equipments that made the carrying and wearing of firearms practical, *Packing Iron* adds substantially to the ever-increasing lore of the West and the study of its specialized artifacts. The author has shown these often unpretentious, workaday items to be justly deserving of a comprehensive, in-depth study.

The description and comparison of military and civilian gunleather are certain to prove of considerable fascination, as will the interpretation of regional artisans and the gear of later Hollywood heroes and western reenactment groups. The liberal use of contemporary accounts, illustrations and photographs is highly informative, adding immeasureably to an understanding of the many

evolutionary and stylistic changes that took place from the mid-nineteenth century to the present day. By clarifying and defining the nomenclature of various forms of leather gear, the author provides the student and collector with a useful guide for recognition of the numerous patterns and styles involved.

Richard Rattenbury's credentials for undertaking this project are formidable. As Curator of History at the National Cowboy Hall of Fame in Oklahoma City, and former curator of the famed Winchester Gun Collection at the Buffalo Bill Historical Center in Cody, Wyoming, he has had the opportunity to closely study and personally handle a great number of these artifacts.

The wealth of material and accompanying illustrations unfolded here shed much new light on these important western accoutrements. It is certain to cause them to be regarded with greater respect and significance. And the collector of these intriguing artifacts is certain to better appreciate their important role as major adjuncts of the weapons they accompanied and protected.

Norm Flayderman
Antiquarian, Author, Consultant
Fort Lauderdale, Florida

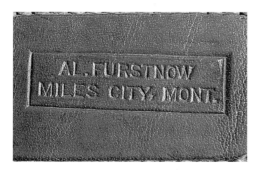

INTRODUCTION

The firearms used in the settlement of the American West, most notably the Colt revolver and the Winchester rifle, have become virtual icons of our frontier mythology. Far less familiar to most contemporary Americans, however, is the variety of military and civilian gunleather that housed this romantic array of weaponry. Yet, these equally ubiquitous pistol holsters, saddle scabbards, cartridge belts and associated equipage were — of necessity — a concomitant facet of the armed westerner's material culture in an unsettled, often hostile environment.

Designed for the carriage and protection of firearms and ammunition, western gunleather evolved during the second half of the nineteenth century in response to technological changes in firearms design and leatherworking processes, to regional adaptations fostered by indigenous saddleries, and to the stylistic interpretations of both makers and users. While considerable diversity and ingenuity were introduced in both military and commercial varieties, only the most utilitarian elements enjoyed appreciable production or longevity. At bottom, pure functionalism remained the constant criteria that dictated the success or failure of basic forms and patterns.

Only in the past dozen years have these historically rich accoutrements attained a sufficient level of interest among students and collectors to merit publication. The greatest attention thus far has focused on military gunleather, for which a large body of primary documentation exists in federal archives. This research potential has resulted in thoroughgoing treatments like Randy Steffen's *The Horse Soldier, 1776-1943* (1979); Stephen Dorsey's *American Military Belts and Related Equipments* (1984); and Scott Meadows' *U. S. Military Holsters and Pistol Cartridge Boxes* (1987).

Civilian gunleather, on the other hand, has thus far been treated in only a scattering of articles and as a part of larger conpendium/price guides such as Joe Goodson's *Old West Antiques & Collectables* (1979); Bill Mackin's *Cowboy and Gunfighter Collectibles* (1989); and Robert Ball and Ed Vebell's *Cowboy Collectibles and Western Memorabilia* (1991). This may be accounted for in the dearth of relevant, primary research materials available on civilian gunleather for the 50 years between 1840 and 1890.

Period photographs constitute the only readily available body of contemporaneous evidence documenting civilian gunleather in the West. Dating from the 1850s onward, such images can be of aid in identifying and delimiting the temporal and geographical range of various gunleather elements. Not until the 1880s does one encounter the first trade literature published by western saddlers (i.e. indigenous gunleather manufacturers), and this resource remains quite sparse prior to 1910. While these illustrated catalogs thus post-date the historic frontier era and represent a period of increasing industrialization and pattern uniformity, they nevertheless are useful in identifying individual product lines and suggesting the characteristics and pricing of a given artisan's or shop's earlier production.

Taking these research considerations into account, much of this book's interpretation — particularly of civilian gunleather   will rely heavily on the study and comparison of the objects themselves. It is hoped that this artifact-centered approach (focusing on the various elements and their individual design, materials, means of construction, style and ornament) will enlarge upon available published sources, and create a framework of developmental typologies and chronologies within the larger context of western material culture. While not confined to a precise time-frame, the treatment of both military and civilian elements will concentrate on the period from the mid-1830s, when Anglo-Americans first entered the trans-Mississippi frontier in appreciable numbers, to the mid-1890s, when the pacification and settlement of the West was complete.

In drawing together and discussing military and civilian gunleather in a single volume, this object study seeks to provide a useful outline of design evolution and stylistic variation. It does not intend to be all-inclusive in scope or definitive in interpretation. Rather it attempts to create a broad overview for the ongoing study of western gunleather as a body of culturally significant artifacts. For these objects not only embody the history and romance of the frontier; their study also reveals evidence about craft technology and commerce in the leatherworking trade, points up the broad cultural range of form and embellishment in utilitarian artifacts, and suggests something of the human values and activities at work among their original users.

Richard C. Rattenbury
Oklahoma City, Oklahoma

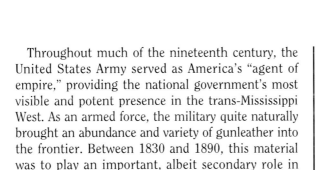

PART ONE

MILITARY GUNLEATHER

Throughout much of the nineteenth century, the United States Army served as America's "agent of empire," providing the national government's most visible and potent presence in the trans-Mississippi West. As an armed force, the military quite naturally brought an abundance and variety of gunleather into the frontier. Between 1830 and 1890, this material was to play an important, albeit secondary role in western pacification and settlement.[1]

Confronted on the Great Plains with vast distances and very mobile adversaries, the army required effective mounted forces to fulfill its mission. The initial contingents, organized as the First and Second Regiments of U. S. Dragoons, took the field in 1833 and 1836, respectively. They were followed in 1846 by the Regiment of U. S. Mounted Riflemen, and in 1855 by the First and Second Regiments of U. S. Cavalry.[2] These mounted troops, armed with an evolving array of horse pistols, revolvers, carbines, musketoons and short rifles, introduced the first relatively uniform patterns of gunleather into the West.

Prior to the Civil War, the military sought to standardize its issue gunleather, then classified as "Horse Equipments." But true pattern uniformity proved elusive for a number of reasons. An obvious hindrance to conformity within a given item, e.g. pommel holsters, stemmed from the military's reliance on more than a half-dozen civilian contractors for fabrication.[3] Continual experimentation with improved weapons and associated gunleather, coupled with periodically revised regulations, also thwarted service-wide uniformity. Writing in 1858, Colonel of

Ordnance H. K. Craig observed:

> ...there is no regularly prescribed pattern for cavalry or dragoon horse equipments, the various patterns in use,...being all experimental. It is very desirable that both the fire-arms and horse equipments for cavalry and dragoon should be regularly prescribed.[4]

Perhaps least conducive to standardization was the military's repeated fluctuation in bureau authority and oversight among the Commissary General of Purchases, the Quartermaster Department and the Ordnance Department during the ante-bellum period.[5]

The exigencies of the Civil War (1861-1865) further complicated efforts toward uniformity, as a plethora of non-regulation gunleather flooded the ranks. Thereafter, the frontier army was, for more than a decade, indifferently equipped through its arsenals with a diversity of material resulting from government parsimony and the ongoing issuance of modified surplus goods.[6] The troops themselves also contributed to a continuing lack of pattern standardization through the frequent adoption of non-regulation, civilian gunleather. Charles King, a veteran officer and early chronicler of the Indian-fighting army, recalled Arizona troopers in 1874 wearing "...revolvers in all manner of cases hung at the hip, the regulation holster, in most instances, being conspicuous by its absence."[7] All of these factors complicate a precise treatment of military gunleather. For the most part, this survey will confine itself to an overview of representative examples.

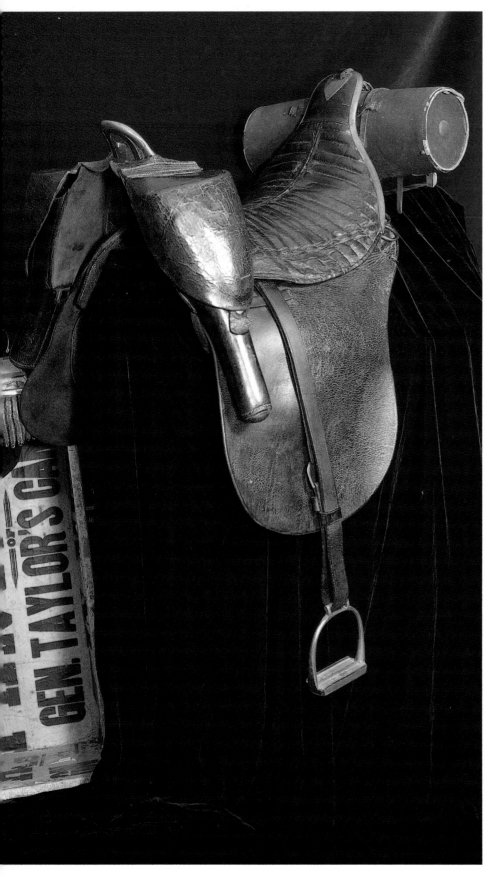

Ringgold pattern dragoon saddle, 1844-1847 with Model 1841 pommel holsters. (Courtesy Don Spaulding Collection. William Manns photo)

POMMEL HOLSTERS

Pommel, or saddle, holsters were the most notable element of military gunleather during the ante-bellum years. Due to the unwieldy size and weight of issue horse pistols and later dragoon revolvers, these "side arms" were carried not on the person, but in substantial holsters mounted at the front of the saddle. Patterned on earlier European and American forms, pommel holsters for both officers and enlisted dragoons had deep, molded bodies that virtually swallowed their intended weapons. Ample covers, or hoods, that latched over the holsters with a strap-and-finial closure, provided additional security and protection against loss and inclement weather.

Ordnance Department literature described early pommel holsters only cursorily. *A System of Tactics*, published in 1834, cited in its equipments inventory:

> **Holsters.** (The upper part called the body, the lower portion [called] the pipe. The right holster [bag] ought to contain a horse shoe, nails, currycomb, and brush, &c., and ought to be six inches wide....)[8]

The 1834 and 1839 *Regulations for the Government of the Ordnance Department* simply listed: "Holsters, pair, with hair, seal skin or patent leather covers, carrying 10 rounds of ammunition."[9] Thus pommel holsters for enlisted dragoons actually consisted of a single holster body on the near (left) side and a utility bag, or pouch, on the off (right) side. Those for commissioned officers, as indicated in later ordnance publications, incorporated a pair of holster bodies for two pistols.

Throughout early production, holster bodies for single-shot, flintlock and percussion pistols were constructed of heavy bridle, or "sole," leather. Cut to pattern, the leather was wet-molded over a symmetrical wooden form and sewn up the back seam. Leather toe plugs, or "bottoms," closed the extremities of the pipes and helped maintain their form. In many instances, the pipe was finished with a brass end cap. Most examples also incorporated a flapped pocket on the upper face of the holster body containing five or six tin tubes for paper-wrapped cartridges. Whether for officers or enlisted men, the two principal elements were joined by a relatively wide leather strap or panel, often having an oval-shaped hole in its center that slipped over the peak of the saddle pommel. Covers of shaped leather, finished with bearskin or "jacked and varnished" to repel moisture, shrouded the tops of the holsters.

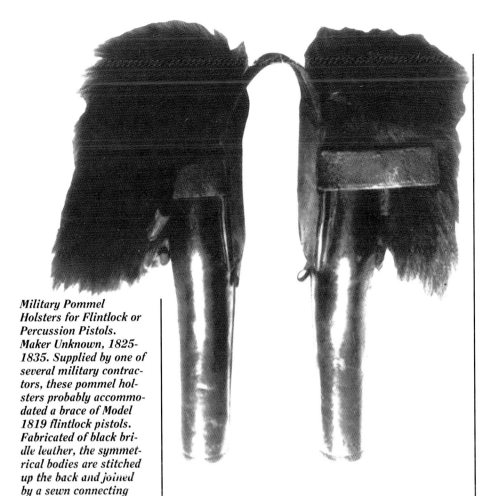

Military Pommel Holsters for Flintlock or Percussion Pistols. Maker Unknown, 1825-1835. Supplied by one of several military contractors, these pommel holsters probably accommodated a brace of Model 1819 flintlock pistols. Fabricated of black bridle leather, the symmetrical bodies are stitched up the back and joined by a sewn connecting leather having a center hole for positioning on the saddle pommel. Bearskin-covered flaps shroud both the tops and the sewn-on cartridge compartments mounted on the upper face of each holster body, while sewn-in leather toe plugs close the pipes. The holsters secured to the saddle by means of two leather surcingle loops sewn at the edge of the upper holster bodies. (Courtesy Scott Meadows Collection)

Military Pommel Holsters for Single-Shot Pistols. Maker Unknown, 1845-1855. Following the regulation pattern of 1841, this set accommodates the U.S. Model 1842 percussion contract pistol by Ira N. Johnson and contains the internal, covered pouch with five tin tubes for carrying .54 caliber paper cartridges. Constructed of black bridle-weight leather, the holsters have brass end-caps and button-finial closures. The wreath and star motif on the end-caps suggests issue to the U.S. Dragoons. (Courtesy Private Collection)

The first detailed description of such gunleather appeared in the 1841 *Ordnance Manual For The Use Of The Officers of the United States Army*, which formalized changes in dragoon equipments made in 1839:

HORSE EQUIPMENTS FOR DRAGOONS — PATTERN OF 1841

HOLSTER: black leather, jacked and varnished; the mouth is stiffened with iron wire covered with leather — a band round the pipe, passing through a loop in a strap attached to the connecting strap.

HOLSTER BAG, for combs, brushes, &c.; mouth strap passing through 2 loops sewed on the bag — 1 buckle and 1 loop for do. — one loop for the bag strap.

CONNECTING STRAP, to which the holster and bag are fastened by thongs; it is doubled and stitched, with an opening in the centre through which the head of the pommel passes. The strap is fastened to the pommel with 2 thongs; the holster being on the near side and the bag on the off side.

HOLSTERS. Pipe, sole leather, black; diameter of cylindrical part 2 in., length of do. 7.5 in.; width of the mouth, 4.7 in.; depth 2.5 in.; whole length, 14.5 in. — pocket, light upper leather, 3.2 in. long, 2.5 in. deep, lined with tin — 5 cylindrical divisions, diameter 0.6 in., each for one cartridge — 1 centre piece to connect the two holsters, light bridle leather, black; mean length about 8 in., width 5.25 in. — 2 straps 14 in. long, 0.6 wide, with 2 buckles, to attach the holsters to the saddle — 2 surcingle loops, light bridle leather, black, 1.5 in. wide, 3.5 in. long, doubled.

HOLSTER COVERS. Black leather; 23 in. long, 9.5 in. wide over the cartridge pocket, 7.5 in. in the middle — straps, 6 in. long, 1 in. wide, to button on the holster.[10]

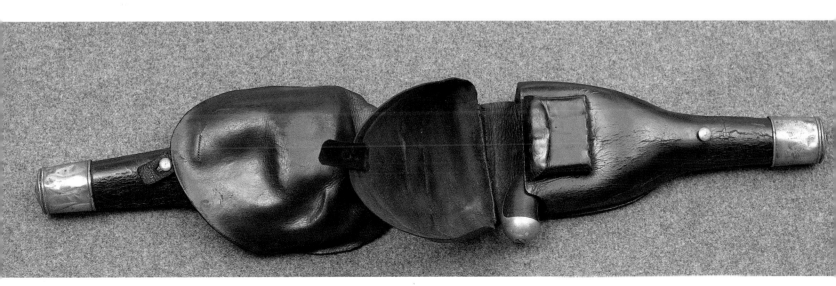

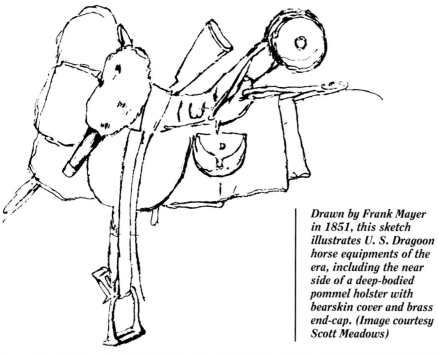

Drawn by Frank Mayer in 1851, this sketch illustrates U. S. Dragoon horse equipments of the era, including the near side of a deep-bodied pommel holster with bearskin cover and brass end-cap. (Image courtesy Scott Meadows)

It can be assumed that pommel holsters manufactured during the 1830s did not differ markedly in form and construction from these specifications, but the use of seal or bearskin in finishing the cover flaps may have been more prevalent.

While not called for in the 1841 Manual, bearskin evidently continued in use to some extent throughout the 1840s. With the 1847 adoption of Grimsley's patented saddle and associated horse equipments, bearskin was again specified for holster covers. By 1850, however, this requirement was discontinued due to an apparent scarcity of bears.[11] Thereafter, covers of molded leather became standard issue.

General Order No. 31 of June 1851 prescribed the dress and equipment for all ranks and branches of the military. The following excerpts from the section entitled "Horse Furniture" give a general description of issue pommel holsters of Grimsley pattern:

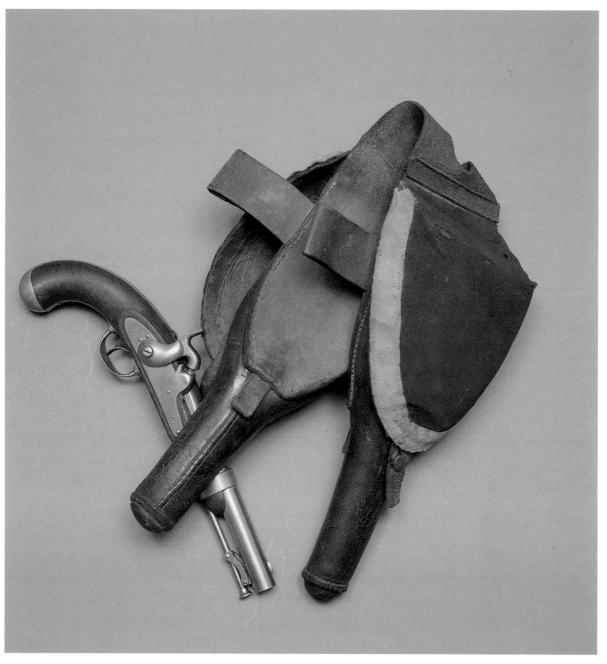

Military Pommel Holsters for Single-Shot Percussion Pistols. Maker Unknown, 1850-1855. Designed in compliance with **The Ordnance Manual For The Use Of The Officers of the United States Army** *of 1850, this dragoon officer's outfit incorporates the specified, 22-inch connecting leather that also forms the back panels of the upper holster bodies. Fabricated of heavy black bridle leather, the symmetrical holsters each have flapped cartridge pockets sewn on the upper face, sewn-in surcingle loops for saddle mounting, and round-bottomed toe plugs. The separate, shaped cover flaps are stitched on and secured with strap-and-finial closures; both are covered with blue wool material and trimmed with a yellow worsted border. With the outfit is a .54 caliber percussion, U. S. Model 1842 contract pistol made by Ira N. Johnson. (Courtesy Private Collection)*

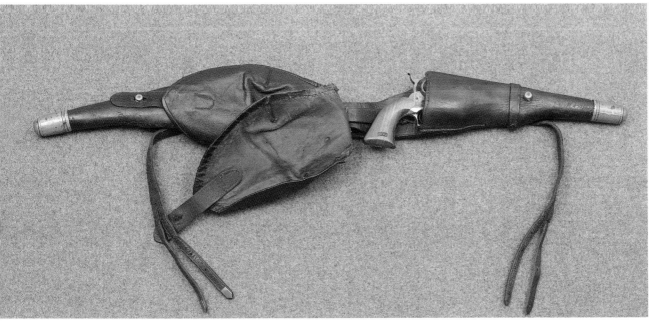

Military Pommel Holsters for Colt Walker and Dragoon Model Revolvers. Possibly Grimsley & Co., St. Louis, Missouri, 1850-1860. One of several contract patterns provided to the U.S. Dragoons, these holsters feature bodies contoured to the revolvers they carried. Constructed of black bridle-weight leather, the outfit has one-piece, lined covers, brass end-caps, and button-finial closures. The accompanying revolver is a .44 caliber percussion, Colt Walker reproduction. (Courtesy Private Collection)

Military Pommel Holster and Utility Pouch for Colt Navy Revolver and Horse Implements. Maker Unknown, 1855-1860. Prescribed under General Order No. 31 of 1851, this combination outfit was issued to enlisted men of dragoons or cavalry for nearly a decade. Constructed throughout of heavy black sole leather, the two principal elements are joined by an extended, double-layered connecting strap that also forms the upper back panel of the holster body. The asymmetrical holster is wire-reinforced at the throat and finished with a plain leather toe plug. The front and back panels of the utility pouch are sewn around the periphery to an expandable gusset "for holding grooming articles." The shaped cover flaps (now missing) laced to the center of the connecting leather and secured with sewn straps to the brass finials. Designed for mounting on a Grimsley pattern saddle, this specimen retains a .36 caliber percussion, Colt Model 1851 Navy revolver.

FOR COMMISSIONED OFFICERS OF DRAGOONS

174. HOLSTERS — black leather, the pipes to have plain brass tips, extending up two inches and a half, to be attached to the saddle and breast strap as in the model.

175. HOLSTER COVERS — black leather, extending two inches below the shoulder of the holster pipe, terminated by a leather strap, one inch wide, strongly sewed to the cover, the strap to button to a brass knob firmly rivetted to the holster.

FOR ENLISTED MEN OF DRAGOONS

185. HOLSTERS — black leather, left side for pistol, right side made in the form of a pouch, for holding grooming articles; attached to the saddle and breast strap as in the model.

186. HOLSTER COVERS — black leather, extending two inches below the shoulder of holster pipe on the left side, and to a corresponding distance on the right side....[12]

A second edition of *The Ordnance Manual For The Use Of The Officers of the United States Army* (1850) again provided detailed specifications for the form and construction of pommel holsters. These remained essentially consistent except that the connecting strap, which was lengthened from eight inches to 22 inches, now also constituted the back panel of the upper holster bodies.[13] This alteration in design actually may have been introduced in the late 1840s with pommel holsters fabricated for the Colt Walker and Dragoon Model revolvers then coming into service. These holsters usually incorporated the extended connecting leather/back panel design.[14]

Pommel holsters for percussion revolvers were manufactured by government contractors throughout the 1850s. The earliest specimens, like their predecessors, were symmetrical in pattern. The vast majority, however, featured an asymmetrical body which was contour-fit to the silhouette of the intended revolver. Such pommel holsters appeared in a variety of regulation and experimental patterns. Pairs for a brace of matched pistols certainly were most common, but unusual combination sets for revolver and single-shot pistol, or a single pistol or revolver with detachable shoulder stock also were fabricated in limited quantities.[15]

Although they served in the West for a quarter century, military pommel holsters were not without their shortcomings. Accessibility to the weapon frequently was difficult, particularly when at a trot or gallop, or when a cloak or blanket was strapped over the rig. But the greatest problem simply involved keeping the holsters fixed to the saddle. Writing in 1852 of service in the Mexican War, a Major Ruff recalled: "So apparent was [this] insecurity that in Mexico the common method adopted by the men was to drive a nail through the [backs of the] holsters into the pommel of the saddle."[16]

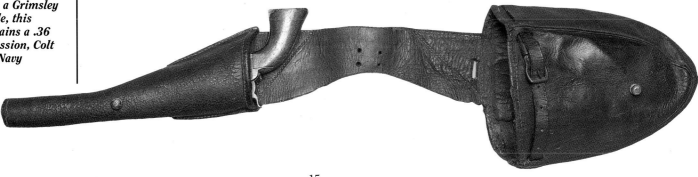

During most of the 1830s and 1840s, pommel holsters typically fastened to the saddle with a strap passing around the pipe, or via two loops that secured to the surcingle of the saddle. The connecting leather was not secured to the peak of the saddle pommel unless a cloak or blanket was strapped over the holsters. Thus, when considerable motion or combat ensued, the holster bodies and connecting leather tended to work upward, riding over the pommel and sometimes actually falling from the saddle. The Grimsley pattern holsters, which attached to and evidently secured the relatively fragile breast straps, presented an even greater incidence of failure and loss.[17]

These problems largely were overcome with the Campbell patent saddle and its associated pommel holsters, which were issued for trial to two squadrons of the First and Second Cavalry Regiments in 1855-1856.[18] The holsters incorporated separate, molded covers which pivoted forward on a brass plate and axle, allowing easy access to the pistols. And, unlike earlier designs, the connecting leather was firmly strapped to the pommel, while the holster bodies were strapped directly to the side-bars of the saddle tree.[19] Unfortunately, this practical pattern was never adopted in full or adapted for use with other issue saddles.

Pommel holsters continued in army service — at least among officers — through the Civil War. But their ultimate demise was recognized as early as 1853 in an inspection report submitted by Lieutenant Colonel W. G. Freeman at San Antonio:

Combination Military Pommel Holsters for Model 1855 Springfield Pistol and Colt Third Model Dragoon Revolver. Maker Unknown, 1855-1856. Manufactured in limited quantities, this outfit was in use among selected companies of U.S. Dragoons during the mid-to late 1850s. Fabricated of black bridle leather, the molded holster bodies are form-fit to their respective weapons (Springfield on the left, Colt on the right), joined by a sewn and riveted connecting leather, and finished with sewn-in leather toe plugs. The detachable cover flaps (now missing) secured to brass closing finials centered on the pouch faces. (Courtesy Norm Flayderman Collection)

Military Pommel Holster and Utility Pouch for Single-Shot Pistol and Horse Implements. Campbell Patent, 1855-1856. Designed expressly for use with the Campbell patent saddle under General Order No. 13 of 1855, this combination rig was issued for trial to one squadron each of the First and Second Cavalry. Fabricated of heavy black bridle leather, the unique feature of this pattern was the swivel-mounted cover that rotated forward to expose the throat of the symmetrical holster body. When closed, the lip of the cover secured beneath an abbreviated flap or "roof-piece" sewn to the connecting leather. The long-bodied holster accommodated the .58 caliber percussion, US. Model 1855 single-shot pistol, while the utility pouch could be used to carry the accompanying shoulder stock. (Courtesy Scott Meadows Collection)

Cases for Colt's Revolver Pistols. It is not safe to carry this [Dragoon Model] pistol in the [pommel] holster, and the practice is universal of wearing it in a leather case attached to the sword, or waist belt. It gives the soldier a feeling of security to carry this arm about his person so that he cannot be separated from it. The leather cases [belt holsters] now used are made, and often indifferently, at the posts. They should be furnished with the pistols.[20]

The military's 1855 adoption of the lighter and more manageable Colt 1851 Navy Model revolver marked the pommel holster's gradual phasing from service among mounted troops. While saddle holsters were produced in limited quantities for this revolver and the later 1860 Army Model, these weapons clearly were best suited to issue with belt-mounted holsters.

Photographed in 1864, this Union officer demonstrates the continuing use of saddle-mounted pommel holsters among commissioned ranks. The holsters appear to be of asymmetrical pattern for Colt Model 1860 Army revolvers and are fitted with brass end caps. The shaped cover flaps secure with strap-and-finial closures. (Image courtesy the Library of Congress and Scott Meadows)

Military Pommel Holsters for Colt Army and Navy Revolvers. Maker Unknown, 1860-1865. A non-regulation pattern for private purchase during the Civil War, this well-made set features contoured holster bodies of heavy saddle-skirting leather with buckled straps and typical brass hardware. The covers have been tarred for increased water resistance; their red border trim suggests use by an artillery officer. The accompanying revolver is a .44 caliber percussion, Colt Model 1860 Army of the period. (Courtesy Private Collection)

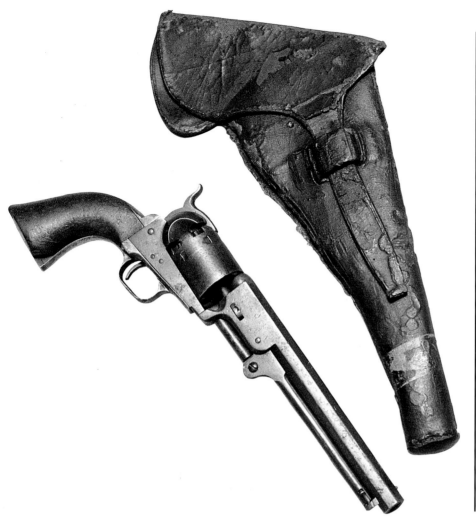

BELT HOLSTERS

Advances in arms technology during the mid-nineteenth century resulted in the design of more compact and less cumbersome revolvers, notably the Colt 1851 Navy Model. The military's adoption of this pistol for mounted troops in 1855 dictated a change in associated gunleather. Writing in 1856, George B. McClellan, then a captain with the First U. S. Cavalry and recently an observer of the Crimean War, remarked: "For my own regiment, armed with revolvers, there need be no [pommel] holster, for the men should follow the Russian system and always carry the pistol on the waist belt."[21] That same year, the army contracted with civilian manufacturers for nearly 3,400 belt-mounted "pistol cases," most patterned for the Colt Navy revolver.[22]

While exceptions were made in experimental forms, regulation military belt holsters invariably were of "left-hand" configuration; that is, the revolver rode with its butt, or grips, projecting rearward when the holster was worn on the left side. The army's standard method of carry, however, required that the holster be worn on the trooper's right side, butt forward. This was necessitated by the use of the saber. As the majority of soldiers were right-handed, the saber and scab-

Military Belt Holster for Colt Model 1851 Navy Revolver. North American Gutta Percha Co., New York, New York, 1855-1856. An experimental design issued to a squadron of the Second Cavalry Regiment in Texas, this rare holster was manufactured of heavy cloth with an overlayer of "vulcanized gutta percha" (a chemically treated plastic resin.) This right-hand pattern features a full-flap closed top with strap-and-tab closure, sewn belt loop, and sewn toe plug. It is accompanied by a .36 caliber percussion, Colt Model 1851 Navy revolver, third variation. (Courtesy Private Collection)

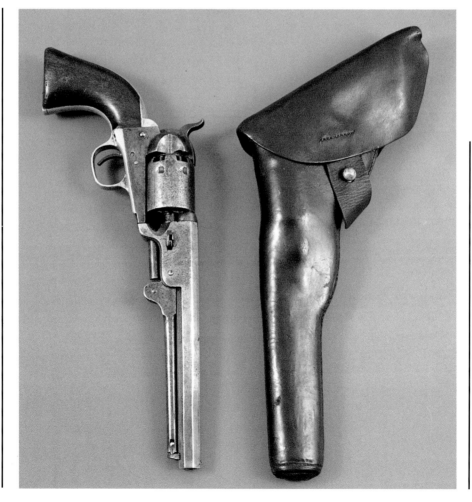

Military Belt Holster for Colt Model 1851 Navy Revolver. Maker Unknown, 1856-1863. An early regulation form, this left-hand holster is closely form-fit to the intended revolver. Fabricated of black bridle-weight leather, the piece has a sewn-on cover flap with strap-and-finial closure, a sewn belt loop reinforced with six copper rivets, and a sewn-in toe plug. The closure strap is straight-sewn and unriveted, indications of early manufacture. A .36 caliber percussion, Colt Model 1851 Navy revolver, fourth variation, accompanies the holster. (Courtesy Scott Meadows Collection)

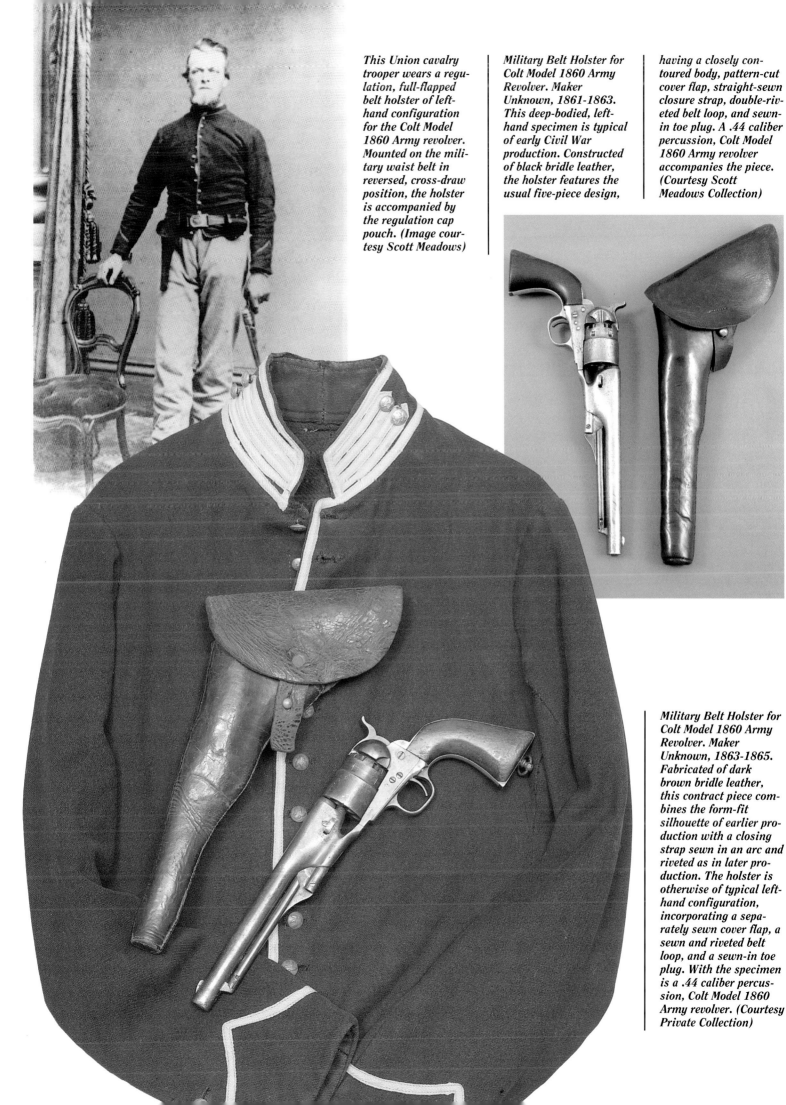

This Union cavalry trooper wears a regulation, full-flapped belt holster of left-hand configuration for the Colt Model 1860 Army revolver. Mounted on the military waist belt in reversed, cross-draw position, the holster is accompanied by the regulation cap pouch. (Image courtesy Scott Meadows)

Military Belt Holster for Colt Model 1860 Army Revolver. Maker Unknown, 1861-1863. This deep-bodied, left-hand specimen is typical of early Civil War production. Constructed of black bridle leather, the holster features the usual five-piece design, having a closely contoured body, pattern-cut cover flap, straight-sewn closure strap, double-riveted belt loop, and sewn-in toe plug. A .44 caliber percussion, Colt Model 1860 Army revolver accompanies the piece. (Courtesy Scott Meadows Collection)

Military Belt Holster for Colt Model 1860 Army Revolver. Maker Unknown, 1863-1865. Fabricated of dark brown bridle leather, this contract piece combines the form-fit silhouette of earlier production with a closing strap sewn in an arc and riveted as in later production. The holster is otherwise of typical left-hand configuration, incorporating a separately sewn cover flap, a sewn and riveted belt loop, and a sewn-in toe plug. With the specimen is a .44 caliber percussion, Colt Model 1860 Army revolver. (Courtesy Private Collection)

bard were carried on the left for relatively easy access in a cross-draw motion. The revolver, carried reversed on the right, was likewise intended to be acquired in a left-hand, cross-draw maneuver when the saber was in use. In actual practice, however, the revolver generally was drawn from the holster with the right hand, palm turned out, in a twisting motion. Although the use of sabers in the field was virtually abandoned by 1875, the military's regulation adherence to the "left-hand" pattern belt holster continued through the remainder of the century.[23]

Military belt holsters typically were constructed of medium-weight black bridle leather in five component elements: the body, cover flap, belt loop, closing strap and toe plug. Like contemporary pommel holsters patterned for revolvers, early belt holsters were characterized by asymmetrical, form-fit bodies that closely followed the silhouette of the intended weapon. Contoured cover flaps, sewn to the back of the upper body, completely shrouded the pistol. The separate belt loop also was sewn to the upper back of the holster body and usually reinforced with six copper rivets. During early production, the flap closure strap was straight stitched to the cover. The toe plug was sewn in at the muzzle to reinforce the lower, "pipe" portion of the body and to preclude debris from entering the revolver's barrel.

Military Belt Holster for Colt Dragoon Model Revolvers. E. Gaylord, Chicopee Falls, Massachusetts, 1863-1865. This regulation, left-hand specimen reflects the continuing issue of Dragoon revolvers during the Civil War. Made of black bridle leather, it incorporates a sewn and riveted belt loop, a separate cover flap with strap-and-finial closure, and a sewn-in toe plug. The use of semi-circular stitching and a reinforcing rivet on the closure strap (as well as the more amorphous main seam contour) date this holster to around 1863, when these design changes were introduced. With the piece is a .44 caliber percussion, Colt Third Model Dragoon revolver. (Courtesy Scott Meadows Collection)

This young Union officer wears a non-regulation, full-flapped military belt holster of right-hand configuration. Probably fit for a Colt Army or Navy Model revolver, the holster utilizes flap-and-finial closure. (Image courtesy Richard F. Carlile Collection and Scott Meadows)

Around 1863 a pattern modification in regulation military holsters was introduced in response to the large variation in pistols procured for Civil War service. The form-fit body design was altered to a more amorphous contour in order to accommodate different revolvers of similar size and shape (particularly the Colt, Remington and Whitney Navy and Army Models, which were purchased in considerable numbers). Concurrently, the attachment of the flap closing strap was strengthened by sewing it on in a semi-circular pattern and adding a reinforcing rivet.[24]

In addition to this fairly standard holster pattern, of which more than 300,000 were made during the Civil War, a variety of non-regulation designs also appeared. These were fabricated by both government contractors and commercial manufacturers for some 48,000 odd revolvers of 15 different makes that were pressed into service. Such "quasi-military" holsters often were form-fit to a particular make of revolver

and, in many instances, were of "right-hand" configuration. They frequently differed as well in quality of leather, cover flap design and means of flap closure.[25] Many of these holsters, pilfered by veterans or sold as government surplus, reappeared in the West among the civilian population following the war.

Descriptive references to regulation military belt holsters prior to and during the Civil War were few and fragmentary. General Order No. 13 of August 1855, which specified the arms and equipment of newly raised cavalry regiments, simply specified:

2. PISTOL. — Colt's Revolver, Navy pattern.

Military Belt Holster for Colt Model 1860 Army Revolver. J. Davy & Co., Newark, New Jersey, 1863-1865. A typical, late Civil War specimen, this left-handed holster is mounted on a Model 1851 Buff Saber Belt with accompanying cap pouch. The rig rests on a Model 1859 McClellan cavalry saddle, which also carries a Civil War-era Spencer carbine in the typical carbine socket or "thimble." (Courtesy Hayes Otoupalik Collection. Image courtesy Blll Munns)

4. PISTOL CASE. — Same as used by the Dragoons; but for one squadron of each regiment, to be made of gutta percha.[26]

The following year, Colonel of Ordnance Craig wrote: "...Colt's revolvers of the light [Navy] pattern are carried in the Army in a pouch, or half-holster attached by a loop to the sabre belt...."[27] By the opening of the rebellion, belt holsters were categorized by the military as "Cavalry Accoutrements" instead of "Horse Equipments," and limited production was undertaken at government arsenals. In the main, however, no clear documentation relevant to specific patterns appeared until the 1870s. During most of that decade, the military still was consumed with the modification and issue of surplus holsters retained from the war.[28]

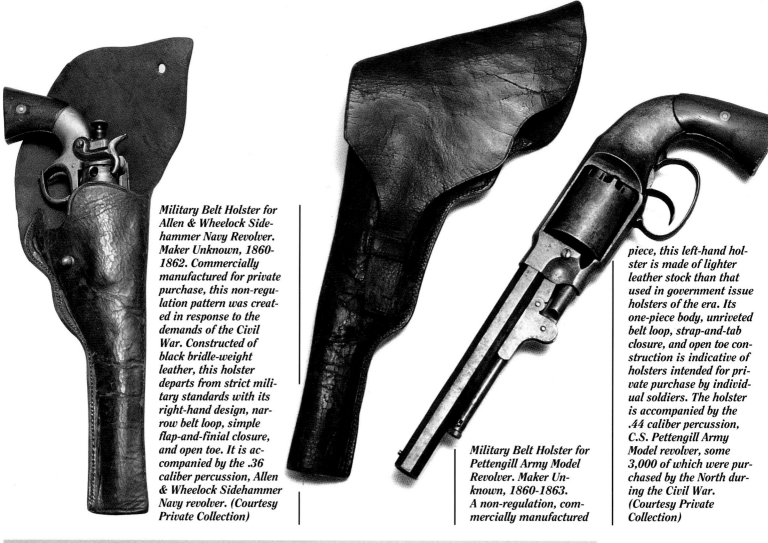

Military Belt Holster for Allen & Wheelock Side-hammer Navy Revolver. Maker Unknown, 1860-1862. Commercially manufactured for private purchase, this non-regulation pattern was created in response to the demands of the Civil War. Constructed of black bridle-weight leather, this holster departs from strict military standards with its right-hand design, narrow belt loop, simple flap-and-finial closure, and open toe. It is accompanied by the .36 caliber percussion, Allen & Wheelock Sidehammer Navy revolver. (Courtesy Private Collection)

Military Belt Holster for Pettengill Army Model Revolver. Maker Unknown, 1860-1863. A non-regulation, commercially manufactured

piece, this left-hand holster is made of lighter leather stock than that used in government issue holsters of the era. Its one-piece body, unriveted belt loop, strap-and-tab closure, and open toe construction is indicative of holsters intended for private purchase by individual soldiers. The holster is accompanied by the .44 caliber percussion, C.S. Pettengill Army Model revolver, some 3,000 of which were purchased by the North during the Civil War. (Courtesy Private Collection)

Military Belt Holster for Starr Model 1858 Army Revolver. Maker Unknown, 1863-1865. A regulation contract pattern of the Civil War era, this left-hand holster was also issued in small quantities to the post-war frontier army. Constructed of black bridle leather, it incorporates the typical full-flap top, strap-and-finial closure, riveted and sewn belt loop, and sewn toe plug. The closing strap is sewn in a semi-circle and riveted, both indications of late Civil War production. Accompanying the holster is the .44 caliber percussion, double action Starr Arms Company revolver of 1858. (Courtesy Private Collection)

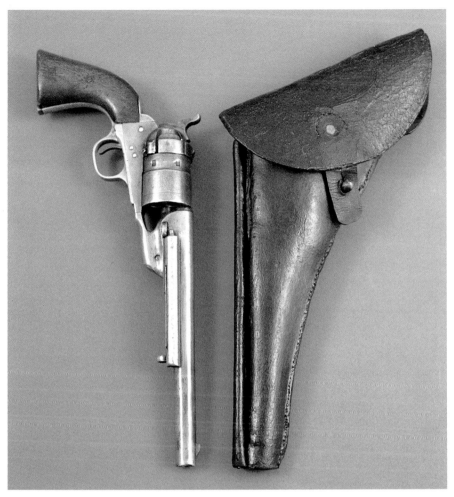

The first of these modifications appeared as the 1872 Pattern Holster, altered at Watervliet Arsenal in New York during 1873 in a quantity of some 1,300. Modifications to this 1863 design incorporated the patented, Hoffman swivel belt loop and a variation of the Tileston wiping rod sleeve. Both contrivances were designed for convenience, but typical of multi-purpose military equipage, they proved unsatisfactory in field use. The Hoffman swivel, which allowed the holster body to rotate a full 360 degrees over the belt loop, resulted in the disappearance of not a few pistols. The wiping rod sleeve, riveted on the front curvature of the holster body, was often removed by the troops as a superfluous hindrance.[29]

An 1874 review board suggested further modifications, as reflected in Ordnance Memoranda No. 18:

> The pistol-holster to be composed of body, strap, and loop for the belt and swivel attachment....The strap to confine the pistol in the holster is to be 2 3/4 inches wide at the widest part, to be sewed to the back of body and fastened in front by a brass button. The loop for the belt to be attached to the body by a swivel-bolt, with head and plate, with stop riveted firmly to loop, and a slot cut in the head into which the stop operates....The swivel attachment allows the holster to move on the belt through an arc of 45 [degrees].[30]

This 1874 Pattern Holster represented something of a design departure with its introduction of the half-flap, top "strap" in lieu of the traditional full cover flap. The half-flap design was considered sufficient protection, as metallic cartridge arms were then standard issue. Unlike earlier patterns, closure was attained not with a strap sewn and riveted to the cover flap, but with a "buttonhole" located in the lower extremity of the truncated, half-flap. The pattern was produced at Watervliet Arsenal in only limited numbers during 1874 and 1875.

With the adoption of the Smith & Wesson Schofield Model revolver in 1875, a further modification in the conformation of the holster body was necessitated to accommodate both this pistol and the Colt Single Action Army Model, already in service. The 1875 Pattern Holster, unchanged from the previous form except for its altered pouch design, was fabricated by Watervliet Arsenal during 1876 and 1877 and totaled some 32,000 units. It was the first pattern to routinely include the embossing of "US" in an oval on the holster, in this instance on the upper body.[31]

Incorporating the modified Hoffman swivel and the "buttonhole" closure from previous production, the 1875 Pattern Holster met with many complaints when issued in the field. The swivel tended to wear and separate, as pointed out in 1877 by Lieutenant James Allison of the Second U. S. Cavalry:

> While wearing one of these [Schofield Smith & Wesson] holsters in the field...I felt my pistol fall from my side and found the holster had

Military Belt Holster for Single Action Cartridge Revolvers and Remington Single-Shot Pistol. Watervliet Arsenal, New York, 1873. Modified from Civil War surplus, this regulation 1872 Pattern Holster introduced the Hoffman swivel belt loop and the attached sleeve for wiping rod. Fabricated of black bridle leather, the left-hand piece has a sewn cover flap with "US" emboss and strap-and-finial closure, and a slightly curvilinear main seam with sewn-in toe plug. The new belt loop is secured to the upper back of the holster body with a brass swivel device that allows the holster to rotate a full 360 degrees over the waist belt. The elongated wiping rod sleeve is sewn closed and riveted to the leading edge of the body. A .44 caliber, Richards conversion of the Colt Model 1860 Army revolver accompanies the holster. (Courtesy Scott Meadows Collection)

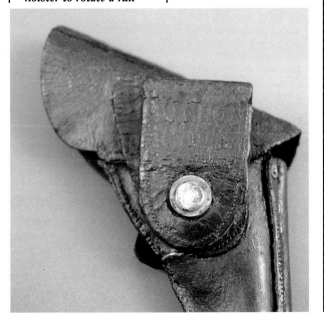

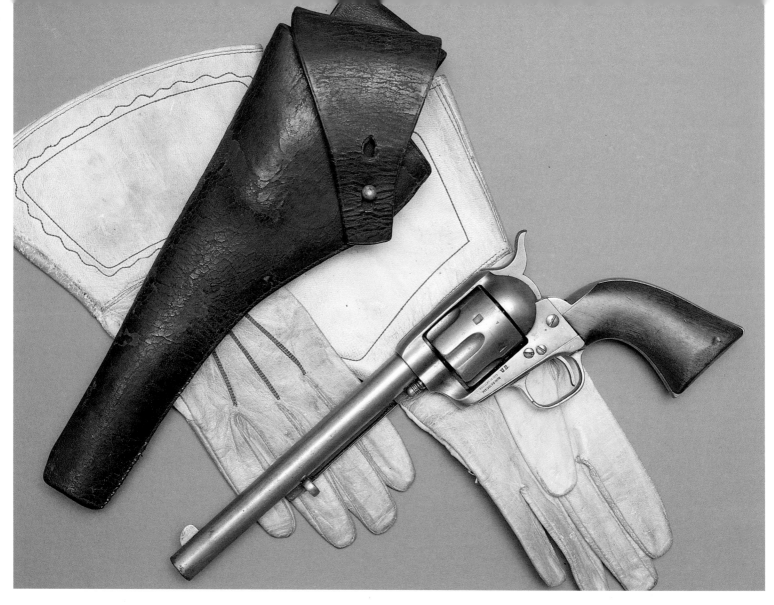

become detached from the loop which still remained on the belt. On the following day, Lieut. Kall, 2nd Cav., while mounted and wearing one of these holsters met with a similar accident, his holster and pistol falling to the ground.[32]

Problems with the half-flap closure also were noted by Major John McGinnis of Rock Island Arsenal: "...if the hole is worn, [it will] cause the flap to unbutton, and allow the pistol to be thrown out by the violent motion incident to fast trotting or galloping."[33] Due to these inherent defects, many of the 1875 Pattern Holsters were further modified by riveting the belt loop fast to the holster body, and by introducing a rounded half-flap incorporating the traditional strap closure with a "hole-and-slit" arrangement for the button finial.

These changes were formally adopted in the 1878/79 Pattern Holster, as specified in part under General Order No. 76 of July 1879:

PISTOL HOLSTER. — of the present pattern without the swivel attachment, which allows the holster to move on the belt through an arc of 45 degrees.[34]

Military Belt Holster for Colt Single Action Army Revolver. Watervliet Arsenal, New York, 1874-1875. Designed to better accommodate the newly adopted, issue side arm, this 1874 Pattern Holster introduced the half-flap cover with narrow, truncated profile and buttonhole-and-finial closure (here modified with an additional, upper buttonhole for greater security). Constructed of black bridle leather, the left-hand design utilized a modified Hoffman swivel belt loop that allowed the body to rotate only about 45 degrees. Accompanying the piece is a government issue, .45 caliber, Colt Single Action Army revolver. (Courtesy Private Collection)

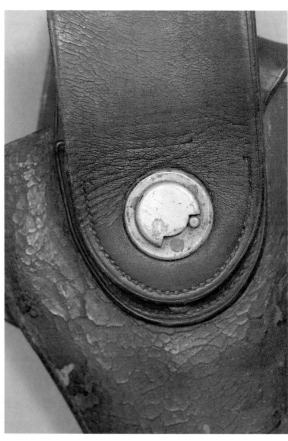

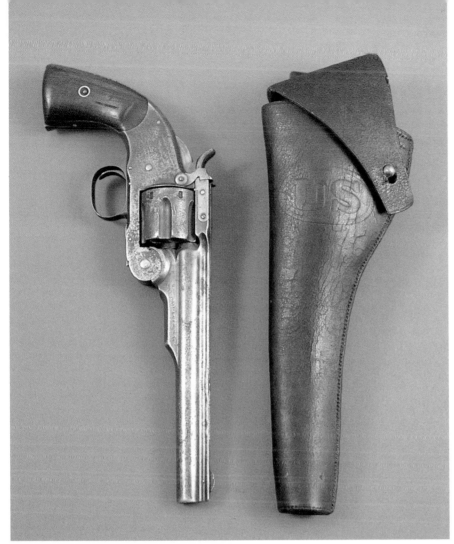

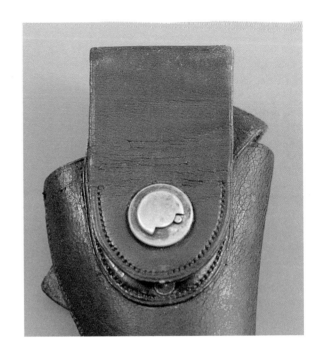

The new pattern thus eliminated the Hoffman swivel, replacing it with a plain, folded belt loop stitched to the holster body and secured with six rivets as in the earlier, Civil War-era design. Although not mentioned in General Order 76, this holster also utilized the rounded half-flap with separate closure strap seen in alterations of the 1875 pattern. The embossed "US" with oval border appeared on the flap. Watervliet Arsenal produced 2,000 such holsters during 1878 and 1879.[35]

Military holster manufacture moved from Watervliet to Rock Island Arsenal in 1881, and a new pattern went into production at the Illinois facility that same year. The 1881 Pattern Holster was fabricated in five variations (as distinguished by belt loop size) and totaled nearly 35,000 units prior to its discontinuance in 1907. This was the holster perhaps most in evidence during the late Indian Wars period in the West.

The 1881 Pattern Holster initially was designed to better accommodate and secure the issue Colt and Smith & Wesson revolvers by means of two "buttonhole" closures situated on a truncated, or straight-bottomed, half-flap reminiscent of the 1874 pattern. The lower left "buttonhole" conformed to the Colt, while that at the upper right fit the Schofield. The Type One variant, of which 4,000 were manufactured in 1881-1882, incorporated a very narrow, stationary loop for mounting on plain waist or saber belts. The "US" emboss reverted again to the upper holster body and remained there throughout the pattern's production.[36]

Military Belt Holster for Colt Single Action Army and Smith & Wesson Schofield Revolvers. Watervliet Arsenal, New York, 1876-1877. Incorporating a modified pouch profile to accommodate the two issue side arms then in service, the 1875 Pattern Holster was otherwise unchanged from the 1874 Pattern. Fabricated of black bridle leather, the left-hand design retained the modified Hoffman swivel belt loop, abbreviated half-flap cover and sewn-in toe plug. This was the first regulation holster regularly embossed with "US" in an oval border. With the piece is a .45 caliber, Smith & Wesson First Model Schofield revolver. (Courtesy Scott Meadows Collection)

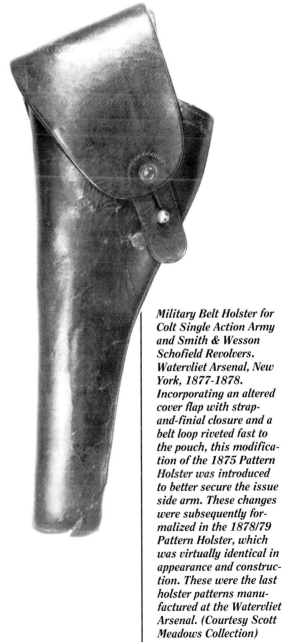

Military Belt Holster for Colt Single Action Army and Smith & Wesson Schofield Revolvers. Watervliet Arsenal, New York, 1877-1878. Incorporating an altered cover flap with strap-and-finial closure and a belt loop riveted fast to the pouch, this modification of the 1875 Pattern Holster was introduced to better secure the issue side arm. These changes were subsequently formalized in the 1878/79 Pattern Holster, which was virtually identical in appearance and construction. These were the last holster patterns manufactured at the Watervliet Arsenal. (Courtesy Scott Meadows Collection)

Military Belt Holster for Colt Single Action Army and Smith & Wesson Schofield Revolvers. Watervliet Arsenal, New York, 1878-1879. The final military holster design produced at Watervliet Arsenal, this 1878/1879 pattern formalized earlier changes made to the unpopular 1875 pattern. A new cover flap shape with strap-and-finial closure was introduced, along with a new belt loop design that canted the toe sharply rearward and was stitched and riveted securely to the body. This specimen carries a .45 caliber, Colt Single Action Army revolver of *government issue and is mounted on the Model 1874 Saber Belt. (Courtesy Hayes Otoupalik Collection. Image courtesy Bill Manns)*

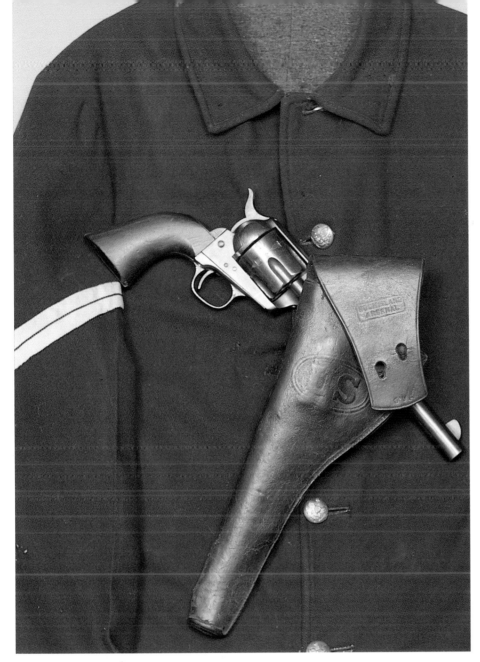

Concurrent with the development of these holsters, the military had adopted the "Prairie" and "Mills" pattern, fabric cartridge belts for carrying carbine and rifle ammunition. Controversy soon arose regarding the adaptation of the holster to these much bulkier belts. The Type Two variant of the 1881 Pattern Holster, which featured a slightly enlarged loop for the plain leather "Cavalry" or Whittemore pattern belt, proved an inadequate compromise. Still, some 4,500 Type Two holsters were made between 1883 and 1885.[37] Many subsequently were retrofitted with larger belt loops.

The desire among troops on the field for a practical cartridge belt/pistol holster arrangement inspired a third variation of the 1881 Pattern Holster, as specified in Ordnance Memoranda No. 29 of 1885/1891:

PISTOL HOLSTER. — Of black leather, 8 1/2 to 9 ounces per square foot, composed of body P, flap C, frog [belt loop] A, and bottom [toe plug] K, and made so that the pistol shall fit neatly into it; to have the letters U.S., surrounded by an oval, stamped in front.....Flap to be sewed and riveted to the back of the body; to have 2 holes with slots for attaching to the button, permitting the use of...either the Colt's or Schofield, Smith & Wesson revolver. The frog [loop] for the belt is sewed and riveted to the flap and body, and is large enough to slip over the empty woven cartridge belt.[38]

This description has led students and collectors to mistakenly identify a "Model 1885" holster which, in fact, the military never so designated.

Military Belt Holster for Colt Single Action Army and Smith & Wesson Schofield Revolvers. Rock Island Arsenal, Illinois, 1881-1882. This regulation 1881 Pattern Holster, Type One, introduced the truncated half-flap with two adjustable buttonholes for finial closure. Fabricated of black bridle leather, the left-hand body has a shallow, riveted and sewn belt loop made to mount only on a plain waist or saber belt. The half-flap carries the Rock Island Arsenal cartouche, while the upper body is embossed with the "US" oval insignia. With the piece is a government issue, .45 caliber, Colt Single Action Army revolver. (Courtesy Private Collection)

Design drawing of the 1881 Pattern Holster as described in Ordnance Memoranda No. 29 of 1885/1891. Note the use of two slotted holes in the half-flap for adjustment to either the Colt Single Action Army or Smith & Wesson Schofield revolver.

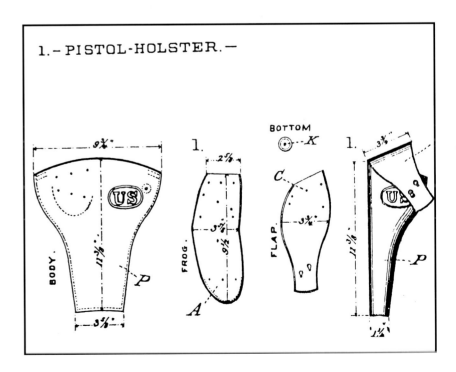

1.— PISTOL-HOLSTER.—

Military Belt Holster with "Mills" Pattern Cartridge Belt. Rock Island Arsenal, Illinois, 1896-1903; and Mills-Orndorff, Worcester, Massachusetts, 1895-1900. Representing "Rough Rider" gun-leather of the Spanish-American War, this rig features the 1881 Pattern Holster (Type Five) modified with a shortened pipe segment to accommodate the so-called Colt "Artillery" revolver with 5 1/2-inch barrel. The holster is mounted on the "Mills" pattern belt for cavalry, fixed with 50 double loops for 100 rounds of .30/40 Krag carbine ammunition and six double loops for 12 rounds of .45 or .38 Colt ammunition. (Courtesy Hayes Otoupalik Collection. Image courtesy Bill Manns)

Variants of the 1881 Pattern Military Belt Holster. Rock Island Arsenal, Illinois 1881-1896. This grouping illustrates the increasing enlargement of the pattern's belt loop for accommodation to issue waist and cartridge belts. From the left: 1) First variation for saber or waist belt; 2) Second variation for "cavalry" or Whittemore belt; 3) Third variation for empty "Mills" pattern cartridge belt; and 4) Fifth variation for the double-looped "Mills" pattern cartridge belt. (Courtesy Hayes Otoupalik Collection)

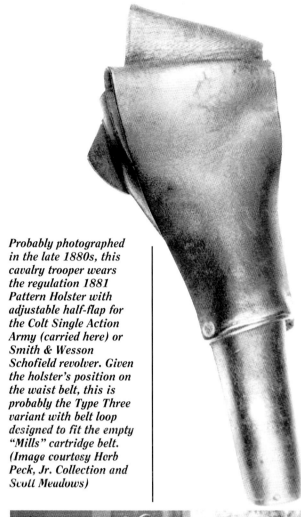

Probably photographed in the late 1880s, this cavalry trooper wears the regulation 1881 Pattern Holster with adjustable half-flap for the Colt Single Action Army (carried here) or Smith & Wesson Schofield revolver. Given the holster's position on the waist belt, this is probably the Type Three variant with belt loop designed to fit the empty "Mills" cartridge belt. (Image courtesy Herb Peck, Jr. Collection and Scott Meadows)

Military Belt Holster for Colt Single Action Army and Smith & Wesson Schofield Revolvers. Rock Island Arsenal, Illinois, 1883. Incorporating the Forsyth modification, this 1881 Pattern Holster has an enlarged belt loop/back skirt designed to accommodate thicker and wider, cartridge-laden belts. Fabricated of black skirting leather, the contoured half-panel is stitched to the holster body at the upper back and secured at the bottom by a riveted strap with a brass harness buckle. The holster is mounted on the Model "1881" Cavalry belt and carries a .45 caliber, Colt Single Action Army revolver.(Courtesy Hayes Otoupalik Collection) Image courtesy Bill Manns)

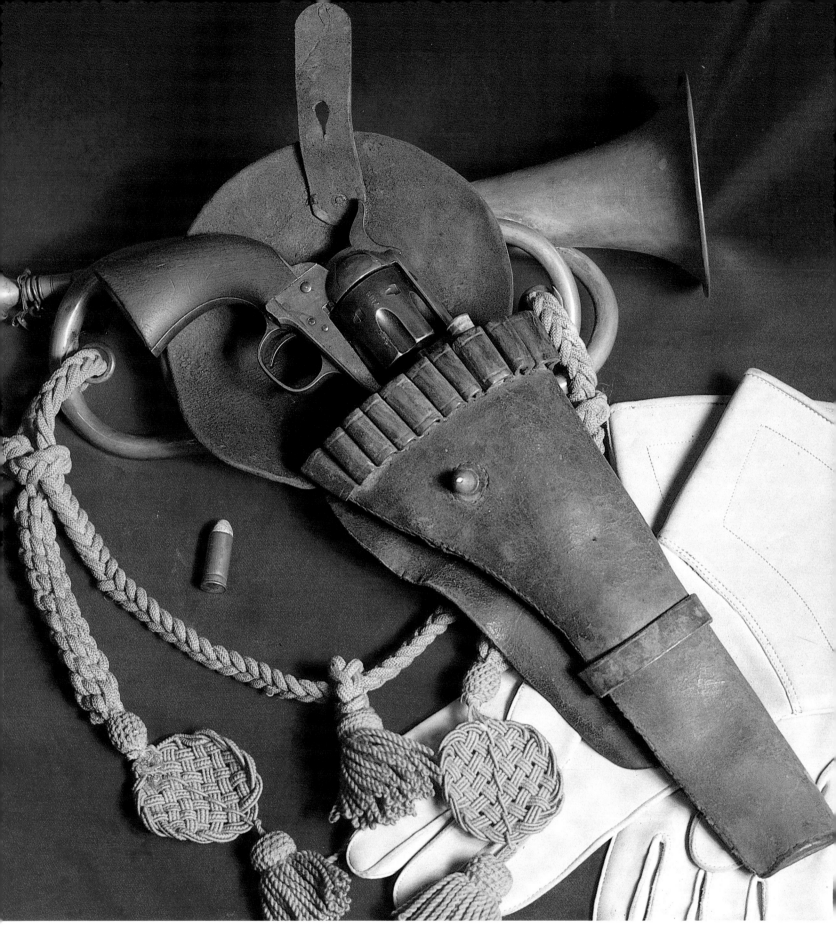

Military Belt Holster for Colt Single Action Army and Smith & Wesson Schofield Revolvers. San Antonio Arsenal, Texas, 1885-1895. This experimental, right-hand design, often credited to Captain James Ropes of the Eighth Cavalry Regiment at Fort Ringgold, Texas, incorporates the extended belt loop/back skirt reminiscent of the civilian "Mexican Loop" holster. Constructed of black bridle-weight leather, it features a full-flap top with strap-and-finial closure, ten sewn-in cartridge loops at the mouth of the holster beneath the flap, and an extended belt loop/skirt attached to the holster body by a single, riveted strap or loop. Accompanying the holster is a government issue, .45 caliber, Colt Single Action Army revolver. (Courtesy Hayes Otoupalik Collection. Image courtesy Bill Manns)

As can be surmised from the last sentence of the specification, this Type Three variant of the 1881 Pattern also was something of a half measure, as it would not readily mount on a belt fully-laden with cartridges. Nevertheless, 10,500 such holsters were fabricated at Rock Island Arsenal between 1885 and 1890; some no doubt were modified with larger belt loops in ensuing years.[39]

The Type Four, 1881 Pattern Holster introduced a still-larger loop designed to pass over the "Mills" belt when completely full of cartridges. In production from 1890 to 1896, some 12,800 such holsters were made. Somewhat beyond the purview of this study, the Type Five variant appeared in 1896 with an even more spacious belt loop to accommodate the larger, double-row "Mills" cartridge belt adopted in 1895.[40]

In addition to these approved holster patterns, a number of experimental forms were devised and field tested between 1880 and 1895; notably the Fechet (1881), Forsyth (1883), Ropes (1883/1890?) and Gaston (1892). In varying degree, these holsters reflected the influence of contemporary civilian gunleather on the western military. In an 1883 letter, Captain J. M. Ropes observed that military holsters were "...much inferior to the holster...which has for years been in use by Texas Rangers, cow-boys, and mounted men generally who carry a pistol for use."[41] Thus, several of these experimental forms incorporated the extended back skirt/belt loop design of the "Mexican Loop" pattern holster (e.g. Fechet, Forsyth and Ropes). Some were of "right-hand" configuration (Fechet and Ropes); while others were of flapless, open-topped pattern (Fechet and Gaston). The latter holster was basically a military interpretation of the classic "California" pattern originated some 40 years earlier.[42]

The army also tested the intriguing, but relatively impractical, Flatau Pistol and Carbine Holder, a pronged metal fixture for suspending issue weapons at the waist belt or from the saddle. It was found inadequate for the rigors of military service in 1883, but met with limited acceptance among civilians in the West.[43] (The device, today commonly known as the "Bridgeport Rig," is described more fully in the section treating civilian gunleather.)

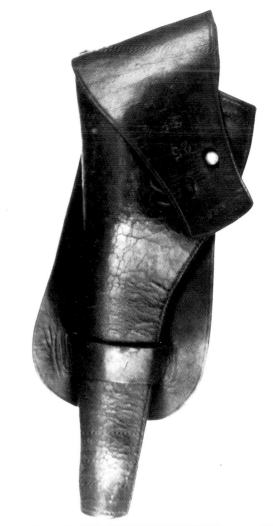

Military Belt Holster for Colt Single Action Army and Smith & Wesson Schofield Revolvers. Maker Unknown, 1890-1900. Obviously copying the civilian, "Mexican Loop" design, this 1881 Pattern holster has been modified to easily mount on bulkier cartridge belts. In lieu of the familiar belt loop, a bulbous, three-quarter-length back skirt is sewn to the upper back of the holster body and secured with a single, integral skirt loop. The style was advocated by several officers (and informally adopted by some troops) in the West, but it was never approved for regular production or issue. (Courtesy Paul Hoffman Collection)

Photographed in the late 1880s at Fort Union, New Mexico, this Sixth Cavalry trooper carries his Colt Single Action Army revolver in a commercially made, "Mexican Loop" pattern holster of right-hand configuration. The informal adoption of such non-regulation gunleather was not uncommon in the Indian-fighting Army. (Image courtesy Fort Davis National Historic Site and Scott Meadows)

31

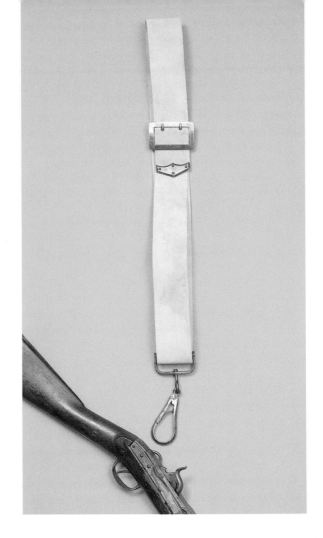

Military Carbine Sling. Maker Unknown, 1840-1850. As specified in the Ordnance Manual of 1841, carbine slings of light buff leather, 2 1/2 inches in width, became regulation issue for dragoon regiments. This specimen features the rectangular, double-claw buckle and riveted and scalloped tip, both of heavy brass. The attached D-ring with swivel and clip-spring hook of polished iron is typical of those used for more than 40 years. Accompanying the sling is a .54 caliber percussion, U.S. Model 1843 Hall-North breech-loading carbine. (Courtesy Private Collection)

Photographed during the mid- to late 1880s, this unknown trooper wears an interesting mix of military gunleather. Hanging over his shoulder is the narrow, 1885 Pattern Carbine Sling as described in Ordnance Memoranda No. 29. His Colt Single Action Army revolver is housed in a Forsyth-modified, 1881 Pattern Holster having an enlarged belt loop/ back skirt secured with a riveted loop. Lastly, his cartridge belt appears to be the arsenal-modified, "1881" Cavalry variation utilizing a woven, "Mills" patent body with sewn-on leather chape and tongue billet secured with a double-frame brass buckle. (Image courtesy Herb Peck, Jr. Collection)

SLINGS, BUCKETS, SOCKETS AND BOOTS

As described above, military gunleather for side-arms afforded abundant protection to the weapon, in addition to providing adequate carriage. This evidently was never a consideration where longarms were concerned. While a variety of gunleather elements were adopted for the carriage of carbines and other shoulder arms, none of these incorporated any provision for shrouding the weapon from the elements or the regular wear and tear inherent in mounted service. The adoption of full saddle scabbards, common among all manner of civilians in the West from the early 1870s, was not undertaken in the military until 1896 with the adoption of the Krag carbine.

Two basic means of carrying shoulder arms among mounted troops were followed in the frontier military. When mounted or dismounted, the weapon was attached to the trooper by means of a sling-and-swivel device which was considered a "Cavalry Accoutrement." When mounted, the weapon also was secured to the saddle by one of several different attachments which came into service over the decades. These included carbine buckets, sockets, loops and boots (short or half-scabbards), and were classified as "Horse Equipments." Here, the long service of the trooper-mounted carbine sling will be treated first, followed by a survey of the various saddle attachments.

Carbine slings evidently were approved issue for the U.S. Dragoons from their inception, but references are scant prior to the 1841 Ordnance Manual. The earliest pattern (1833-1838?) probably was not unlike the contemporary musket sling issued to infantry. Fabricated of white buff leather, the carbine sling measured about 55 inches in length by 1 1/4 or 1 1/2 inches in width. Worn according to regulation, it crossed over the torso from left shoulder to right hip, where a brass swivel-and-snap fixture captured the sling ring or bar on the left side of the carbine. This early sling design probably was adjusted to length by means of a brass claw hook with leather keeper.[44]

During the late 1830s, a wider sling pattern was adopted to reduce chafing of the trooper's shoulder and neck. This change was specified in the 1841 Ordnance Manual:

> CARBINE SLING, buff leather. Length 56 in., width 2.5 in. — 1 buckle and 1 tip, brass — swivel and D with roller, iron, bright, 2.62 in. wide — link and hook, iron — guard-spring, steel.[45]

This pattern was specified again in General Order No. 31 of 1851, except that the leather was changed to a blackened buff finish. With General Order No. 13 of 1855, leather of smooth black finish was adopted. This established the pattern and basic attributes of

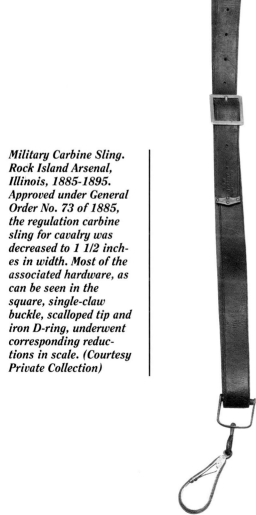

Military Carbine Sling. Rock Island Arsenal, Illinois, 1885-1895. Approved under General Order No. 73 of 1885, the regulation carbine sling for cavalry was decreased to 1 1/2 inches in width. Most of the associated hardware, as can be seen in the square, single-claw buckle, scalloped tip and iron D-ring, underwent corresponding reductions in scale. (Courtesy Private Collection)

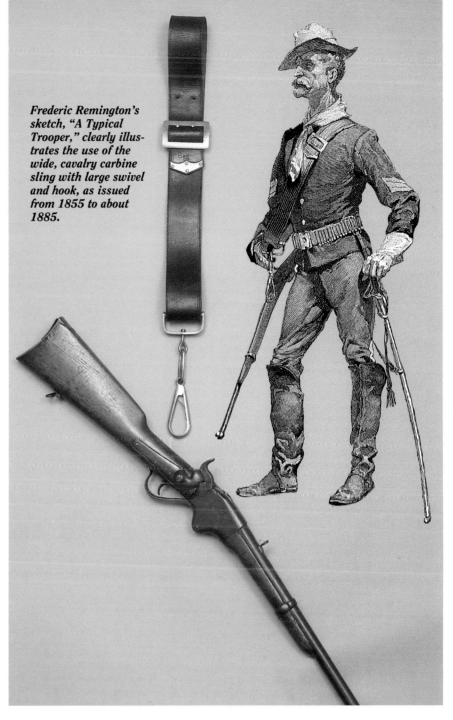

Frederic Remington's sketch, "A Typical Trooper," clearly illustrates the use of the wide, cavalry carbine sling with large swivel and hook, as issued from 1855 to about 1885.

Military Carbine Sling. Watervliet Arsenal, New York, 1855-1885. The classic carbine sling of the Civil War and later Indian Wars, this pattern was specified in General Order No. 13 of 1855. Constructed of black collar-weight leather, the sling proper is 2 1/2 inches wide and fixed with a rectangular, double-claw brass buckle and riveted brass tip. The attached D-ring with roller bar and clip-spring hook are made of polished iron. With the sling is a Spencer repeating carbine with modified, buckhorn rear sight. (Courtesy Private Collection)

the carbine sling utilized by mounted troops during the Civil War and well into the Indian Wars era.[46]

During 1872 and 1873 an experimental "brace system" to support the waist belt was tested by elements of the Seventh Cavalry. It incorporated a modified and shortened carbine sling that "...fastened to the brace in the rear, and buckled or hooked to the brace in front, forming a loop under the right arm to carry the swivel that holds the carbine."[47] Considered too cumbersome, the outfit was not adopted. The last modification of the regulation carbine sling was introduced in 1885 and described in Ordnance Memoranda No. 29 of 1891 under Cavalry Accoutrements:

> CARBINE SLING AND SWIVEL of black collar leather, 8 1/2 to 9 ounces per square foot, with brass bar buckle and tip. Swivel of iron with D and roller; link and hook of iron; guard spring of steel.[49]

In this modification, the buckle was altered from the large, rectangular form to a smaller, double-frame pattern; not specified was an evident narrowing of the sling leather to 1 1/2 inches. This 1885 Pattern Carbine Sling remained in service into the 1890s, as did many of the earlier, Civil War-era pattern issued to units in the West.

The carbine bucket was the first saddle attachment issued to mounted troops for securing shoulder arms (typically the Hall breech-loading carbine) on horseback. No examples of those issued to the U. S. Dragoons during the 1830s are known, nor is any specific documentation available.[49] One may assume, however, that they were similar in form and dimension to the pattern specified in the 1841 *Ordnance Manual For The Use Of The Officers of the United States Army*:

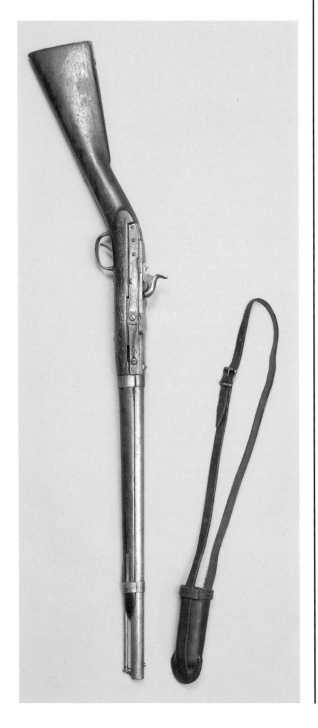

This 1851 sketch by Frank Mayer portrays the typical U. S. Dragoon horse equipments of the period. Note the use of the carbine bucket, or "boot," retaining the muzzle of the carbine, and the associated "carbine strap" securing the weapon at the wrist. The items probably are those specified with the Grimsley pattern saddle. (Image courtesy Scott Meadows)

Military Carbine Bucket. Watervliet Arsenal, New York (?), 1847-1860. This rare carbine bucket probably is the design adopted for the Grimsley saddle in 1847 and described in General Order No. 31 of 1851. Fabricated of black sole leather, the bucket is formed from a single pattern-cut and molded piece that is stitched along the bottom seam and around the mortised "drag" at the toe. A single leather band is sewn around the mouth of the bucket, providing loops on either side. The mounting strap, which attached to the right-front side bar ring of the saddle, passes through the side loops and toe mortise of the bucket and secures with a single iron roller buckle. A .54 caliber percussion, U.S. Model 1843 Hall-North carbine accompanies the piece. (Courtesy Private Collection)

HORSE EQUIPMENTS FOR DRAGOONS — PATTERN OF 1841

CARBINE BUCKET, sole leather, jacked like the holster; it is made of two pieces, with a band sewed round the mouth and mortise in the lower part — the bucket strap 1 inch wide, with 1 buckle and 2 loops: it passes through the mortise and through 2 loops in the band of the bucket, and is attached to the saddle by passing under a thong tied to the connecting strap [of the pommel holsters] and to the lacing of the seat.

CARBINE BUCKET, sole leather, black: diameter 1.5 in., length of front part 6 in., back part 7.5 in. - strap, heavy bridle leather, black, 1 in. wide, 22.5 in. long, clear of the bucket; the strap passes round the sides and bottom of the bucket.[50]

Issued with the bucket was a "carbine strap" fixed with a buckle and two loops. This item attached to the saddle in the same manner as the bucket, and secured to the wrist of the carbine stock while the carbine muzzle rode downward in the bucket.

With the adoption of the Grimsley horse equipments in 1847, the carbine bucket, by then referred to as a "boot," remained the same except that it attached to the saddle on a ring and staple fixed on the right side bar. The carbine strap was specified at 28 inches in length by 3/4 of an inch in width, with an oval brass buckle. The description of the "Carbine Strap and Boot" appearing in General Order No. 31 of 1851 reiterated this pattern. The equipment evidently remained in service among mounted troops in the West up to, and perhaps past, the adoption of the McClellan saddle in 1859.[51]

The adoption of the McClellan saddle and its associated horse equipments introduced the carbine socket, a new and greatly simplified means of carrying the issue shoulder arm when mounted. Termed a "carbine thimble" in military literature, the device was briefly described in the 1861 Ordnance Manual:

CARBINE-THIMBLE. — 1 strap; 1 buckle No. 10A sewed to the socket: the thimble is buckled to the D-ring [securing the girth straps] on the off [right] side of the saddle.[52]

Constructed of black harness leather, the socket was about 9 inches in outside circumference, 2 1/2 inches in width, 2 3/4 inches in diameter at top and bottom, and presented a slight "hourglass" profile. The securing strap passed around the narrower, center area and was fixed with an iron, double-frame buckle, usually having a japanned or blued finish.

Military Carbine Socket. Watervliet Arsenal, New York, 1860-1880. Used extensively by mounted troops in the West for more than 20 years, the carbine socket, or "thimble," provided a simple means of carriage. Constructed of heavy harness stock, the socket itself is double-layered and flared at top and bottom for ease of insertion and withdrawal. The mounting strap of bridle leather is riveted and sewn at the center of the socket and fixed with a double-frame bridle buckle of japanned iron. (National Cowboy Hall of Fame Collection)

Accommodating the Model 1855 Springfield carbine and such secondary martial arms as the Burnside, Joslyn, Merrill, Sharps and Spencer, the carbine socket saw extensive service during the Civil War and among the ten regiments of cavalry serving in the West throughout much of the Indian Wars period. Its use, in concert with the shoulder sling, was alluded to in Ordnance Memoranda No. 13 of 1872:

With the mounted soldier, the weight of the carbine, to a great degree, is sustained by the socket fixed to the saddle, being merely steadied by the sling; when he is dismounted, the carbine is carried "at will", either on the shoulder, behind the back...while held by the sling, or in the hand...[53]

Military Carbine Socket. Watervliet Arsenal, New York, 1880-1885. Adopted under General Order No. 76 of 1879, the Hartman split-spring socket was designed for fast release of the issue, Springfield carbine. The body incorporates a circular element of spring steel having a narrow, bevelled opening at the front. This is sheathed in heavy, sewn collar leather and mounted with a double-riveted strap fixed with a double-frame harness buckle of brass. The spring tension in this specimen is too great to easily free the weapon by pushing it through the opening. (Courtesy Private Collection)

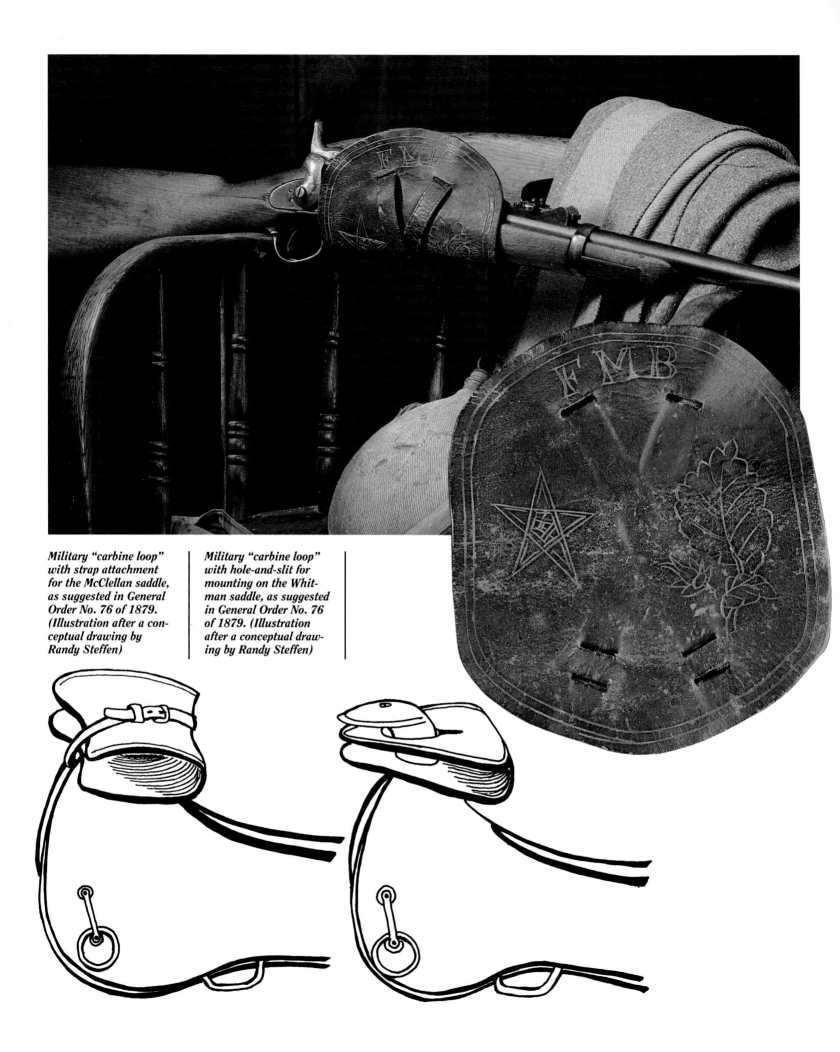

Military "carbine loop" with strap attachment for the McClellan saddle, as suggested in General Order No. 76 of 1879. (Illustration after a conceptual drawing by Randy Steffen)

Military "carbine loop" with hole-and-slit for mounting on the Whitman saddle, as suggested in General Order No. 76 of 1879. (Illustration after a conceptual drawing by Randy Steffen)

Under General Order No. 76 of 1879, the Hartman split-spring socket was adopted. Designed for quick release of the issue, Springfield "Trapdoor" carbine without drawing it clear of the socket, this innovative device incorporated an unclosed, spring steel body sheathed in leather and secured with a single buckled strap. The review board recommending the new pattern observed that "... it possesses decided advantages...in the facility with which the carbine can be liberated by simply pressing the carbine outward, a great safeguard were a rider to be thrown with his carbine slung." [54]

Concurrent with this equipment change, the army also adopted a "carbine loop," or sleeve, which was designed to carry the weapon at the front of the saddle in a lateral attitude. General Order No. 76 provided the following rationale for its use:

> While retaining the carbine socket the Board has placed a carbine loop [on] the pommel, believing that to be the most convenient place to carry the carbine on scouts and long marches. In fact, this is the universal custom of horsemen on the frontier, both white and Indian, and in many cavalry regiments company officers permit their men to carry their carbines in a similar way. [55]

Two variations evidently were trialed and issued: one a contoured, folded and sewn leather sleeve that secured to the pommel with a strap and buckle; the other a folded and sewn loop of triangular pattern with a "hole-and-slit" through both layers that slipped over the horn of the 1879 Pattern Whitman saddle.[56] The extent to which these two variations of the carbine loop were issued remains unclear, but no surviving examples are known to the author.

The Hartman split-spring socket was supplanted in 1885 by the Carbine Boot, a contoured sleeve of stiff leather that strapped on the off side of the saddle rigging. Patterned much like a short, open-ended saddle scabbard, this new equipment actually appeared in improvised form during the late 1870s and early 1880s. The first regulation pattern, approved under General Order No. 73 of 1885, measured 11 1/2 inches in length and incorporated double mounting straps, a slightly flared throat profile, and a swell along the leading edge of the body accommodating the rear sight of the "Trapdoor" carbine. Some examples, fit for earlier McClellan saddles with rear side bar rings, were suspended on an adjustable, buckled strap. Most specimens, however, employed a straight, double-holed strap that suspended from the cantle saddlebag stud of the McClellan saddle then in common issue.[57]

Following initial field trials, the Carbine Boot was modified in 1886-1887. To better accommodate the carbine's Buffington rear sight, the body was lengthened to 13 5/8 inches and the impressed swell was moved downward. The leading edge of the throat was flared outward and reinforced with a curved brass plate to protect the rear sight leaf when the weapon

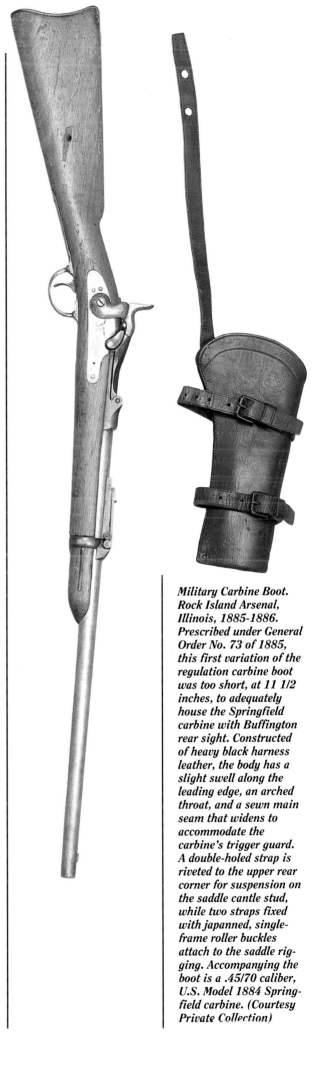

Posed in the mid-1880s, this trooper wears a Forsyth modification of an 1881 Pattern Holster on a modified, "1881" Cavalry cartridge belt. His Springfield "Trapdoor" carbine is deeply seated in the early, short pattern of the 1885 Carbine Boot. Note the absence of the flared profile and brass reinforcing plate at the leading edge of the throat, and the protrusion of the Buffington rear sight beyond the bottom of the boot. (Image courtesy Scott Meadows)

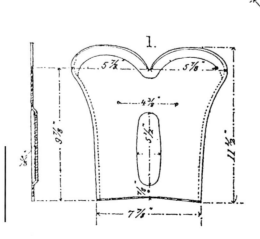

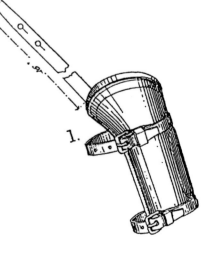

Design drawing of the early, short variation Carbine Boot as approved under General Order No. 73 of July 1885.

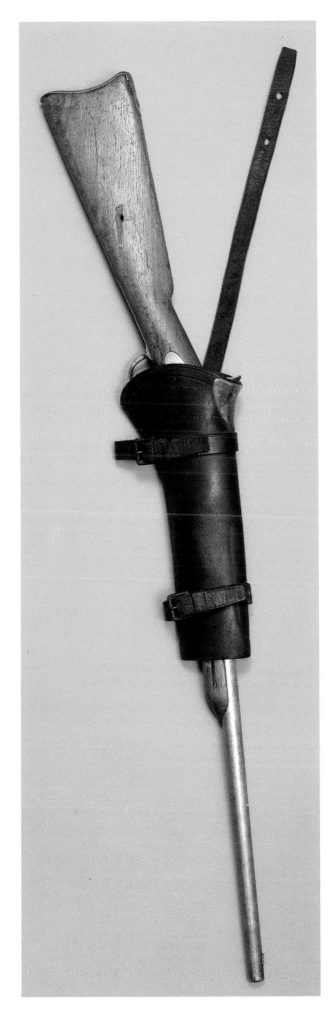

Military Carbine Boot. Rock Island Arsenal, Illinois, 1887-1895. As specified in Ordnance Memoranda No. 29 of 1891, this second variation of the regulation carbine boot was redesigned to better accommodate the Springfield carbine with Buffington rear sight. Lengthened to 13 5/8 inches, the leading edge of the body incorporates a lower sight swell and a flared profile at the throat that is reinforced with a triangular brass plate for easier insertion of the weapon. The double-holed suspension strap is riveted near the leading edge so that the boot hangs in a more vertical attitude, while the rigging straps are spaced further apart for greater stability. The boot holds a .45/70 caliber, U.S. Model 1884 Springfield carbine with Buffington rear sight. (Courtesy Private Collection)

was inserted into the boot. The suspension strap also was moved so that the boot held the carbine in a near vertical position behind the trooper's right leg and seat.[58]

The revised pattern was described in Ordnance Memoranda No. 29 of 1885/1891 under Horse Equipments:

> CARBINE BOOT AND STRAPS. The boot of thick harness leather, 13 5/8 inches in length and 2 1/4 inches interior diameter at the lower end. The opening at the upper end 5 1/8 inches long by 3 inches wide, shaped so as to embrace the carbine just in front of the trigger guard and have a swell pressed in the front to allow for the projection of the rear sight. A triangular piece of leather is inserted in the front of the boot to cause it to flare so as not to catch the rear sight leaf when inserting the carbine. A curved brass plate made of No. 14 sheet brass is riveted on the boot to secure this shape....The boot is suspended from the saddle-bag stud by a strap with 2 holes near the end for adjusting the height of the boot, and riveted to the front part of the boot on the under side....The boot is fastened to the rear girth strap and girth-strap ring, off side, with two 7/8-inch straps with iron roller buckles....[59]

Designed to more securely retain the weapon in movement and lessen the weight on the trooper's shoulder sling, the Carbine Boot was a half-step toward the full saddle scabbard. The device served in the West through the remainder of the Indian Wars and was phased from service during the late 1890s with the adoption of the saddle scabbard for the Krag carbine.

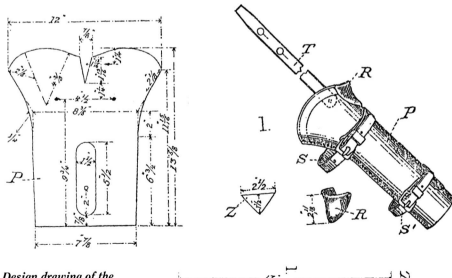

Design drawing of the standard, long variation Carbine Boot as prescribed in 1886 and described in Ordnance Memoranda No. 29 of 1891.

Military Cartridge Pouch/Box for Musket or Carbine Ammunition. Maker Unknown, 1825-1835. No doubt furnished by a civilian contractor, this specimen probably pre-dates dragoon service in the West. The body is formed from two, round-bottomed panels of light-weight black bridle leather. These are sewn around the mid-seam, creating a soft, bag-like compartment below the wooden cartridge block insert. Drilled for 24 paper-wrapped cartridges of .69 caliber, the slightly concave insert block is nine inches long at the back and three inches deep. A broad, pattern-cut cover flap of heavier bridle leather is sewn on at the upper back and secures with a slit strap and square leather button (now missing). Two loops are sewn on the upper back of the box for belt mounting. (Courtesy Private Collection)

CARTRIDGE BOXES AND BELTS

Equipage for the carriage and protection of small arms ammunition was an ancillary, but important element of military gunleather in the frontier West. Although looped belts fitted with tinned metal tubes for paper-wrapped cartridges were trialed in the army prior to 1800, this means of carrying ammunition remained impractical until dependable, self-contained metallic cartridges were developed during the 1860s.[60] Thus, throughout the first two-thirds of the nineteenth century, the belt-mounted cartridge box served as the principal means of carrying ammunition among both cavalry and infantry troops. With the adoption of metallic cartridge arms, the use of multi-looped cartridge belts gradually gained favor in the military, first during the Civil War and then among western troops in the late 1860s.

Both methods of carrying ammunition presented advantages and disadvantages. The flap-covered cartridge box afforded greater protection from the elements to its rather delicate, paper or linen-wrapped cartridges. However, if not tightly packed in the box, these could be damaged or broken when on the move, while early copper-cased metallic cartridges were easily battered — and noisy — in similar circumstances. The cartridge box also concentrated weight and bulk in a limited area on the waist belt and was of comparatively limited capacity, usually accommodating only 20 to 30 rounds for the carbine.[61]

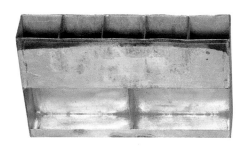

Military Cartridge Box for Pistol Ammunition. Maker Unknown, 1835-1840. Made on contract, this early specimen does not comply precisely to standard specifications. In lieu of the typical, wooden block insert drilled for paper-wrapped cartridges, this box utilizes 13 tubes of soldered tin to retain the ammunition. Fabricated of black bridle leather, the body is mounted with two sewn-on belt loops and has a full-profile cover flap with embossed border ornament and an insignia disc (now missing). (Courtesy Scott Meadows Collection)

Military Cartridge Box for Pistol Ammunition. Allegheny Arsenal, Pennsylvania (?), 1840-1850. As prescribed in the 1841 Ordnance Manual, this regulation pistol cartridge box introduced the "US" oval flap plate of cast

brass and the compartmented insert liner of soldered tin for packaged cartridges of .54 caliber. Fabricated of black bridle leather, the body is sewn around the end panels and has two sewn and riveted belt loops on the back. The interior

and exterior cover flaps are sewn on across the upper back of the body; the exterior flap is slightly scalloped along its lower edge and secures with strap-and-finial closure. The contemporary carbine cartridge box was slightly

larger in scale, but otherwise identical in design. With minor alterations for changes in ammunition, both boxes served through the Civil War years. (Courtesy Private Collection)

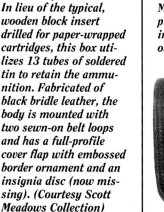

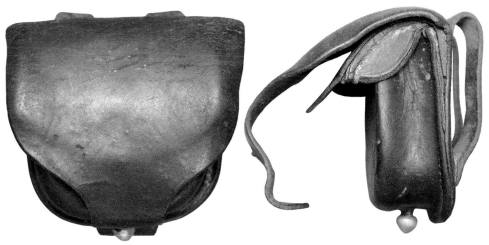

In contrast, full cartridge belts generally accommodated 40 to 50 rounds and distributed the weight evenly around the body. While appreciated in combat, this increased carrying capacity could be a liability in other circumstances. Tom Horn, a military scout and interpreter in Arizona, recalled that "...a hundred rounds of 45-70 cartridges weighs eleven pounds when you first put them on, and at the end of twenty days,...about as much as a small-sized locomotive." [62] But cartridge belts also provided readier access and more secure and silent carriage, decided advantages when operating in the field. On the debit side, they afforded less protection from the elements and allowed some disfiguration of the lead bullets at the nose of the cartridges. [63]

Perhaps most detrimental, both cartridge boxes and early belts promoted the formation of verdigris, a waxy green residue common where copper and brass cases contacted leather. This residue tended to slow the withdrawal of cartridges from belt loops and, with either means of carriage, could make the chambering of a live round difficult and the extraction of a spent casing impossible — serious drawbacks in the midst of battle! As will be seen, the military, after some false starts, largely eliminated this problem with the adoption of cartridge belts which were fabricated of canvas or cotton webbing. [64]

Mounted troops of the 1830s were issued two cartridge boxes — one for carbine ammunition, the other for pistol loads. As with other dragoon equipments from the period, descriptive documentation

was cursory. The 1834 Regulations for the Government of the Ordnance Department merely inventoried the items and cited capacities of 30 and 12 rounds, respectively. Both boxes probably were constructed of black, bridle-weight leather and contained wooden blocks bored to receive the appropriate number of paper-wrapped cartridges in separate holes of proper diameter. Both incorporated a pair of sewn back loops for belt mounting and utilized leather cover flaps with an embossed eagle motif and strap-and-finial closure. [65]

Changes in design and appearance were introduced around 1840, as reflected in an 1839 Board of Officers report:

> ...the Board recommends that the Cavalry or Carbine Cartridge Box, new pattern, be adopted and that...instead of having the leather [flap] stamped or embossed as heretofore, be marked with the U.S. mark in brass.... The Board [also] recommends...the expediency of rejecting the wooden box [insert block], and substituting therefore the tin case and method of delivering cartridges to the soldier in packages. [66]

These recommendations were acted upon for both carbine and pistol cartridge boxes, introducing the oval "US" flap plate and a compartmented tin liner. Formal specifications appeared in the 1841 Ordnance Manual:

> CARBINE CARTRIDGE BOX, light bridle leather, black — Exterior length 7 in., width 1.3 in., height in front 5 in. — inner cover 4 in. wide — flap 7.5 in. deep, 8.5 in. wide at bottom, 8 in. at top where it is connected with the box — pocket for implements — strap 1 in. wide — button, brass, on the bottom of the box — lining, tin, edges turned over; 2 lower divisions, each 2.6 in. deep and 3.4 in. wide, to contain a bundle of 10 cartridges, (musket calibre;) 5 upper divisions, each 1.35 in. square, to contain 4 cartridges — plate, brass, oval, 2.8 in. long, 1.6 in. wide, lettered U.S. [67]

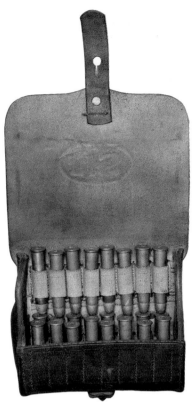

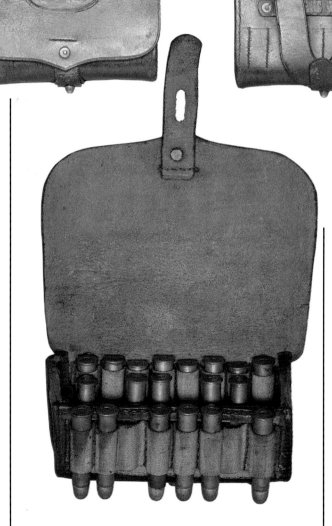

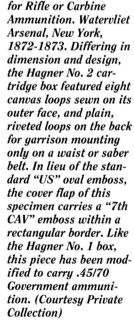

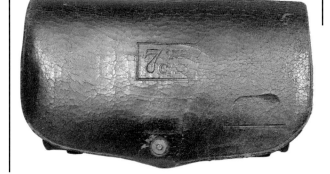

Military Cartridge Box for Rifle or Carbine Ammunition. Watervliet Arsenal, New York, 1872-1873. Originally designed for the experimental Infantry Brace System, the Hagner No. 1 cartridge box was field tested by the cavalry but was rapidly supplanted by the Dyer cartridge pouch and "Prairie" belt. *Fabricated of black bridle leather, the body consists of a single, pattern-cut piece (forming the cover flap, back, bottom and half-front) sewn around double-layered end panels. A horizontal strap on the back allows adjustment of the Y-shaped belt loop for mounting on either a waist belt or wider car-*tridge belt. *Both the belt loop and flap closure strap secure to a brass finial at the bottom. Like most specimens, the 24 sewn canvas loops in this piece were modified at Rock Island Arsenal to accommodate the .45/70 Government rifle cartridge. (Courtesy Private Collection)*

Specifications for the pistol cartridge box designated somewhat smaller dimensions throughout for "rifle calibre" ammunition, but were otherwise identical in pattern and construction.

Around 1845 a belt-mounted pouch for percussion caps was developed and issued to both infantry and mounted troops. Constructed of black bridle leather, it had inner and outer cover flaps, twin belt loops, and a lining of sheeps wool. More than 375,000 such cap pouches were fabricated during the Civil War to specifications laid down in the 1862 Ordnance Manual. Thousands of these were reissued, in original or modified form, as *pistol cartridge boxes* to cavalry units in the West during the Indian Wars era. Serving well into the 1890s, these ersatz cartridge boxes were intended to carry 12 loose rounds of .44 or .45 caliber ammunition for Colt and Remington Army conversions or the Single Action Army Colt or Schofield Smith & Wesson revolvers, respectively.[68]

Between 1840 and the close of the Civil War, the regular carbine and pistol cartridge boxes underwent several changes in dimension and compartmentation in response to changes in ammunition for newly adopted weapons. But the basic patterns remained in service into the early 1870s. Under Ordnance Memoranda No. 13 of 1872, the carbine cartridge box was reduced in capacity to 24 rounds, while the modified cap pouch/cartridge box, described above, was specified for pistol ammunition.

In 1874 the round-bottomed, Dyer pattern cartridge pouch with expandable gusset was adopted for both carbine and pistol ammunition, but modified cap pouch/cartridge boxes continued to be substituted for pistols. As described in Ordance Memoranda No. 18 of 1874, both items were to be constructed of black collar leather with sheepskin linings and cover flaps having the "US" oval emboss. Concurrently, an initial step toward the use of cartridge belts appeared

Military Cartridge Box for Rifle or Carbine Ammunition. Watervliet Arsenal, New York, 1872-1873. Differing in dimension and design, the Hagner No. 2 cartridge box featured eight canvas loops sewn on its outer face, and plain, riveted loops on the back for garrison mounting only on a waist or saber belt. In lieu of the standard "US" oval emboss, the cover flap of this specimen carries a "7th CAV" emboss within a rectangular border. Like the Hagner No. 1 box, this piece has been modified to carry .45/70 Government ammunition. (Courtesy Private Collection)

Military Cartridge Pouch for Carbine Ammunition. Rock Island Arsenal, Illinois, 1874-1876. As specified in Ordnance Memoranda No. 18 of 1874, this Dyer Pattern Cartridge Pouch was designed to carry 40 rounds of .45/70 Govt. ammunition. Constructed of black collar leather, the piece incorporates round-bottomed, front and back panels (the latter with integral cover flap) that are lined with sheepskin and sewn around an expandable gusset leather. Two belt loops are riveted and sewn on the pouch back, while the "US"-embossed cover flap secures with an escutcheoned, tab-and-finial closure. The Dyer pouch was rapidly replaced in the field by the 1876 "Prairie" cartridge belt. (Courtesy Private Collection)

with adoption of the 20-round, Hazen pattern cartridge loop attachment that slid over the waist belt.[69]

By the mid-1870s, cartridge boxes for carbine ammunition were being supplanted in the field by cartridge belts, but they remained in garrison service through the 1890s. The last of these was the McKeever pattern box, first trialed in 1874 and officially approved for infantry service only in General Order No. 76 of 1879. The basic pattern was described in Ordnance Memoranda No. 29 of 1891:

CARTRIDGE BOX

The McKeever cartridge box, made of black collar leather, 8 1/2 to 9 ounces per square foot, is made in 2 parts connected by a leather hinge working over a brass rod, which passes through the [bottom] ends of the box and is secured by a brass oval riveted on each end. A swell is pressed in the right-hand end of the box for carrying a screwdriver. A brass button is riveted on [the top] front of box, a billet with a slitted hole on back for closing box. Two waist belt loops riveted and sewed on back of box. The cartridges are held in webbing loops sewed to a drab duck bellows, 10 in each section of the box. The bellows allow the cartridges to incline forward when the box is open. The letters U.S., surrounded by an oval, stamped on front of box.[70]

Military Cartridge Box. Watervliet Arsenal, New York, 1880-1890. First trialed in 1874 with the experimental Palmer Brace System, the McKeever cartridge box was issued in several variations for infantry garrison duty. This relatively scarce specimen utilizes back bellows and cartridge loops of Mills-type, integrally-woven cotton webbing in standard, 20-round capacity. Fabricated of black collar leather, the box is constructed in two, open-faced sections joined by a brass hinge rod at the bottom; the right side panels have a swelled contour to hold a small dismounting tool for rifle or carbine. Two belt loops are riveted and sewn on the back panel, and the box is closed at the top by an escutcheoned billet and brass finial. (Courtesy Author's Collection)

These boxes varied somewhat in dimension over the years, but typically measured 6 7/8 inches in length, 4 1/2 inches in height, and 1 3/4 or 1 7/8 inches in width. The top billet, or strap sometimes utilized a brass escutcheon for more secure closure. The McKeever pattern cartridge box remains in service today with the ceremonial guard at Arlington National Cemetery.[71]

Although multi-looped belts for metallic cartridges were not formally adopted by the military until 1876, they were in unofficial use among western troops for a decade previous (and no doubt originated during the Civil War). Sometimes referred to as "thimble belts" or "Fair Weather Christian Belts," these early, non-regulation cartridge belts differed considerably in pattern, often copying designs popular with civilian scouts, hunters and frontiersmen. Usually constructed of bridle-weight leather, or a combination of leather and canvas, most secured with a military belt plate and incorporated from 30 to 50 loops for the .50 or .45 caliber carbine ammunition then in issue.[72]

Captain Anson Mills, an early promoter of cartridge belt adoption in the army, portrayed the typical genesis of the non-standard form at Fort Bridger, Wyoming Territory, in 1866:

> Our equipment consisted of the regular old-fashioned cartridge box for paper cartridges to be carried in tin cases inside the leather boxes, and were wholly unsuited for metallic cartridges.... the metallic ammunition carried in these tin boxes rattled loudly, and were even noisy when carried by men on foot.

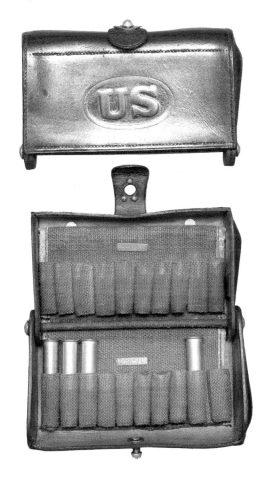

So I devised a belt, which the post saddler manufactured out of leather, with a loop for each of the fifty cartridges. The men wore these belts around their waists, and they proved much more comfortable and efficient than any other method of carrying cartridges.[73]

These belts naturally were subject to verdigris formation on the cartridges, but their use continued unabated until the army adopted a more suitable, regulation issue. As late as 1874, Charles King encountered such "homemade" equipage worn by an Arizona soldier: "...his waist was girt with a rude 'thimble-belt', in the loops of which were thrust scores of copper cartridges for carbine and pistol."[74]

As noted earlier, the Hazen pattern, sliding cartridge loop was the military's first, tentative move toward the official adoption of a regulation cartridge belt. Designed by Colonel William B. Hazen and first tested in 1867, this 20-round waist belt attachment was approved and described in Ordnance Memoranda No. l8 of 1874:

Two for each belt, each consisting of a strip of black bridle-leather, 7 3/4 inches long and 1 7/8 inches wide. To one side is sewed a piece of black collar-leather, making 12 loops for carbine-cartridges, to the other side is sewed three loops for the belt, one 5/8 inches wide at each end, and one in the middle 1 inch wide; between these [belt] loops are formed eight loops for carbine-cartridges, four on each side of the center loop. Each attachment thus contains twenty cartridges in a double row of loops.

The Board have recommended the addition of the [Hazen] cartridge loops, to be used with or without the [Dyer] pouch, so arranged as to distribute the weight of a large amount of ammunition [40 rounds total] as equally as possible upon the belt. These have been tested for a long time upon the frontier, and are used now by many in that locality.[75]

The Hazen attachment was manufactured in limited quantities at Watervliet and Benecia Arsenals. Like the non-regulation cartridge belts already in the field, it was constructed entirely of leather and permitted continual verdigris formation, an inherent vice ultimately unacceptable to the military.[76]

Still, the obvious preference among western troops for some form of cartridge belt remained pervasive, as witnessed in 1875 by an officer at Fort Laramie, Wyoming Territory:

...for field use, there is nothing equal in my opinion, to the thimble belt either in point of convenience or comfort, and all men taking the field provide themselves with it, if allowed to exercise their own judgement.[77]

The Ordnance Department finally succumbed to such admonitions in the fall of 1876, authorizing adoption of the first official U. S. military cartridge belt.

The impetus for this decision resulted in part from a field report rendered by Captain of Ordnance O. E. Michaelis in September of 1876 from the Military Department of Dakota:

...The prairie or loop belt is universally demanded, and is always worn by both Infantry and Cavalry....Colonel Miles of the 5th Infantry, informed me that his recruits, on the passage up the Missouri, were so anxious to obtain these belts that they sacrificed their suspenders in making them.

A belt, to fulfill all the necessary conditions, should offer no leather surface to the cartridges, for otherwise verdigrising will invariably ensue. It should be made of a leather body (the present waist belt will answer the purpose) covered with white duck, with loops of the same material attached.

I was very favorably impressed by a pattern of the loop belt worn by some companies of the 7th Cavalry. I understand that it is the invention of one of the company saddlers.[78]

Military Cartridge Belt. Field Alteration, 1870-1875. Originally manufactured as a plain waist or saber belt by Horstmann Brothers of Philadelphia, this specimen was modified by a post saddler or individual trooper for the carriage of self-contained ammunition. Constructed of black bridle leather, the body has an interior billet-and-claw arrangement for waist adjustment and secures with an 1851 Pattern Sword Belt Plate. Thirty-seven loops, or "thimbles," have been stitched around the belt face to accommodate .45 caliber carbine or pistol rounds. Sometimes referred to as "Fair Weather Christian Belts," such field alterations were quite common prior to the issue of the regulation "Prairie" pattern cartridge belt in 1876. (Courtesy Arizona Historical Society - Southern Arizona Division, Tucson)

Seeking to obviate the verdigris problem, this so-called Model 1876 "Prairie" belt had a leather body entirely sheathed in drab canvas and faced with sewn-on loops of varnished canvas. A double-layered tongue billet of black bridle leather extended beyond the canvas-covered body about 12 inches, securing at the opposite end in a double-frame buckle of varnished brass.

The Type One variant of the Model 1876 cartridge belt, fabricated in 5,000 units at Watervliet Arsenal during the winter of 1876-1877, typically measured 45 1/2 inches in length (including the buckle) and 2 1/16 inches in width. It accommodated 54 rounds of .45 caliber rifle or carbine ammunition in loops 1 3/4 inches in height. Acceptance among troops in the field was immediate and overwhelming, and the pattern gained widespread popularity with civilian buffalo hunters as well. Late in 1877, the Type Two variant of the "Prairie" belt went into production at Watervliet in 10,000 additional units. To better secure the cartridges and protect the uniform from lead residue, the loops were increased to 2 inches in height and the belt body to 2 1/2 inches in width.[79]

These belts were not intended or designed to carry additional equipage, such as the issue holster. Consequently, the pattern underwent a variety of field and arsenal modifications. Typical among cavalry troops was the attachment of a secondary billet or strap on either the interior or exterior of the belt at

Military Belt Holster with Field-Made Cartridge Belt. Makers Unknown, 1865-1875. This non-regulation rig combines a full-flapped, right-hand holster with an early, all-leather "thimble belt" looped for pistol cartridges. Fabricated of black, bridle-weight leather, the holster is of typical, commercial contract style with a sewn and riveted belt loop, flap-and-finial closure, semi-contoured main seam and sewn-in toe plug. The cartridge belt is constructed of black bridle leather with stitched-on loops of like material and utilizes the 1851 Pattern Sword Belt Plate for closure. With the outfit is a .44 caliber, Richards conversion of the Colt Model 1860 Army revolver. (Courtesy Herb Peck, Jr. Collection)

the billet end. Stitched or riveted in place, this leather had sufficient free length to mount the holster, pistol cartridge pouch or hunting knife scabbard, either singly or in combination. (For infantry, three metal rings were riveted and stitched into the lower edge of the belt to hang the bayonet scabbard; an additional 10,000 such belts, recognized as the Type Three variant, were fabricated in 1878 and first trialed by infantry units at Fort Abraham Lincoln, Dakota Territory.) Other variations of the military "Prairie" belt included an issue of 300 with loops for .50 caliber ammunition intended for auxiliary services like scouts and packers; and the rare Unger pattern belt fitted with double cartridge loops arranged one above the other.[80]

Although the Model 1876 cartridge belt represented a distinct advance in ammunition carriage, it did possess some defects. Specified with 54 cartridge loops, it often was too large for typically slim-waisted cavalry troopers; many were shortened and rebilleted to a capacity of 47 to 50 rounds. Worse, the loops tended to wear and separate from the canvas backing, resulting in the loss of cartridges. Anson Mills, still pursuing the ultimate cartridge carrier, overcame these problems with a belt fabricated entirely of loomed cotton webbing. This innovation incorporated integrally-woven cartridge loops that were inherently stronger than the sewn type, and utilized a "clip-on" belt plate and keeper adjustable for length.[81]

Lightweight, strong and comparatively inexpensive, the "Mills" pattern cartridge belt was recommended for adoption in 1879 under General Order No. 76:

> ...the board is very favorably impressed with the means devised by Major Anson Mills, 10th Cavalry, for weaving the cartridge belt and recommends it for adoption by the Ordnance Department in their manufacture.[82]

The first such belts, issued in mid-1880, actually were manufactured by the Gilbert Loom Company of Worcester, Massachusetts, under a five year contract for 40,000 units. Thereafter, production continued at Mills' own Worcester facility, under the direction of T. C. Orndorff, for the remainder of the century.[83]

The "Mills" patent cartridge belt issued in the West during the late Indian Wars era was of tan coloration and typically measured 39 inches in length by 3 inches in width. Forty-five cartridge loops, usually 2 1/4 inches in height, accommodated either of the .45 Government rounds for the issue carbine or rifle.[84] The belts generally were differentiated by their association with the various "H" pattern belt plates used for closure. While not clearly documented or defined in existing sources, at least four such plates were pertinent to the western military:

First Pattern — a comparatively narrow, two-piece plate of stamped sheet brass with raised "US" insignia in a recessed oval surrounded by a smooth field and raised peripheral border; circa 1880-1881. Split-front type; the left edge of the keeper forms the left border of the plate when secured. Unmarked; believed manufactured by Mills company. Height, circa 3 5/8 inches: width. circa 2 3/8 inches.

Second Pattern — a two-piece, cast brass plate with raised "US" in a recessed oval and having a raised peripheral border with beveled edge; circa 1882-1883. Split-front type with sliding rods on back belt ports for tightening the belt body. Unmarked; believed arsenal-manufactured. Height, circa 3 3/4 inches; width, circa 2 3/8 inches.

Third Pattern — a two-piece, cast and pressed brass plate with raised "US" insignia within a raised oval border and having a raised beveled edge; circa 1884-1885. Split-front type with same belt port/sliding rod system as in Second Pattern. Unmarked; believed arsenal-made. Height, circa 3 3/4 inches; width, circa 2 3/8 inches.

Fourth Pattern — a wider, one-piece plate of stamped sheet brass with raised "US" in a recessed oval and having a raised peripheral border with rounded edge; circa 1887-1895. Solid-front type with wide, integral tongue or hasp securing in a sheet brass end-piece. Marked: ANSON MILLS, PAT. FEB. 1, 1881/T. C. ORNDORFF SOLE MANF./WORCESTER, MASS./U.S.A. Height, circa 3 1/8 inches; width, circa 2 3/4 inches.[85]

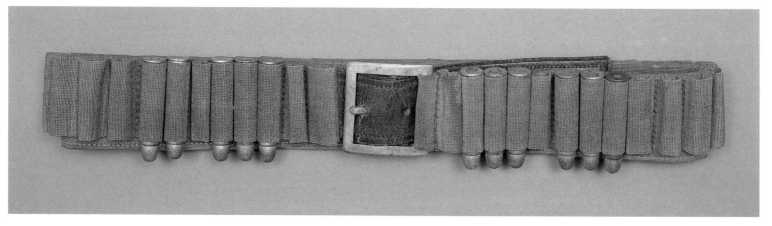

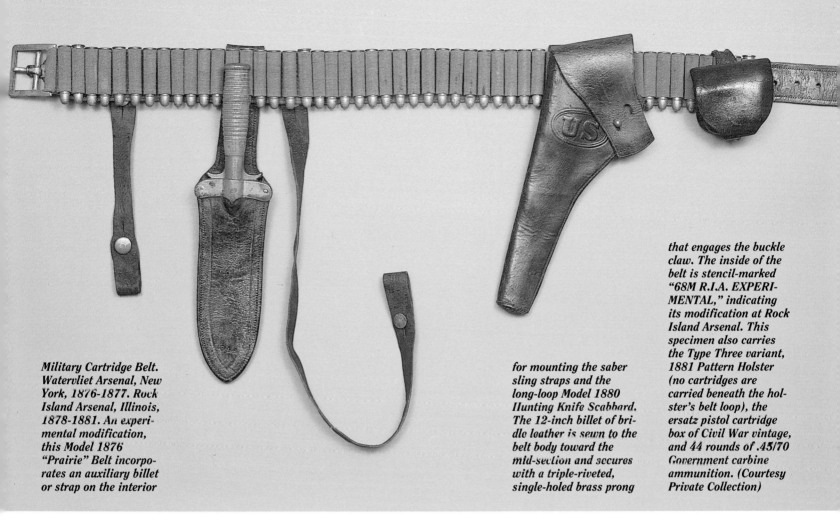

Military Cartridge Belt. Watervliet Arsenal, New York, 1876-1877. Rock Island Arsenal, Illinois, 1878-1881. An experimental modification, this Model 1876 "Prairie" Belt incorporates an auxiliary billet or strap on the interior for mounting the saber sling straps and the long-loop Model 1880 Hunting Knife Scabbard. The 12-inch billet of bridle leather is sewn to the belt body toward the mid-section and secures with a triple-riveted, single-holed brass prong that engages the buckle claw. The inside of the belt is stencil-marked "68M R.I.A. EXPERIMENTAL," indicating its modification at Rock Island Arsenal. This specimen also carries the Type Three variant, 1881 Pattern Holster (no cartridges are carried beneath the holster's belt loop), the ersatz pistol cartridge box of Civil War vintage, and 44 rounds of .45/70 Government carbine ammunition. (Courtesy Private Collection)

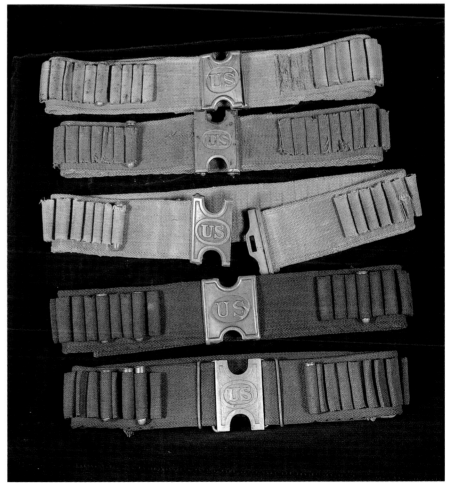

"Mills" Patent Cartridge Belts with Variant Plates. Top to bottom: (1) Tan web belt with First Pattern, Mills-manufactured plate, circa 1880; (2) Tan web belt with Second Pattern, arsenal-manufactured plate, circa 1882; (3) Tan web belt with Third Pattern, arsenal-manufactured plate, circa 1884; (4) Blue web belt with Fourth Pattern, Mills-manufactured plate, circa 1888; and (5) Blue web belt with Fifth Pattern, arsenal-manufactured plate, circa 1894. (Courtesy Hayes Otoupalik Collection. Image courtesy Bill Manns)

47

Military Cartridge Belt. T. C. Orndorff, Worcester, Massachusetts, 1887-1895. Constructed of loomed cotton, this "Mills" pattern belt incorporates 50 integrally-woven cartridge loops and the Fourth Pattern (1887), stamped "H" plate with "US" emboss. The belt body is pierced with 13 unequally spaced grommets for thong or hanger mounting of the hunting knife sheath, revolver holster, etc. Three grommets are spaced vertically at each end of the body so that two belts could be thong-laced to make a 100-round bandoleer. (Courtesy Private Collection)

Military Cartridge Belt. Rock Island Arsenal, Illinois, 1881-1887. A regulation alteration of the standard "Mills" cartridge belt with brass closure plate and keeper, this Model "1881" Cavalry Belt was especially adapted for mounted service. The body of typical webbed fabric is mounted with sewn-on, billet and chape leathers for closure in a double-frame brass buckle similar to that used on the earlier, "Prairie" pattern belt. A brass hook for dismounted carriage of the saber is fixed on the lower edge of the body with a double-riveted chape. As specified in Ordnance Memoranda No. 29 of 1885/1891, the belt is of No. 1 size, having 45 integrally-woven loops for the .45/70 Govt. cartridge. (Courtesy Private Collection)

During the early 1890s, beyond the purview of this treatment, a fifth, cast belt plate was introduced about concurrent with the appearance of the simpler, "C" type closure of brass wire. At the same time, belts of dark blue fabric, often having riveted brass end-tips, came into service.[86]

As suggested by the rapid succession of design changes in the first three "Mills" belt plates, these evidently proved somewhat unserviceable, particularly for mounted troops. The problem no doubt lay in the method of closure, which utilized a relatively insecure, single hasp-and-slot arrangement of comparatively small size. Consequently, between 1881 and 1887, several thousand "Mills" pattern belts were modified especially for cavalry use by Rock Island Arsenal. The issue plates and keepers were replaced with stitched-on leather billets and chapes for closure with double-frame brass buckles.[87]

This modified, "Mills" cavalry belt was described in Ordnance Memoranda No. 29:

WOVEN CARTRIDGE BELT

The belt is of a uniform gray [sic] color. At the left-hand end is sewed a black leather chape, embracing in its fold a brass bar buckle and the belt. At the right-hand end a billet with a leather lining. The chape and billet, where joined to the belt, to be of its full width, then abruptly narrowed down to 1 1/2 inches and placed close to the cartridge loops....The belt to be manufactured in 2 sizes, and issued to troops in equal proportions, unless otherwise called for.No. 1, with 45 loops. No. 2, with 50 loops.[88]

In general appearance, these altered cartridge belts were very reminiscent of the earlier "Prairie" pattern. Issued in two variations, the so-called Model "1881" Cavalry Belt utilized a buckle virtually identical to the "Prairie" variety, while the Model "1886" version had a buckle of round brass stock with rounded corners. Ultimately, the closure problem on regular "Mills" cartridge belts was overcome with the 1887 pattern belt plate, which employed a larger, curved hasp that "locked" firmly into the keeper.

In its adoption of various gunleather elements, the U. S. Military revealed both practical and impractical characteristics. From the 1830s through the 1850s, when the standing army was relatively small, it was generally responsive to improvements in arms technology and readily adopted appropriate leather equipage whenever possible. Belt-mounted pistol holsters, for example, rapidly supplanted the use of pommel holsters during the late 1850s. But, as observed earlier, this "experimenting" attitude resulted in a continuing absence of true pattern standardization.

Conversely, while constrained after the Civil War by tight budgets and mounds of surplus material, the military was overly conservative in its selection of practical gear. This was perhaps nowhere more apparent than in the failure to adopt a full, saddle-mounted carbine scabbard for cavalry service prior to the mid-1890s. Nevertheless, the army left a rich legacy of gunleather in the frontier West.

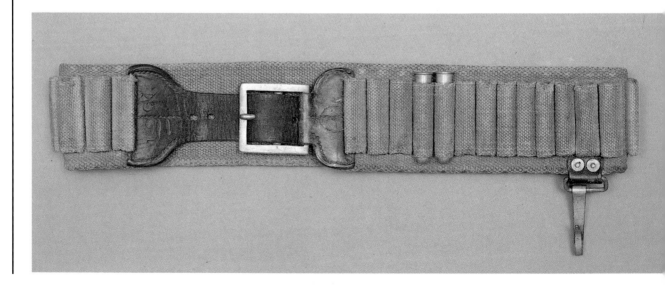

Military Cartridge Belt. T. C. Orndorff, Worcester, Massachusetts, 1882-1883. Developed by Major Anson Mills, the "Mills" pattern woven cartridge belt was adopted by the U.S. military in 1880 and issued in various forms into the twentieth century. The body of loomed cotton webbing has 45 integrally-woven cartridge loops and is fitted with the Second Pattern (1882) cast "H" plate with "US" emboss. Note that the plate is the split-front type with full belt ports and adjustable tightening rods, perhaps manufactured at Springfield Arsenal. (Courtesy Gene Autry Western Heritage Museum, Los Angeles)

*Yellow Coyote, a Chiricahua Apache scout photographed around 1886, displays two variations of the "Mills" patent, woven cartridge belt. At top is a field-modified version with stitched and riveted leather billets secured with a single-frame, roller buckle. Immediately below is a regulation, all fabric version with the Third Pattern, "H" plate with "US" emboss. Both belts are fully loaded with .45/70 Govt. rounds for the Model 1873 Springfield carbine.
(Image courtesy Herb Peck, Jr. Collection)*

PART TWO

CIVILIAN GUNLEATHER

Between 1830 and 1860, increasing numbers of civilians penetrated the inhospitable and often hostile reaches of the trans-Mississippi West. Whether they were Santa Fe traders, Texas settlers, California gold seekers or Oregon emigrants, these independent agents of "Manifest Destiny" approached the frontier with a plethora of weaponry. Ranging from single-shot, pepperbox and early revolving cylinder pistols to the ubiquitous American rifle in its Kentucky, mid-western and plains variations, this armament was accompanied by an equally diverse panoply of attendant gunleather.

Following the Civil War, continuing migration and the widespread incursion of railroads into the West brought rapid change. New mining districts opened, cattle droving flourished, town building boomed and lawlessness held sway in many areas. New repeating arms, notably the various Colt revolvers and Winchester rifles and carbines, were adopted whole-sale by many characters in this nascent society. Unsettled conditions throughout much of the West guaranteed that guns and gunleather would remain essential elements of civilian material culture well into the 1890s.[1]

Unlike military equipage, the gunleather employed by civilians in the West was not subject to imposed standards of uniformity. Rather, much early material was characterized by its diversity in form and quality. As early as the 1850s, however, isolated regional artisans were crafting and establishing wholly-new gunleather patterns that were better suited to frontier conditions. These indigenous western creations, particularly the "California" pattern belt holster, generally surpassed eastern and military forms both in utility and aesthetic character. Even prior to the coming of the railroads, such "native" material proliferated fairly rapidly over various regions of the West.

While cognizant of the requirements of their often rough-and-ready clientele, frontier gunleather makers also were responsive to advances in the design technology of arms and ammunition. The production of practical cartridge belts and carbine and rifle scabbards, coupled with the formulation of the innovative "Mexican Loop" pattern holster, were all indicative of adaptation to such change. By the late 1880s, with increasing cohesion in communication and commerce, basic gunleather elements and patterns had become nearly universal throughout the West, differing only in individual interpretations of style and embellishment.[2]

Eastern leather goods manufacturers and commercial supply houses provided inexpensive gunleather to westerners throughout the latter half of the nineteenth century, invariably offering a selection of articles closely patterned on indigenous frontier forms. But arguably the best and most sought-after gunleather in the West was fabricated by the many saddleries scattered over the still-unsettled plains and mountains. Although gunleather was but a sideline to the saddle trade, these artisans usually supplied custom-patterned goods typified by superior materials, design and craftsmanship.

By the 1880s, the best of these saddleries had established regional markets and most had commenced stamping their gunleather with maker's marks or cartouches. The more successful and enterprising saddlers generally offered a number of styles of holsters, scabbards and cartridge belts, often providing gradations in leather quality and degree of ornamentation. For the most talented, or pragmatic, such as H. H. Heiser and S. D. Myres, gunleather nearly supplanted saddles as the mainstay of business.[3] As in Part One, this survey of civilian gunleather presents a broad overview of representative specimens.

John Woodhouse Audubon's watercolor sketch, "The Forty-niner," portrays the civilian use of saddle-mounted pommel holsters for the carriage of pistols among overland gold seekers in the Southwest. The pair on the left appear to be of asymmetrical design for large-frame revolvers and are fixed with end caps. Those on the right suggest symmetrical construction of para-military design. (Image courtesy The Southwest Museum, Los Angeles, California)

POMMEL HOLSTERS AND POMMEL BAG-HOLSTERS

In the decades prior to the Civil War, civilians on the frontier had recourse to a variety of large-bore, single-shot handguns generically referred to as "horse pistols," "dragoon pistols" or "holster pistols." These hefty, often cumbersome weapons, which were popular in running buffalo from horseback as well as for defense, typically were carried in pairs in saddle-mounted pommel holsters. No doubt inspired by the military, civilians certainly were utilizing pommel holsters during the 1830s, thus introducing one of the first commercially made gunleather elements into the West.[4]

Following the Oregon Trail in 1846, Francis Parkman noted that pommel holsters often were included in the equipage of overland travelers:

> His outfit, which resembled mine, had been provided with a view to use rather than ornament. It consisted of a plain, black Spanish saddle, with holsters of heavy pistols, a blanket rolled up behind, and the trail rope attached to his horse's neck hanging coiled in front.[5]

Parkman's observation was reiterated by Englishman William Kelly, who departed for California in the early 1850s with a party "...well equipped, each man carrying in his belt a revolver, a sword, and bowie-knife; the mounted men having besides a pair of holster-pistols and rifle slung from the horn of their saddles...."[6]

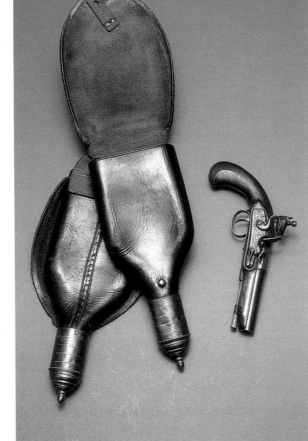

Para-Military Pommel Holsters for Single-Shot Pistols. Maker Unknown, 1835-1845. A non-regulation pattern for private purchase, this rather diminutive set is designed to hold a pair of medium-sized flint or percussion pistols. The molded holster bodies are constructed of black bridle-weight leather with brass end-caps, and have sewn-on covers with strap-and-finial closures. The accompanying pistol is a .41 caliber, flintlock reproduction by G. Thomson, c. 1950. (Courtesy Private Collection)

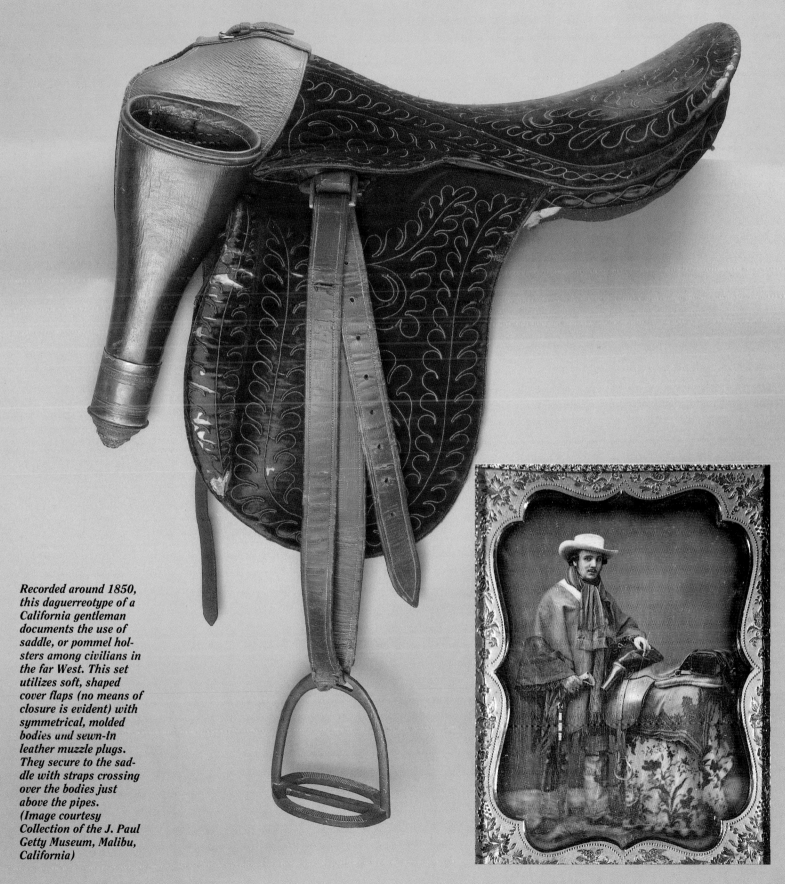

Para-Military Pommel Holsters for Single-Shot Horse Pistols. Maker Unknown, 1840-1845. Acquired by Captain James Donaldson while serving in the Mexican War, this riding saddle and pommel holster outfit probably was made for a gentleman officer. The holster bodies are constructed of lightweight, red morocco leather sewn over molded, paste-board forms with wire-reinforced throats and brass end-caps. The holsters are without cover flaps and provide no apparent means for securing them. (National Cowboy Hall of Fame Collection)

Recorded around 1850, this daguerreotype of a California gentleman documents the use of saddle, or pommel holsters among civilians in the far West. This set utilizes soft, shaped cover flaps (no means of closure is evident) with symmetrical, molded bodies and sewn-in leather muzzle plugs. They secure to the saddle with straps crossing over the bodies just above the pipes. (Image courtesy Collection of the J. Paul Getty Museum, Malibu, California)

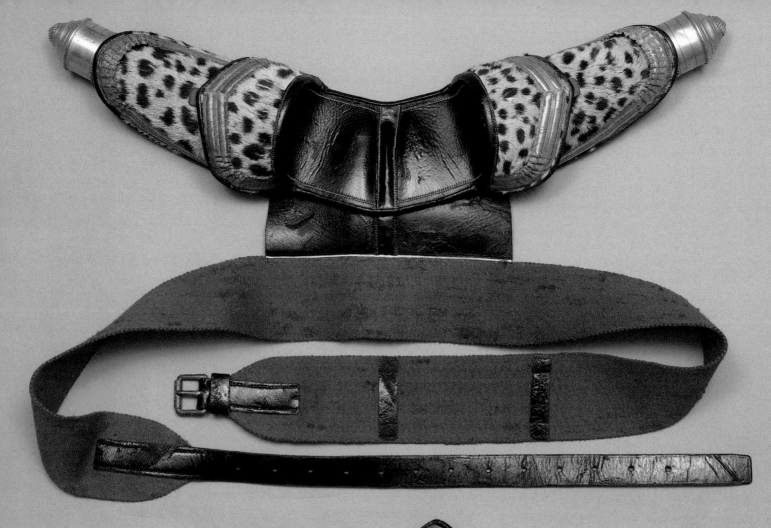

Civilian Pommel Holsters for Single-Shot Pistols or Colt Dragoon Model Revolvers. Maker Unknown, 1850-1860. *Probably crafted in southern California for a gentleman of means, this set is semi-military in design but made of fair russet leather. The molded holster bodies are constructed of heavy saddle-skirting with brass end-caps and button finials. The separate, one-piece cover is pattern-shaped and decorated with a hand-carved floral motif over a punch-dot background. (Courtesy Private Collection)*

Para-Military Pommel Holsters for Medium-Sized Percussion Pistols. Maker Unknown, 1845-1855. *Probably of Mexican origin, this diminutive outfit combines unusual design and embellishment. Fabricated of russet skirting leather, the symmetrical holster bodies are stitched to a rectangular connecting strap of black patent leather, which in turn is sewn to a tightly woven surcingle of red wool. Both the shaped cover flaps and the facing panels of the holsters are finished with leopard skin and bordered with silver bullion trim. Decorative end caps of nickel silver complete the ornamentation. Secured directly to the horse via the surcingle, this colorful rig probably was used in conjunction with a light riding, or pad saddle. (Courtesy Museum of the Horse)*

Westering civilians no doubt often employed pommel holsters of military origin — or patterns that closely paralleled martial forms. Commercial leather goods manufacturers like Thornton Grimsley of St. Louis and Main & Winchester of San Francisco, both of which produced pommel holsters on contract for the army, also probably supplied like material to overland traders, emigrants and gold seekers. Others, such as Rice & Childress of San Antonio, presumably followed suit in providing saddle-mounted holsters to the "ranging companies" of Texas and to other frontiersmen in the Southwest.[7]

Like their military cousins, civilian pommel holsters incorporated form-molded, symmetrically contoured bodies that encased the intended pistols almost entirely. (The later adoption of asymmetrical holster bodies by the army appears to have been coincident in the commercial trade.) Shaped cover flaps shrouded the upper holster bodies, while brass end caps usually enclosed the extremities of the pipes. Unlike the single holster and utility pouch pattern common to the military, however, civilian pommel holsters typically combined two holster bodies joined either with an integral or separately sewn connecting leather. The use of russet leather also frequently appeared in lieu of the army's uniform issue of black-dyed leather.

By the mid-1850s, commercially made, civilian pommel holsters fabricated in the Southwest often reflected a degree of Mexican influence in styling and embellishment. Surviving examples suggest that these well-made, finely ornamented specimens probably were intended to outfit gentlemen riders rather than hard-bitten frontier types. An example of the proliferation of this cultural borrowing appears in the para-military pommel holsters that accompanied a presentation saddle made in 1862 by E. L. Gallatin of Denver for Colonel Jesse Leavenworth.[8]

With the increasing availability of revolving cylinder handguns during the 1850s, most civilians in the West quickly adopted belt-mounted holsters, particularly for the compact Colt Navy revolver. But, for those denizens of the frontier who felt a continuing need for additional firepower, pommel holsters remained in service for at least another decade. Early Arizona pioneer John Cremony, who lived among the Apache Indians during the 1850s and 1860s, later recalled going armed with "...four Colt's six-shooters, two in my saddle-holsters and two in my belt, with a

Civilian Pommel Holsters for Colt Model 1851 Navy Revolvers. Maker Unknown, 1855-1865. Of stylish design, this set incorporates asymmetrical, form-molded bodies stitched to a pierced and contoured connecting leather that also forms the upper back panels of the holsters. Fabricated of black bridle leather, the outfit has separate, sewn-on cover flaps with strap-and-finial closures and small, heart-shaped motifs stitched on the faces. Brass end caps finish the pipes. (Courtesy the Smithsonian Institution)

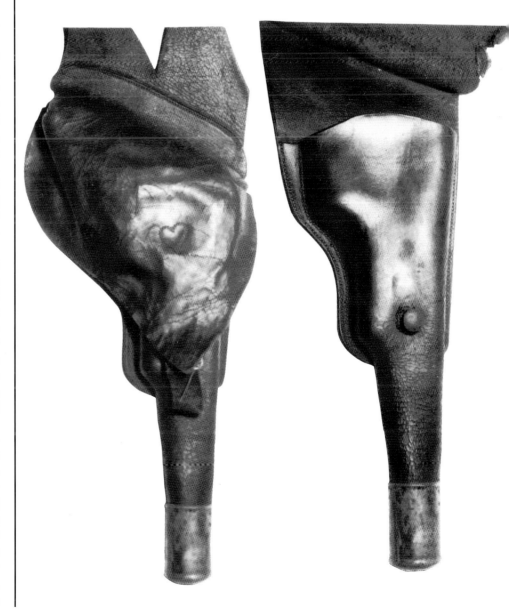

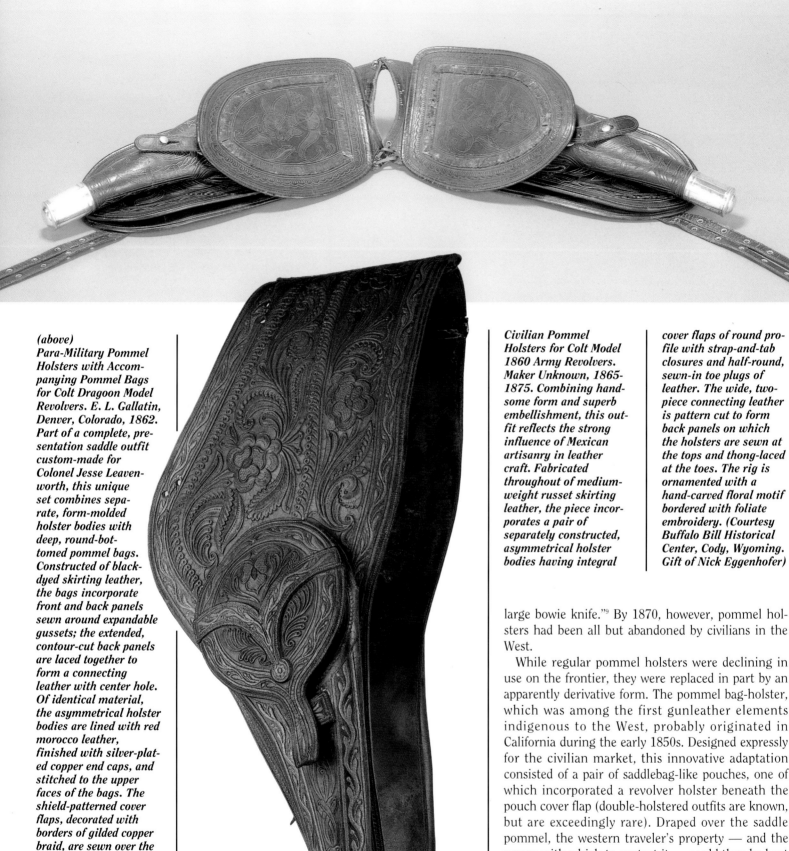

(above)
Para-Military Pommel Holsters with Accompanying Pommel Bags for Colt Dragoon Model Revolvers. E. L. Gallatin, Denver, Colorado, 1862. Part of a complete, presentation saddle outfit custom-made for Colonel Jesse Leavenworth, this unique set combines separate, form-molded holster bodies with deep, round-bottomed pommel bags. Constructed of black-dyed skirting leather, the bags incorporate front and back panels sewn around expandable gussets; the extended, contour-cut back panels are laced together to form a connecting leather with center hole. Of identical material, the asymmetrical holster bodies are lined with red morocco leather, finished with silver-plated copper end caps, and stitched to the upper faces of the bags. The shield-patterned cover flaps, decorated with borders of gilded copper braid, are sewn over the mouths of the bags and holsters and secure with strap-and-finial closures. All surface elements are incised and carved with finely executed floral and border ornamentation. (Courtesy Colorado Historical Society)

Civilian Pommel Holsters for Colt Model 1860 Army Revolvers. Maker Unknown, 1865-1875. Combining handsome form and superb embellishment, this outfit reflects the strong influence of Mexican artisanry in leather craft. Fabricated throughout of medium-weight russet skirting leather, the piece incorporates a pair of separately constructed, asymmetrical holster bodies having integral cover flaps of round profile with strap-and-tab closures and half-round, sewn-in toe plugs of leather. The wide, two-piece connecting leather is pattern cut to form back panels on which the holsters are sewn at the tops and thong-laced at the toes. The rig is ornamented with a hand-carved floral motif bordered with foliate embroidery. (Courtesy Buffalo Bill Historical Center, Cody, Wyoming. Gift of Nick Eggenhofer)

large bowie knife."[9] By 1870, however, pommel holsters had been all but abandoned by civilians in the West.

While regular pommel holsters were declining in use on the frontier, they were replaced in part by an apparently derivative form. The pommel bag-holster, which was among the first gunleather elements indigenous to the West, probably originated in California during the early 1850s. Designed expressly for the civilian market, this innovative adaptation consisted of a pair of saddlebag-like pouches, one of which incorporated a revolver holster beneath the pouch cover flap (double-holstered outfits are known, but are exceedingly rare). Draped over the saddle pommel, the western traveler's property — and the means with which to protect it — could thus be kept in convenient proximity. The pommel bag-holster was of sufficient utility that Wells Fargo & Company evidently purchased a number for use in its mail service to the scattered mining camps of the Mother Lode country.[10]

Sometimes referred to as cantenas,[11] pommel bag-holsters usually were constructed of medium-weight

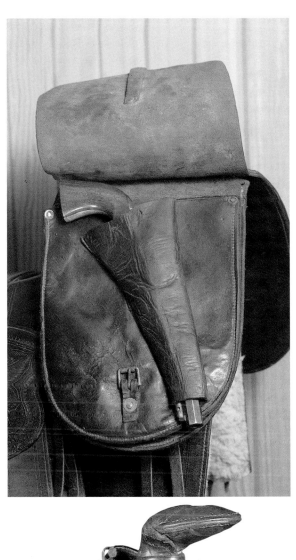

Civilian Pommel Bag-Holster for Colt Model 1849 Pocket Revolver. Main & Winchester, San Francisco, California, 1850-1860. Made for the commercial market, this pommel bag-holster, or cantana, features a "half-pouch" holster beneath the right cover flap. Constructed of dark russet skirting leather in the manner of regular saddlebags, the piece has two expandable bags with separate covers ornamented in incised-line floral motif. These elements are joined at the top seam by a laced thong closure designed to slip over the saddle pommel horn. The cover straps are secured with copper rivets and fixed with single-frame iron roller buckles. Accompanying the piece is a .31 caliber, Colt Model 1849 Pocket revolver. (Courtesy Bill Mackin Collection)

(left)
Pommel Bag-Holster for Colt Model 1851 Navy Revolver. Main & Winchester, San Francisco, California, 1850-1860. Another early variant in the Main & Winchester line, this rather diminutive pommel bag-holster set incorporates a very typical, incised and carved floral motif with multiple border elements. Fabricated of medium-weight russet skirting leather, the bags, connecting leathers and cover flaps are of standard design. The sewn-in holster body is contour-fit to the intended weapon and features a straight throat and open toe. It holds a .36 caliber percussion, Model 1851 Colt Navy revolver. (Courtesy R.M. Bachman Collection. Image courtesy Bill Manns)

Pommel Bag-Holster for Medium-Frame Revolvers. Victor Earnshields Saddlery, Marysville, California, 1865-1875. Prominently stamped with a "Wells Fargo & Co." inscription, this rig probably saw service in the gold fields of northern California. Fabricated of medium-weight russet skirting leather, the gusseted bags are deep and square-bottomed with a tapered half-holster sewn on the right, off side face. Unlike most specimens, the cover flaps are sewn and thong-laced to the connecting leather and cover the bags only partially. Adorned with a fern frond border ornament, the covers secure with riveted straps that engage rectangular, double-frame harness buckles. (Image courtesy George T. Jackson)

(left and opposite page) Pommel Bag-Holster for Colt Model 1851 Navy Revolver. Main & Winchester, San Francisco, California, 1860-1870. An interesting departure from the typical Main & Winchester product, this handsome set incorporates unusual, recurved cover flaps with fine border tooling around richly hand-carved floral and foliate fields. Manufactured of medium-weight russet skirting material, the pouch bodies are of familiar design, while the cover flaps differ in being buckled behind the saddle horn instead of thong-laced. Still in superb condition, the outfit accommodates a .36 caliber percussion, Colt 1851 Navy revolver. (Courtesy R.M. Bachman Collection. Image courtesy Bill Manns)

This cut from Main & Winchester's circa 1898 wholesale catalog illustrates their more embellished pommel bag-holster outfits, or cantenas. These examples differed little in construction from those of 40 years earlier. A plain, edge-creased variant also was available for $4.50.

MAIN & WINCHESTER : SAN FRANCISCO, CAL.   71

SADDLE CANTENAS.

When ordered with Saddle will be stamped to match. They can be detached and the Saddle is complete without them. For illustration of application see Saddles No 141 and 142, page 3. Saddles No 090 and 091 page 18, Saddle No 110, page 43 of this catalogue

No. 2 Saddle Cantena.
No 2, Full Flower Raised Stamp, black Angora goat flaps, pockets with gusset, off side pocket has pistol holster under flap
per pair $12 00

No. 5 Saddle Cantena.
No 5, Full Flower Raised Stamp, black Angora goat flaps, pockets with gusset, off side pocket has pistol holster under flap
per pair $9 00

No. 3 Saddle Cantena.
No 3 Full Flower Raised Stamp, pockets with gusset, off side pocket has pistol holster under flap   per pair, $9 00

russet skirting leather. The typically round-bottomed pouches were formed with front and rear panels sewn around the periphery to an expandable gusset for increased capacity. The back panels extended above the pouch bodies to form half of the thong-laced connecting leather, which usually was shaped with a center hole to slip over the saddle horn. Separate, full-profile cover flaps shrouded the pouches and secured with riveted, strap-and-buckle closures. The holster, consisting of either a half- or whole-body design, was contoured to the intended revolver and sewn (and sometimes riveted) to the outer face of the off (right) side pouch. In most instances, the weapon was completely hidden from view when the pouch cover flap was secured.

From its probable birthplace in Gold Rush-era-California, the pommel bag-holster rig dispersed throughout the West during ensuing decades. Known, maker-marked specimens provide some indication of both the regional migration and stylistic evolution of the type. Main & Winchester of San Francisco, which may have devised the form, certainly was among the earliest and most prolific manufacturers. Surviving examples of its work, dating from the mid-1850s and 1860s, typically were fitted for Colt's 1849 Pocket and 1851 Navy revolvers. The pouch cover flaps usually were embellished in relatively full coverage with incised-line or hand-carved floral motifs, although flaps finished with angora goat hair or seal skin were available as well.[12]

By the 1870s and 1880s, inter-mountain and plains saddlers, such as W. L. Pickard & Son of Salt Lake City, The Denver Manufacturing Company and H. H. Heiser of Denver and S. C. Gallup of Pueblo, were fabricating pommel bag-holsters of similar pattern. Sometimes a bit larger in scale, these later gun-leather products typically accommodated the Colt Single Action Army revolver or a pistol of like proportion. Due to the size of the weapon, usually having a 7 1/2-inch barrel, these outfits often utilized a holster body that protruded somewhat beyond the bottom of the supporting pouch and cover flap. While full, carved or stamped ornamentation was available, most late-nineteenth-century specimens generally featured only a simple, rolled borderline tracing the periphery of the cover flaps and connecting leathers.[13]

Although the pommel bag-holster offered little advantage over roomier saddlebags and more accessible belt holsters, it apparently enjoyed a limited popularity in western regions into the 1890s. The venerable Main & Winchester firm carried four variations of the cantena in its 1898 product line, ranging in price from $4.50 to $12.00 depending on style and embellishment. And, as late as 1900, the R. T. Frazier saddlery of Pueblo offered "Cantinas, full raised stamped, with Holster [or]...plain finished, with Holster" for $6.00 and $4.00, respectively. By the latter year, however, the pommel bag-holster clearly had outlived both its utility and its market in the then, largely settled West.[14]

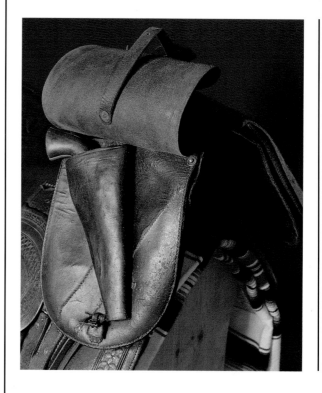

Pommel Bag-Holster for Colt Model 1851 Navy Revolver. Main & Winchester, San Francisco, California, 1865-1875. Yet another specimen of Main & Winchester leathercraft, this set incorporates a sewn-in half-pouch holster with typical gusseted bags and full-profile, foliate and floral-carved cover flaps secured by roller buckles. (Courtesy Richard Ellis Publications. Paul Goodwin, Photographer)

Pommel Bag-Holster for Small and Medium-Frame Revolvers. J. P. Mason, Sacramento, California, 1860-1870. Stamped in four places with the maker's cartouche, this outfit actually was used by an express company rider in the California mining country. Constructed of dark russet skirting leather, the cantenas are of typical design and feature a tapered, non-contoured holster body on the off-side pouch. The holster retains a .36 caliber percussion, Colt Model 1862 Police revolver with 4 1/2-inch barrel. (Courtesy R.M. Bachman Collection)

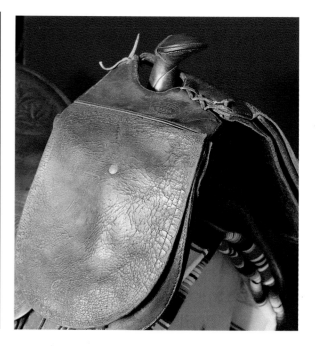

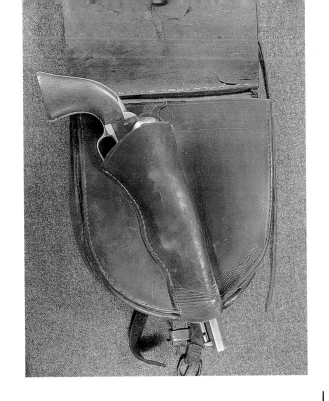

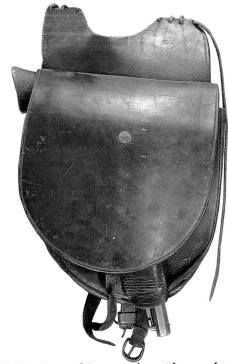

Pommel Bag-Holster for Colt Model 1851 Navy Revolver. Maker Unknown, 1865-1875. Completely unembellished, this comparatively inexpensive outfit is typical of small saddlery production during the late percussion era. Fabricated of medium-weight russet leather and of simple design, the set incorporates a sewn-on half-pouch holster with a slightly arched throat profile and contoured main seam. The flap closure straps secure with relatively atypical, small brass harness buckles. (Courtesy John E. Fox Collection)

Civilian Pommel Bag-Holster for Colt Single Action Army Revolver. H. H. Heiser Saddlery, Denver, Colorado, 1880-1890. Designed much like saddlebags, this pommel bag-holster outfit incorporates a contour-fit holster beneath the right flap. Constructed of dark russet harness leather, the piece has two expandable pouches joined by thong-laced connecting panels and covered by flaps ornamented with rolled border lines and Heiser's "Triple H" trademark. The holster body is secured by two copper rivets and features an arched throat profile, sewn main seam, and open toe. Closure straps are attached with copper rivets and fixed with single-frame iron roller buckles. The holster contains a .38 caliber, Colt Single Action Army revolver with 7 1/2-inch barrel. (Courtesy Bill Mackin Collection)

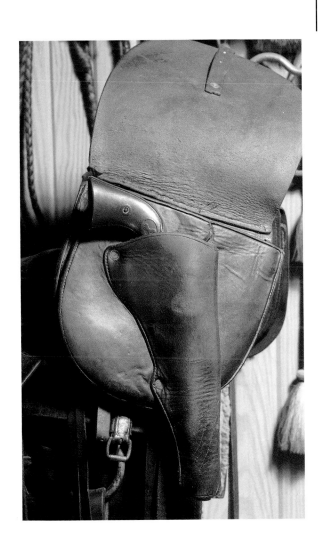

Civilian Pistol Holster with Plain Waist Belt. Makers Unknown, 1840-1850. This relatively rare assemblage is representative of eastern-made gunleather introduced into the West during the era of Manifest Destiny. Constructed of stiff black bridle leather, the right-hand, open-topped holster has a sewn main seam and open toe. Two vertical slits in the back of the upper body are used for belt mounting in lieu of a separate loop. The waist belt, made of light bridle leather, utilizes a single-frame, japanned harness buckle and a separate tongue billet (riveted on the inside) for closure. With the outfit is a .44 caliber percussion, Kentucky-pattern pistol made by Truitt Brothers, Philadelphia. (Courtesy Private Collection)

Eastern Belt Holsters In The West

While substantial "horse pistols" were perhaps most obvious on the early frontier, smaller single-shot pistols, pepperboxes and revolvers also were commonplace among westering civilians. These weapons typically were thrust beneath a waist belt or carried in a pocket. But illustrative evidence indicates that, at least by the mid-1840s, such handguns also were conveyed in belt-mounted holsters. By the early 1850s, even the large Walker and Dragoon Colts sometimes were housed in holsters that slipped over a waist belt. Throughout most of the ante-bellum period, the majority of this gunleather was supplied by eastern manufacturers and brought into the West by emigrant settlers, traders and prospectors.[15]

Decidedly rare and invariably unmarked, early belt holsters reveal little information for comparison and classification. The most rudimentary form — actually not a true holster — consisted of an open-ended leather loop or sleeve fixed vertically on the face of a relatively wide waist belt. Retaining a single-shot or pepperbox pistol about the upper barrel, such a rig provided ready access but little protection from the elements. Much more common were separate holsters, or "pistol cases," which mounted over the belt through two vertical slits cut in the upper back of the holster body, or by means of a sewn and/or riveted back-loop.

The copiously armed gentleman in this early 1850s daguerreotype carries what appears to be an Allen & Thurber pepperbox pistol in a rare and unusual, proto-holster. The "holster" consists of a folded and sewn leather belt loop that extends below the belt and is fixed with a circular leather socket of sufficient diameter to accommodate the barrel cluster. Such a socket-type design probably was peculiar to pepperbox arms. (Image courtesy John McWilliams Collection)

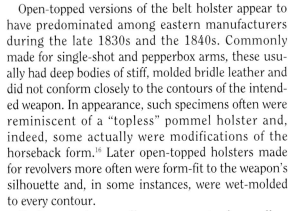

This late 1840s daguerreotype captures a young adventurer whose armament includes a brace of Allen or Marston pepperbox pistols housed in molded, open-topped belt holsters with concave throats and sewn-in toe plugs. (Image courtesy Herb Peck, Jr., Collection)

Open-topped versions of the belt holster appear to have predominated among eastern manufacturers during the late 1830s and the 1840s. Commonly made for single-shot and pepperbox arms, these usually had deep bodies of stiff, molded bridle leather and did not conform closely to the contours of the intended weapon. In appearance, such specimens often were reminiscent of a "topless" pommel holster and, indeed, some actually were modifications of the horseback form.[16] Later open-topped holsters made for revolvers more often were form-fit to the weapon's silhouette and, in some instances, were wet-molded to every contour.

Early examples usually were open-toed as well as open-topped. By the late 1840s, however, toe plugs were introduced to strengthen the holster body against collapse and preclude debris from entering the muzzle of the pistol. (Over time, such an arrangement actually served to collect debris entering at the throat of the pouch.)

By the early 1850s, belt-mounted holsters having full cover flaps were rapidly supplanting the open-topped variety, and this new form was to predominate among eastern gunleather manufacturers for the next several decades. Invariably patterned for the many revolvers then gaining favor, these flap-topped holsters were designed to better secure the weapon and protect it from moisture and dirt that might foul the cylinder. While it has been argued that these civilian flap holsters copied U. S. military designs, photo-

This daguerreotype from the mid-1840s portrays a young militiaman(?) carrying a brace of single-shot percussion pistols. The weapons are retained within open-ended leather sleeves sewn to the face of a plain leather waist belt. A precursor of true pistol holsters, this rudimentary rig was of civilian, rather than military, origin. (Image courtesy Herb Peck, Jr. Collection)

Photographed around 1850, the young Californian on the right carries a silver-mounted quirt and a hefty, Colt Walker revolver worn in cross draw position. The weapon is retained in a full-flapped, civilian belt holster (the cover flap has been folded back) with straight throat, contoured main seam, cross-strap closure and open toe. (Image courtesy Dr. William Schultz Collection)

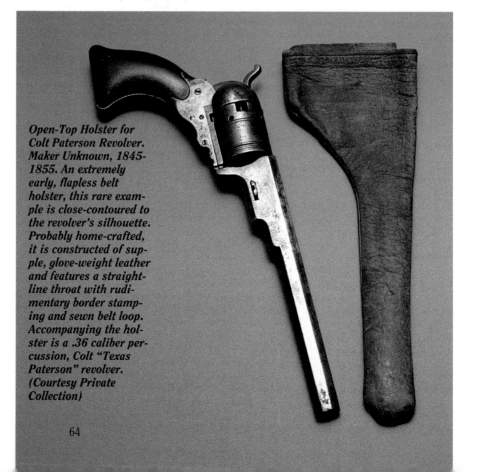

Open-Top Holster for Colt Paterson Revolver. Maker Unknown, 1845-1855. An extremely early, flapless belt holster, this rare example is close-contoured to the revolver's silhouette. Probably home-crafted, it is constructed of supple, glove-weight leather and features a straight-line throat with rudimentary border stamping and sewn belt loop. Accompanying the holster is a .36 caliber percussion, Colt "Texas Paterson" revolver. (Courtesy Private Collection)

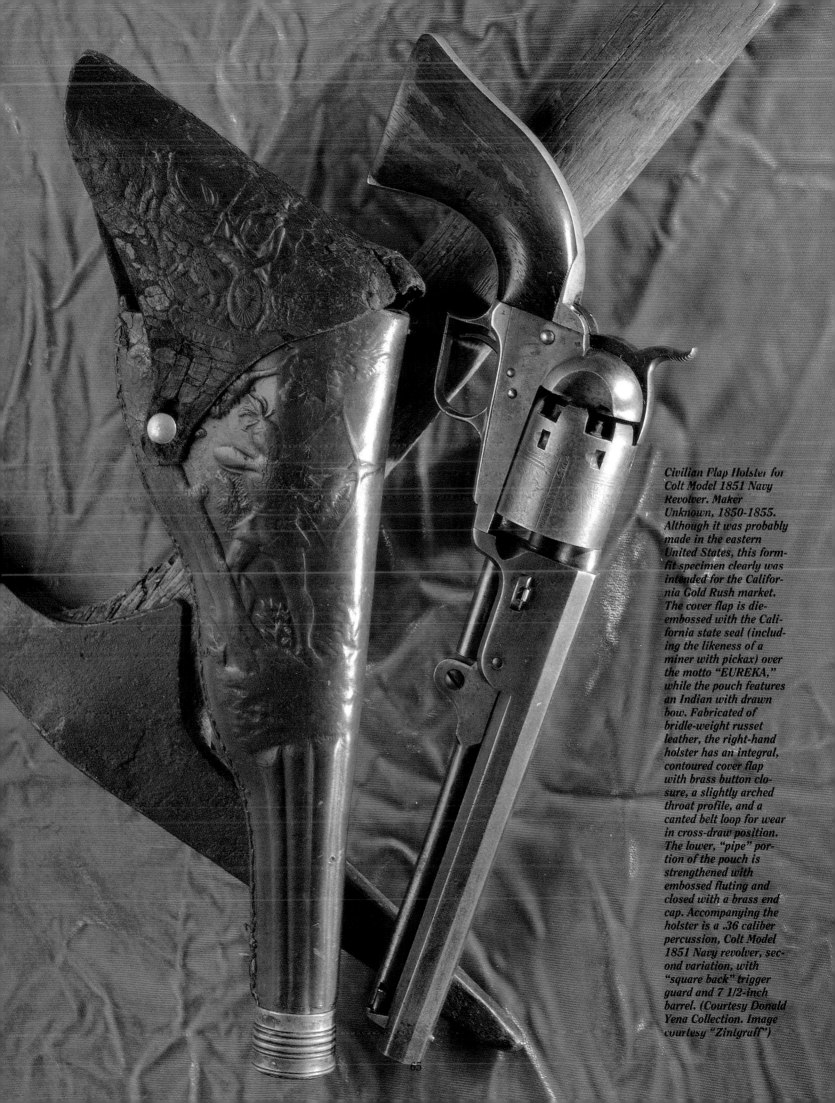

Civilian Flap Holster for Colt Model 1851 Navy Revolver. Maker Unknown, 1850-1855. Although it was probably made in the eastern United States, this form-fit specimen clearly was intended for the California Gold Rush market. The cover flap is die-embossed with the California state seal (including the likeness of a miner with pickax) over the motto "EUREKA," while the pouch features an Indian with drawn bow. Fabricated of bridle-weight russet leather, the right-hand holster has an integral, contoured cover flap with brass button closure, a slightly arched throat profile, and a canted belt loop for wear in cross-draw position. The lower, "pipe" portion of the pouch is strengthened with embossed fluting and closed with a brass end cap. Accompanying the holster is a .36 caliber percussion, Colt Model 1851 Navy revolver, second variation, with "square back" trigger guard and 7 1/2-inch barrel. (Courtesy Donald Yena Collection. Image courtesy "Zintgraff")

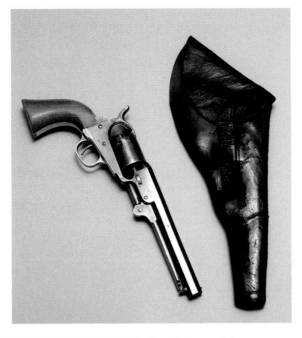

Civilian Flap Holster for Colt Model 1849 Pocket Revolver. Maker Unknown, 1850-1860. This early, contour-fit belt holster is of the style carried by ante-bellum gold seekers and overland emigrants. Constructed of black bridle-weight leather, it has a full flap secured with a strap-and-tab closure and features a sewn-in toe plug. The piece is accompanied by the .31 caliber percussion, Colt Model 1849 Pocket revolver. (Courtesy Private Collection)

graphic and artifactual evidence clearly indicates that the earliest commercial versions pre-dated any standardized army adoption and were of simpler, two- or three-piece construction. By the 1860s, however, eastern-made flap holsters for the civilian market certainly had taken on many attributes of their martial cousins.[17]

The earliest of these covered holsters had deep, relatively form-fit bodies with integral, pattern-cut flaps. Variations with separate, sewn-on cover leathers were not unknown, but evidently were quite rare. Those made for large-frame revolvers, such as the Walker and Dragoon Colts, sometimes were open-toed, while those for the Navy Colt and smaller pistols generally were fitted with sewn-in toe plugs. A cross-strap sewn on the face of the upper holster body typically secured the cover flap. This strap retained either the lower, tapered portion of the flap itself, or a leather tab or strap sewn on the inside of the flap's extremity.

By the opening of the Civil War in 1861, the eastern-made, commercial flap holster paralleled the military form in most respects, and thousands were manufactured during the conflict to accommodate a wide range of personal sidearms and odd, army contract revolvers. Closely contoured to the intended weapon, these para-military holsters typically had sewn-in toe plugs and utilized the flap-and-finial, or strap-and-finial, closure method common to the martial form. The commercial variety differed from the military pattern, however, in frequently employing a "right-hand" configuration and in utilizing a lighter grade, often russet-colored leather. Hundreds of these civilian flap-topped holsters, whether for large army and navy revolvers or smaller pocket models, migrated west with their martial counterparts during the immediate post-war years.[18]

Well-armed for an overland trek, this gent from the late 1840s carries a Colt Transition Walker or First Model Dragoon revolver in an open-topped, straight-throated and toe-plugged belt holster that has been wet-molded to the weapon's every contour. A second, open-topped belt holster with a molded, almost tubular pouch retains a bag-handled single-shot or pepperbox pistol. (Image courtesy Western Reserve Historical Society, Cleveland, Ohio)

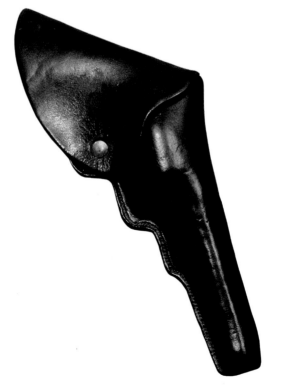

Civilian Flap Holster for Colt "Root" Model Revolver. Maker Unknown, 1860-1865. The product of an eastern leather goods manufactory, this diminutive, right-hand specimen probably carried a Union soldier's personal sidearm. Constructed of stiff, russet bridle leather, the piece is patterned on contemporary military designs, having a molded and contour-fit body with full, upswept cover flap and sewn-in toe plug. The belt loop, however, consists merely of a narrow, sewn strap. The flap is secured with a copper button-finial. Many such holsters were brought west in the immediate post-war years; few survived in this condition. (Courtesy Lacey and Virginia Gaddis Collection)

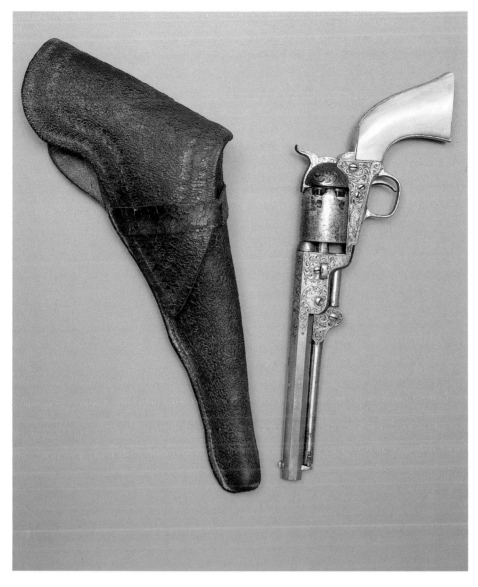

Eastern leather goods manufacturers continued to produce flap-topped belt holsters for the remainder of the century and beyond. By the late 1860s, some were offering "transitional" patterns with half-flap covers in lieu of the typical, full-flap design. Later examples, patterned for metallic cartridge revolvers, presented more amorphous contours with rounded, sewn-through toes and flaps of varying profile that secured with finial or snap closures. By the mid-1870s, some of these holsters appeared with rudimentary ornamentation in the form of sewn, stamped or rolled border motifs on both the body and cover flap.[19]

While they were carried west in large numbers during the percussion era, commercially made, flapped belt holsters evidently met with little appreciation among those seasoned frontiersmen who desired ready access to their arms. As one keen observer, bound across the plains in 1857, recorded:

> ...so frequent were assassinations that each man traveling on the prairie, as soon as he perceived another approaching him, slipped [loosened] his six-shooter to have it most convenient to his hand. Of course, the flap of the holster, placed to protect the pistol from rain, had long before been cut off; it was preferable to suffer a little rust on the weapon rather than run the risk of losing a fraction of a second in drawing it.[20]

An appreciable number of these eastern belt holsters evidently were altered to meet the demands of their new environment by the simple expedient of cutting off their cover flaps, thus creating another type of "transitional" holster pattern. Many others, however, survived in the West with their protective flaps intact.[21]

Civilian Flap Holster for Large-Frame Revolver. Maker Unknown, 1855-1865. Ornamented with double rows of border stamping, this graceful example typifies the civilian flap holster in the immediate ante-bellum period. Constructed of medium skirting leather, the holster has an unusual, upswept and elongated flap, the point of which makes secure closure beneath a strap running across the upper body. With the holster is a .36 caliber percussion, Colt Model 1851 Navy revolver with ivory grips and scroll engraving. (Courtesy Private Collection)

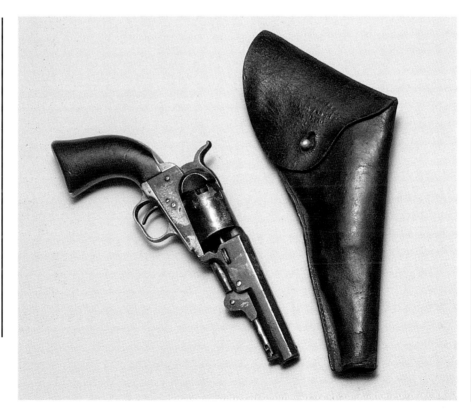

Civilian Flap Holster for Colt Model 1849 Pocket Revolver. B. Kittridge & Co., Cincinnati, Ohio, 1860-1865. Incorporating design elements typical of military holsters of the era, this piece probably was marketed to accommodate a Civil War soldier's personal sidearm. Constructed of black bridleweight leather, it is contoured to the revolver and has a riveted belt loop, flap-and-finial closure, and a sewn-in toe plug (now missing). Accompanying the holster is a .31 caliber percussion, Colt Model 1849 Pocket revolver. (Courtesy Private Collection)

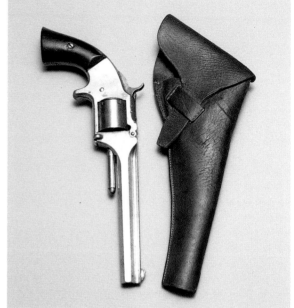

Posed in the late 1850s, this fellow wears a flap-topped, civilian belt holster with straight throat and sewn toe. The cover flap has been turned back to better show off the Colt Model 1849 Pocket revolver, which is reversed in the holster with the trigger guard riding up on the throat. (Image courtesy Herb Peck, Jr. Collection)

Civilian Flap Holster for Smith & Wesson Model No. 2 Army Revolver. Maker Unknown, 1865-1870. This contoured, right-hand holster is typical of commercial production for early, small-frame, metallic cartridge revolvers. Constructed of russet bridle leather, it utilizes a simple flap/strap-and-tab closure and is open-toed. Accompanying the holster is the .32 caliber, Smith & Wesson Model No. 2 Army revolver. (Courtesy Private Collection)

As will be seen in the following segment, full-flapped belt holsters also were fabricated by early frontier saddlers during the ante-bellum period. But, whether produced in the East or the West, this gun-leather pattern was a marginal form on the frontier by 1870. Westerners clearly preferred open-topped holsters; few, if any, frontier leather artisans produced the flapped variety during the remainder of the nineteenth century.[22] Of more than 45 western saddlers surveyed, none except Hamley, Heiser, Main & Winchester, and Marden offered flap-covered belt holsters in their mail order catalogs between the late 1890s and 1930. This record suggests a prevailingly negative market in the late-nineteenth-century West. And indeed, by the 1880s, flapless belt holsters dominated the western market to such an extent that eastern manufactories and outfitting houses commenced copying indigenous frontier patterns for sale in their gunleather lines.[23]

Civilian Flap Holster for Remington Army and New Model Army Revolvers. Maker Unknown, 1862-1865. This closely form-fit piece probably was manufactured to fill the shortfall in regulation military holster production during the Civil War. Constructed of dark russet bridle-weight leather, the holster originally had a sewn belt loop and strap-and-finial closure. It is accompanied by the .44 caliber percussion, Remington New Model Army revolver. (Courtesy Private Collection)

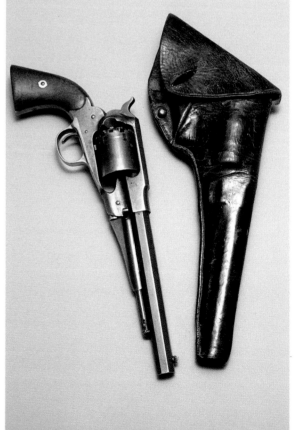

Civilian Flap Holster for Small-Frame Revolvers. Maker Unknown, 1875-1885. A commercial product of eastern manufacture, this right-hand specimen is fabricated of black-dyed, pebble-grained leather with a full suede lining and stitched floral ornament. It incorporates a sewn-on belt loop, flap-and-finial closure, and a sewn-in toe plug. While the accompanying .38 caliber, Colt Pocket conversion fits the holster perfectly, it appears that a pistol with an ejector rod was long associated with the piece. (Courtesy Phil Spangenberger Collection. Photo by Charlie Rathbun)

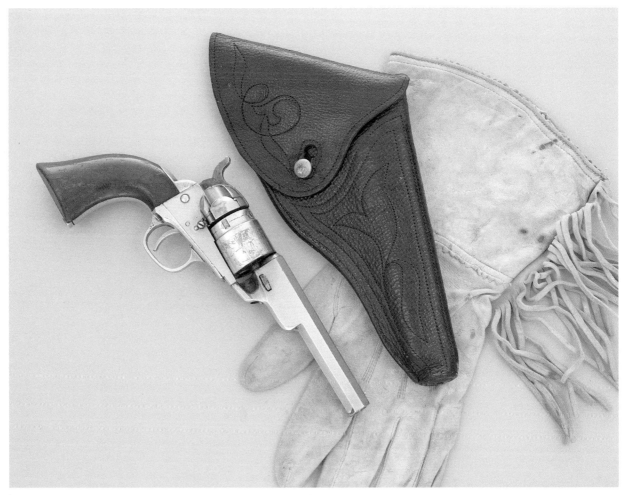

Transitional Half-Flap Holster for Colt Model 1851 Navy Revolver. Maker Unknown, 1860-1870. The product of an eastern outfitting house, this left-hand, half-flap belt holster suggests a transition from full-flapped to open-topped forms in the civilian market. Fabricated of bridle-weight russet leather, the deep-bodied pouch is fairly closely contoured to the weapon and has a sewn main seam and belt loop with an open toe. Unlike contemporary "California" patterns, the throat profile precludes ready acquisition of the trigger area. The half-flap cover leather shrouds the cylinder area and secures the weapon by means of a cross-strap sewn on the face of the pouch. The holster holds a .36 caliber percussion, Colt Model 1851 Navy revolver, third variation, with checkered ivory grips. (Courtesy Lacey and Virginia Gaddis Collection)

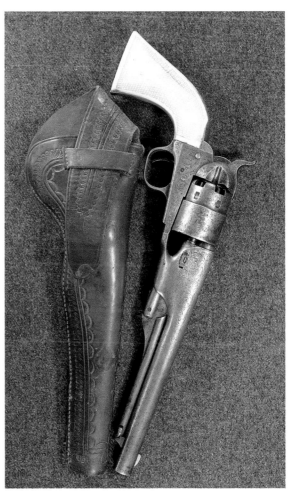

Transitional Half-Flap Holster for Colt Model 1860 Army Revolver. Maker Unknown, 1865-1875. Presenting a very slim, contoured profile, this right-hand specimen is constructed of russet, bridle-weight material with an integral, pattern-cut half-flap. The pouch has a slightly arched throat profile, sewn main seam and open toe. A rolled and stamped border element of fronds and decorative arcs is applied to both the major elements. With the holster is a .44 caliber percussion, 1860 Colt Army revolver with 8-inch barrel and checkered ivory grips. (Courtesy John E. Fox Collection)

Buffalo hunters Bill Tilghman (left) and Jim Elder (right) wear civilian and military, full-flap belt holsters for large-frame revolvers in this circa 1874 photograph. Note that Elder has folded the holster flap into his waistband to better expose his weapon. Both holsters are mounted on early, all-leather cartridge belts; Elder's appears to be of non-regulation military derivation with an officer's belt plate. (Image courtesy Western History Collections, University of Oklahoma Library)

Transitional Half-Flap Holster with "Mexican Loop" Alteration. Maker Unknown, 1865-1875. A true hybrid form, this civilian half-flap holster has been modified to accommodate a larger cartridge belt by the addition of a "Mexican Loop" pattern back skirt. Fabricated of medium-weight russet leather, the left-hand pouch is fully lined with smooth red morocco leather and ornamented with an incised, foliate and vine motif. Of typical design, the holster body incorporates an arched throat, sewn-on closure strap, contoured main seam, and open toe. The unusually contoured, full-profile back skirt is sewn to the upper back of the holster body and secures the pouch with two widely spaced, integral loops. Accompanying the holster is a .44 caliber percussion, Colt Model 1860 Army revolver with full 8-inch barrel. (Courtesy Robert W. Smith Collection)

Transitional Open-Top Holster for Colt Whitney-ville-Hartford Dragoon Revolver. Maker Unknown, 1850-1860. Deep and closely contoured, this right-hand holster features a quarter-flap with strap-and-tab closure to amply secure the revolver. Constructed of russet bridle-weight leather, the piece has the square, or straight-line, throat profile typical of contemporary military and civilian flap holsters. Accompanying the holster is a .44 caliber percussion, Whitneyville-Hartford Dragoon, or "Transition Walker," revolver. (National Cowboy Hall of Fame Collection)

"Half-Pouch" Belt Holster for Smith & Wesson No. 2 Army Revolver. Maker Unknown, 1865-1875. Constructed of medium-weight russet skirting leather, this unusual holster design features a contour-fit, "half-pouch" body sewn to a wide, artfully scalloped skirt or back panel. The body has a shallow recurved throat profile and an open toe, while the skirt has a separate belt loop secured with six japanned rivets. Accompanying the holster is a .32 caliber, Smith & Wesson Model No. 2 Army revolver. (Courtesy Phil Spangenberger Collection)

Transitional Half-Flap Holster for Colt Model 1862 Pocket Navy Conversion. Maker Unknown, 1870-1875. Incorporating an extra long, tapered half-flap that is integral with the holster, this piece presents a compact yet graceful silhouette. Fashioned of dark russet bridle-weight leather, the right-hand body has a high arched throat profile, recurved main seam with open toe, and double slits for belt mounting. With the holster is a .38 caliber, Colt Pocket Navy conversion with ivory grips and 4 1/2-inch barrel. (Courtesy R. M. Bachman Collection. Image courtesy Bill Manns)

This mid-1870s carte-de-visite photo captures a Mexican gentleman wearing a deep, full-flapped civilian belt holster with strap-and-tab closure and sewn-in toe plug for what appears to be an ivory-stocked, Smith & Wesson American revolver. The holster is mounted on a low-slung, military-style belt, while a pistol cartridge belt with harness buckle girds the "pistolero's" waist. (Image courtesy Herb Peck, Jr. Collection)

Civilian Flap Holster for Large-Frame Cartridge Revolvers. Maker Unknown, 1875-1885. A later example, this flapped holster is rather amorphous in contour to accommodate a variety of similarly proportioned, large-frame revolvers. Constructed of black bridle leather, it is unusual in having the recurved throat profile common to the open-top holsters then most popular in the West. The piece is accompanied by a .44 caliber, Forehand & Wadsworth New Model Army revolver. (Courtesy Private Collection)

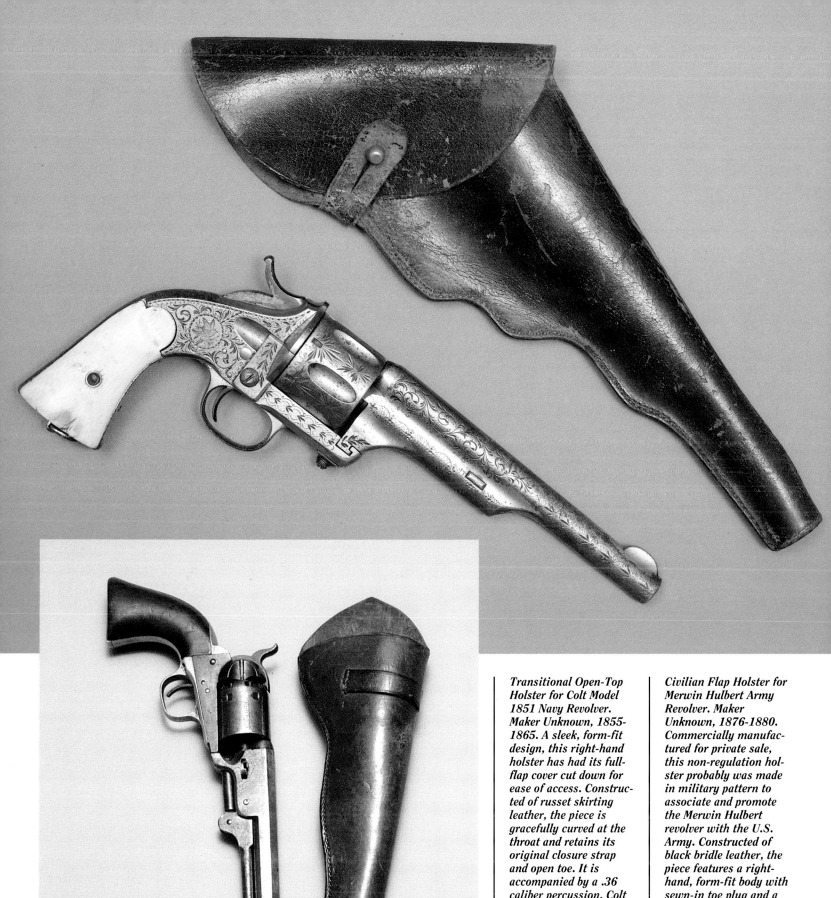

Transitional Open-Top Holster for Colt Model 1851 Navy Revolver. Maker Unknown, 1855-1865. A sleek, form-fit design, this right-hand holster has had its full-flap cover cut down for ease of access. Constructed of russet skirting leather, the piece is gracefully curved at the throat and retains its original closure strap and open toe. It is accompanied by a .36 caliber percussion, Colt Model 1851 Navy revolver, fourth variation. (Courtesy Private Collection)

Civilian Flap Holster for Merwin Hulbert Army Revolver. Maker Unknown, 1876-1880. Commercially manufactured for private sale, this non-regulation holster probably was made in military pattern to associate and promote the Merwin Hulbert revolver with the U.S. Army. Constructed of black bridle leather, the piece features a right-hand, form-fit body with sewn-in toe plug and a full-flap top with strap-and-finial closure of unusual arrangement. Accompanying the holster is the .44 caliber, Merwin Hulbert Army revolver, which was never adopted by the military. (Courtesy Private Collection)

"California" Pattern Holster for Colt Model 1851 Navy Revolver. Maker Unknown, 1850-1855. An early example of the "California" open-top style, this right-hand holster has a deep, very slender body that is contour-fit to its revolver. Constructed of medium-weight russet skirting leather, the piece is adorned with a hand-tooled, "fern frond" border motif and has an atypical, slightly arched throat profile. (Note that the trigger guard area has been left untooled; it could be removed to create an abrupt recurve without disrupting the existing ornamentation.) Typical of the type, the holster has a riveted and sewn belt loop, and a sewn main seam and toe plug. (Courtesy Lacey and Virginia Gaddis Collection)

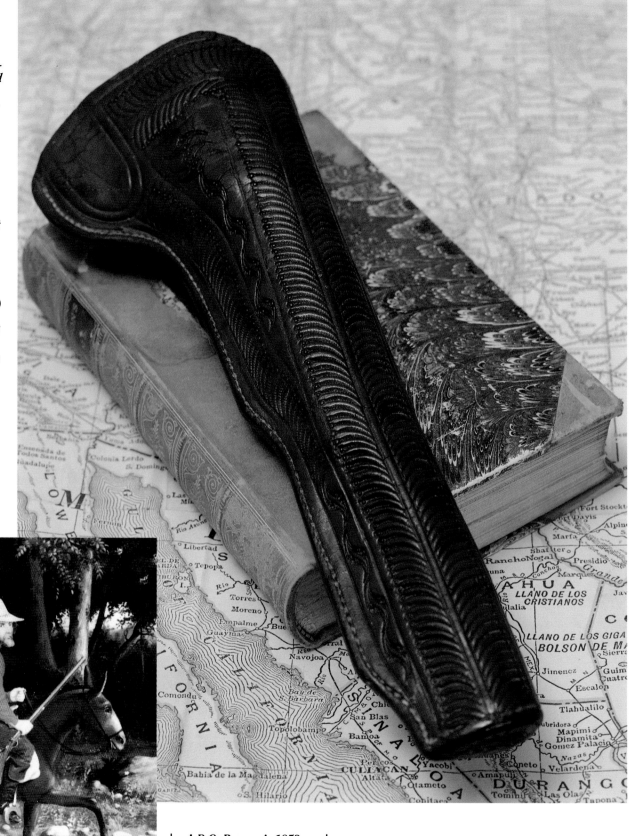

A.D.O. Browere's 1853 narrative painting, "The Lone Prospector," illustrates the use of an open-topped, "California" pattern belt holster by a miner. (Image courtesy National Cowboy Hall of Fame and Western Heritage Center)

"CALIFORNIA" PATTERN HOLSTERS

Although commercial belt holsters of eastern origin played an important role in the ante-bellum West, they sometimes were unobtainable in isolated areas and, when available, frequently proved unsuitable for the rigorous and occasionally violent frontier environment. These deficiencies were remedied by pioneer saddlers, who set up shop in scattered settlements and burgeoning towns throughout the West from the early 1850s onward. Responding to their new-found markets, these emigrant tradesmen gradually developed custom-crafted gunleather that was better adapted not only to the intended weaponry, but also to the functional requirements of their rough-hewn clientele.[24] The first such indigenous western holster, which appeared as a discrete regional variation during the Gold Rush era of the early 1850s, was the gracefully contoured "California" pattern.[25]

Apparently the collective inspiration of Anglo saddlers in upper California, this distinctive holster design evolved in both full-flapped and open-topped configurations. Leather working firms like Main & Winchester and L. D. Stone Company, established in San Francisco in 1849 and 1852, respectively, created

"California" Pattern Holster for Colt Model 1851 Navy Revolver. Maker Unknown, 1850-1855. A well-finished, open-topped "California" holster, this right-hand example presents a slim, closely contoured silhouette. Constructed of dark russet skirting leather, the pouch is fully lined with a smooth, red Morocco leather. The holster body incorporates the classic, sewn-in toe plug and triple-recurved throat profile exposing the revolver's hammer and both sides of the trigger guard area. The belt loop is riveted and sewn. The holster is fully ornamented in a hand-cut, open foliate motif over a vertical, hash-lined ground. With the holster is a .36 caliber percussion, Colt Model 1851 Navy revolver, third variation, with ivory grips. (Courtesy Lacey and Virginia Gaddis Collection)

"California" Pattern Holster for Colt Dragoon Revolver. Maker Unknown, 1850-1860. A fine "California," open-top holster, this right-hand piece is form-fit to its intended revolver. Constructed of dark russet skirting leather, it has the double-recurved throat profile typical of this holster pattern and features a crudely incised floral motif on the body, sewn and riveted belt loop, and sewn toe plug (now missing). The holster is accompanied by a .44 caliber percussion, Colt Third Model Dragoon revolver. (Courtesy Private Collection)

the handsome, silhouette pattern in response to the hordes of prospectors who relied on their own protection in lawless placer camps like Helltown, Lousy Level and Murderers Bar along the western slope of the Sierra Nevada range. Custom-sized to accommodate Colt's widely popular 1851 Navy revolver, as well as the big Dragoon and smaller Pocket models, these often finely embellished "California" holsters were an established form by 1855.[26]

Usually fabricated of good quality, medium-weight russet skirting leather, "California" pattern belt holsters incorporated deep, form-fit bodies designed to snugly retain their deadly cargo. The earliest examples, particularly those for the Colt Navy, were quite slender in profile and often precisely contoured to the pistol's loading lever and trigger guard configuration. Later examples (circa 1860 and after) typically featured a more curvilinear main seam contour, but most still were fitted to but one revolver model and barrel length.

Sewn-in toe plugs commonly were employed on early holsters to strengthen and maintain the form of the slender "pipe" area of the pouch, while later examples often had rounded, sewn-through toes. A generally shallow, leather loop was sewn and/or riveted to the upper back of the holster pouch for mounting on a plain waist belt. The pattern was produced in both "right-" and "left-hand" configurations in about equal numbers.[27]

Surviving examples in public and private collections suggest that fewer than one in ten "California" holsters were made with protective cover flaps; by the mid-1860s, fabrication of the flapped variation had virtually ceased. These western flap holsters differed from their eastern counterparts in subtleties of form

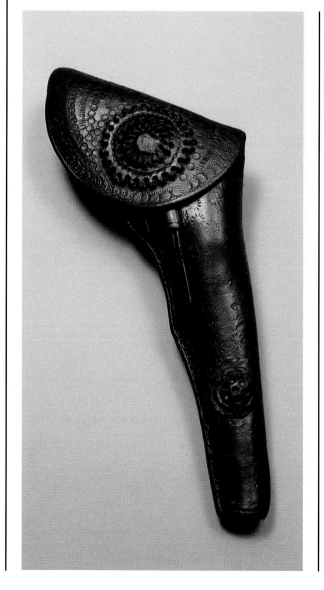

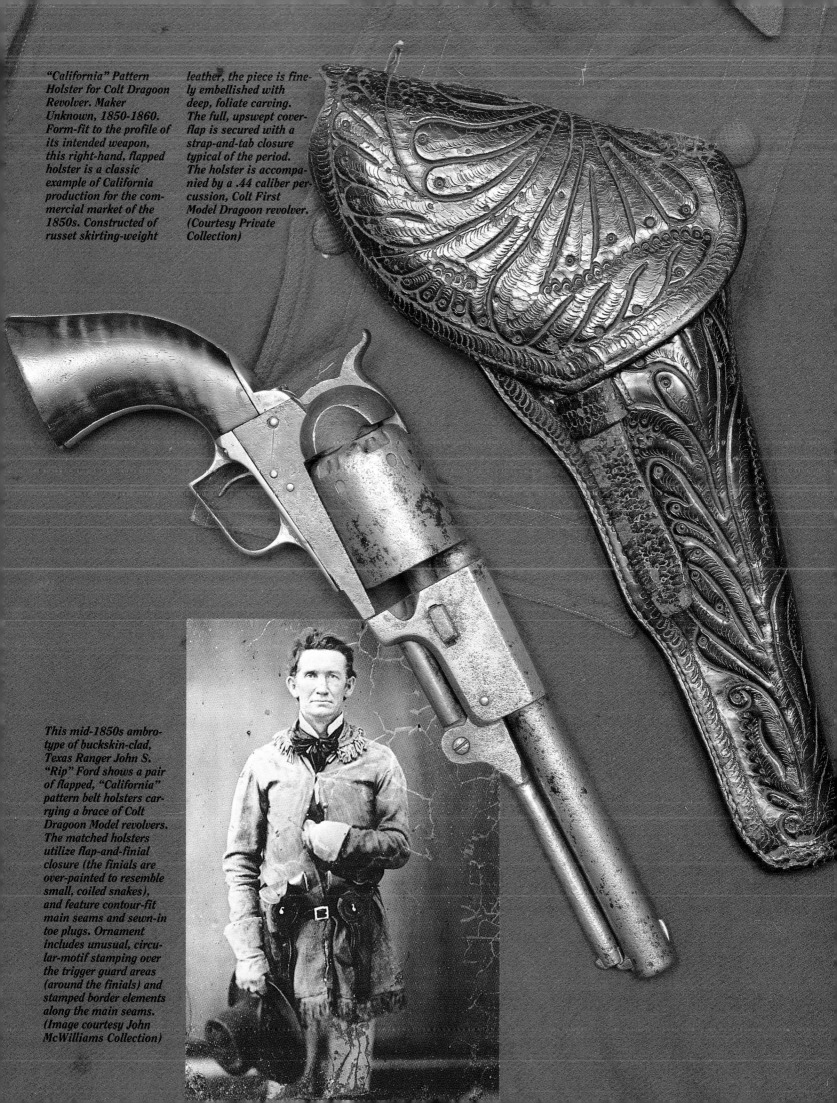

"California" Pattern Holster for Colt Dragoon Revolver. Maker Unknown, 1850-1860. Form-fit to the profile of its intended weapon, this right-hand, flapped holster is a classic example of California production for the commercial market of the 1850s. Constructed of russet skirting-weight leather, the piece is finely embellished with deep, foliate carving. The full, upswept cover-flap is secured with a strap-and-tab closure typical of the period. The holster is accompanied by a .44 caliber percussion, Colt First Model Dragoon revolver. (Courtesy Private Collection)

This mid-1850s ambrotype of buckskin-clad, Texas Ranger John S. "Rip" Ford shows a pair of flapped, "California" pattern belt holsters carrying a brace of Colt Dragoon Model revolvers. The matched holsters utilize flap-and-finial closure (the finials are over-painted to resemble small, coiled snakes), and feature contour-fit main seams and sewn-in toe plugs. Ornament includes unusual, circular-motif stamping over the trigger guard areas (around the finials) and stamped border elements along the main seams. (Image courtesy John McWilliams Collection)

and line, in leather weight and quality, in scale (most were sized for Dragoon or Navy Colts) and, perhaps most, in their distinctive embellishment (discussed below). Most specimens incorporated pattern-cut flaps that were integral with the holster body. Like the eastern, commercial form, most utilized a closure method in which the narrow flap extremity, or an attached tab leather, secured beneath a cross strap sewn on the upper pouch face.

While the flap-covered "California" holster was perhaps the rarest form made in the West, it was the open-topped "California" pattern which truly established a new design standard in frontier gunleather. The rapid acceptance and ongoing popularity of the open-topped form certainly had more to do with prevailing frontier conditions than with any technological advances, as percussion ignition (always subject to moisture degradation) remained the standard throughout the 1850s and 1860s. Clearly, the most

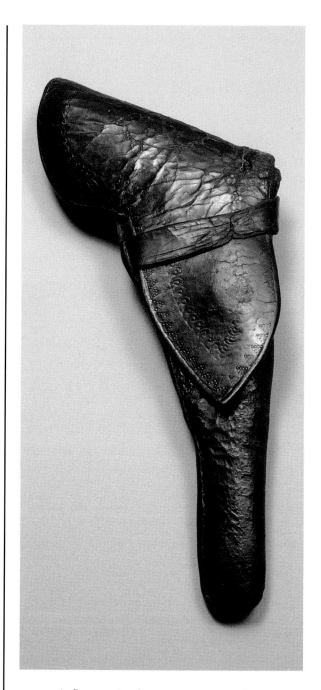

"California" Pattern Holster for Colt Dragoon Revolver. Maker Unknown, 1855-1860. A full-flapped variation of the "California" style, this right-hand specimen is semi-contoured to the lines of its intended revolver. The one-piece, pattern-cut body and cover flap are fabricated of dark russet skirting leather with sewn main seam running through the toe. The large, upswept cover flap is retained by a full-width leather strap sewn at the front main seam and riveted at the back. The separate belt loop also is riveted to the upper rear of the holster body. The periphery of the cover flap is ornamented with stamped border patterns around a large sunburst motif at upper center. (Courtesy Lacey and Virginia Gaddis Collection)

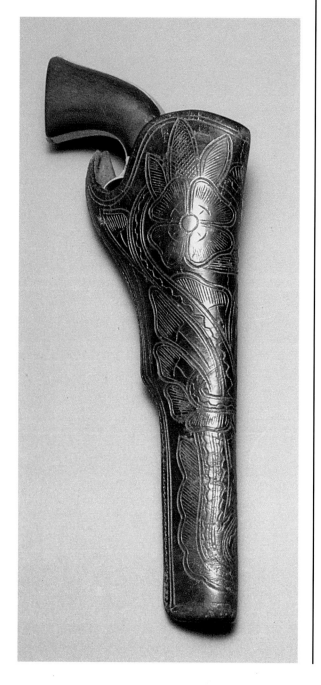

"California" Pattern Holster for Colt Model 1851 Navy Revolver. Maker Unknown, 1855-1865. Exhibiting the lavish, incised-line floral and vine embellishment typical of the style, this right-hand example is representative of western, open-top holsters in the ante-bellum era. Constructed of dark russet skirting leather, the piece has the characteristic, double-recurved throat design with riveted belt loop, contoured main seam, and sewn-in toe plug (now missing). With the piece is a .36 caliber percussion, Colt Model 1851 Navy revolver, fourth variation. (Courtesy Bill Mackin Collection)

potent influence in the westerner's preference for flapless belt holsters was the widely perceived, often very real need for instant access to one's weapon. This was nowhere more apparent than in the unsettled, sometimes lawless mining districts of California, Montana and Colorado, where the open-topped "California" belt holster found hundreds of devotees well prior to the availabilty of dependable, metallic cartridge arms and ammunition.[28]

The open-topped "California" holster certainly was most notable for its introduction of the distinctive S-curve, or recurved profile at the throat of the pouch. While some specimens were made with straight or arched throats, the great majority incorporated a variation of the pleasing curvilinear design. Intended to shroud the revolver's cylinder and percussion caps while allowing ready acquisition of the grip and trigger area, this practical feature appeared with either a single recurve on the face of the pouch or, more

"California" Pattern Holster for Colt Model 1851 Navy Revolver. Main & Winchester, San Francisco, California, 1855-1865. A classic example of the "California" design, this right-hand holster was made by perhaps the earliest and best-known practitioner of the style. Constructed of medium-weight russet skirting leather, the piece incorporates a triple-recurved throat profile that is extremely deep at the *upper, leading edge. The body is relatively uncontoured along the main seam and has a separate, stitched-on belt loop and a sewn-in toe plug. The holster is beautifully hand-carved in a flowing, foliate and floral pattern within a clean border element. A .36 caliber percussion, 1851 Colt Navy revolver accompanies the specimen. (Courtesy R.M. Bachman Collection. Image courtesy Bill Manns)*

often, with a double, parallel recurve at both the front and back. In many instances a third dip in the throat line was introduced at the upper, leading edge to expose the revolver's hammer spur as well. The recurved throat profile was a classic design innovation in western gunleather. Both functional and attractive, it has been widely utilized in holster design from the mid-1850s to the present day.[29]

"California" pattern holsters also were remarkable as the first to routinely incorporate elements of decorative enhancement in their finish. From their inception up into the Civil War years, a select few were fitted with ornamental brass or, in rare instances, silver toe caps in the manner of pommel holsters. Far more typical (and perhaps indicative of Mexican influence

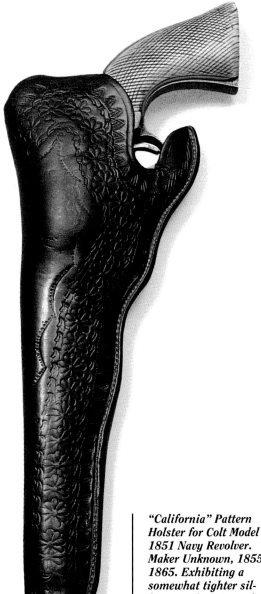

"California" Pattern Holster for Colt Model 1851 Navy Revolver. Maker Unknown, 1855-1865. This fine, right-hand specimen is distinguished by its deep and finely executed, foliate-carved decoration. Constructed of dark russet, medium-weight skirting material, the holster has a triple-recurved throat, semi-contoured main seam, sewn-in muzzle plug, and separate belt loop stitched on the upper back. It holds a .36 caliber percussion, Colt Model 1851 Navy revolver with 7 1/2-inch barrel. (Courtesy R.M. Bachman Collection)

"California" Pattern Holster for Colt Model 1851 Navy Revolver. Maker Unknown, 1855-1865. Exhibiting a somewhat tighter silhouette along its welted main seam, this left-hand "California" holster represents a handsome interpretation of the form. Constructed of black skirting leather, the body has a fairly abrupt, double-recurve at the throat, riveted and sewn belt loop, and sewn-in toe plug. The wide border embellishment is hand-stamped and consists of floral rosettes, fronds and sawtooth elements with scalloped lines at the interior. A .36 caliber percussion, Colt Model 1851 Navy revolver, third variation, with incised ivory grips accompanies the piece. (Courtesy Lacey and Virginia Gaddis Collection)

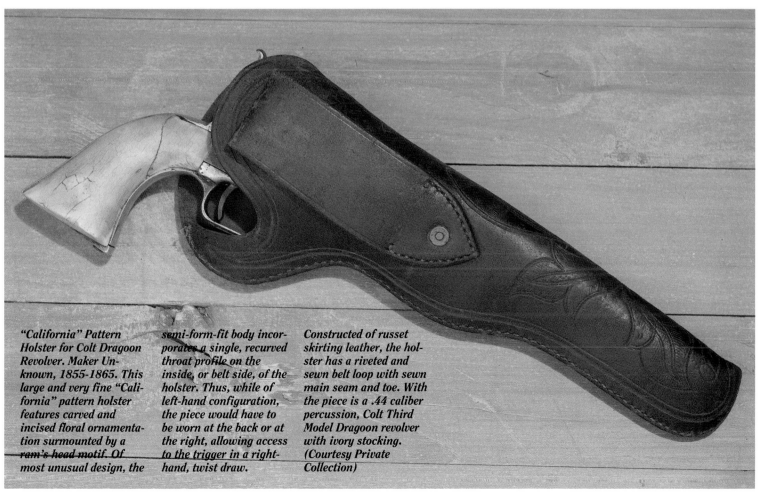

"California" Pattern Holster for Colt Dragoon Revolver. Maker Unknown, 1855-1865. This large and very fine "California" pattern holster features carved and incised floral ornamentation surmounted by a ram's head motif. Of most unusual design, the semi-form-fit body incorporates a single, recurved throat profile on the inside, or belt side, of the holster. Thus, while of left-hand configuration, the piece would have to be worn at the back or at the right, allowing access to the trigger in a right-hand, twist draw. Constructed of russet skirting leather, the holster has a riveted and sewn belt loop with sewn main seam and toe. With the piece is a .44 caliber percussion, Colt Third Model Dragoon revolver with ivory stocking. (Courtesy Private Collection)

"California" Pattern Holster for Colt Navy Model Revolvers. Maker Unknown, 1860-1865. Slim and graceful in line, this right-hand "California" holster is contour-fit and features the typical, double-recurved throat pattern (here having the small up-curved portion at the trigger guard removed for easier access). Constructed of bridle-weight russet leather, the body is border stamped with a "sun burst" motif and features a riveted belt loop and sewn-in tow plug. With the piece is a .36 caliber percussion, Colt Model 1851 Navy revolver, fourth variation, with ivory stocking. (Courtesy Private Collection)

"California" Pattern Holster for Colt Model 1862 Police Revolver. W.H. Watkinds & Co., Salem, Oregon, 1862-1865. Fitted to a Colt Police pistol with 6 1/2-inch barrel, this right-hand specimen is fabricated of medium-weight russet skirting stock with a wide border ornament of scalloped, fern-frond motif. The holster body presents a classic silhouette with its double-recurved throat and contoured main seam. Differing from the norm, the piece has an open toe and a sewn panel with double slots for belt carriage. (Courtesy Dr. Georg Priestel Collection)

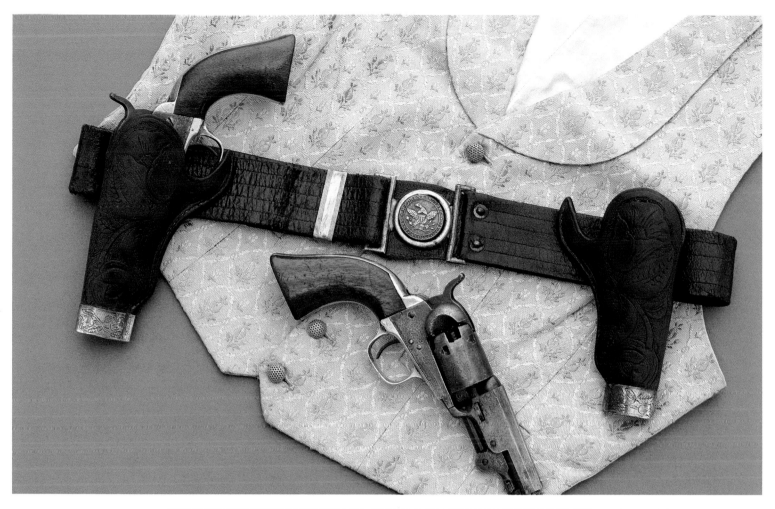

"California" Pattern Holsters with Para-Military Waist Belt. Main & Winchester, San Francisco, California; Cohen & Brother, San Francisco, California, 1860-1865. Carrying provenance traceable to San Francisco's Barbary Coast, this unique outfit is truly imbued with western history. Fabricated of black-dyed skirting leather, the diminutive holsters incorporate triple-recurved throat profiles, sewn belt loops and closely contoured main seams. The pouches are tooled in foliate and floral motif and are finished with end caps of engraved silver. With the rig is its original pair of .31 caliber percussion, Colt Model 1849 Pocket revolvers with 3-inch barrels and modified rammers. (Courtesy Herb Lyman Collection. Photo by Charlie Rathbun)

This Civil War-era photograph of three of Quantrill's guerillas illustrates the widespread distribution and popularity of the "California" pattern holster during the mid-1860s. The fellow at right grasps the toe of a form-fit pistol scabbard having the double-recurved throat profile characteristic of the style. (Image courtesy the Library of Congress)

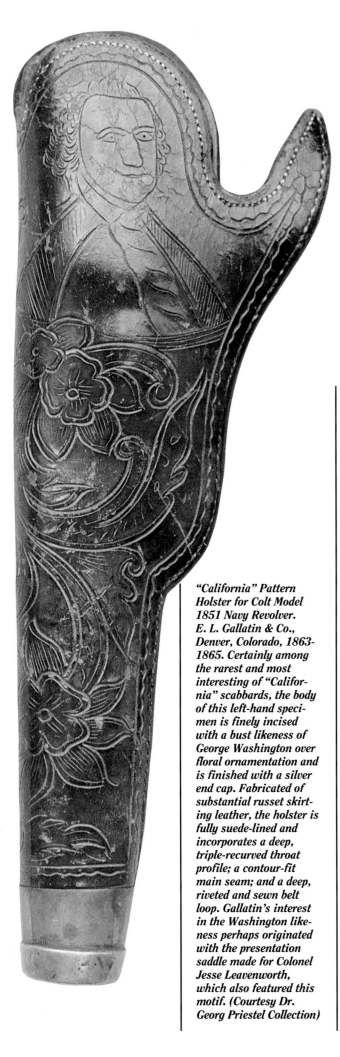

"California" Pattern Holster for Colt Model 1851 Navy Revolver. E. L. Gallatin & Co., Denver, Colorado, 1863-1865. Certainly among the rarest and most interesting of "California" scabbards, the body of this left-hand specimen is finely incised with a bust likeness of George Washington over floral ornamentation and is finished with a silver end cap. Fabricated of substantial russet skirting leather, the holster is fully suede-lined and incorporates a deep, triple-recurved throat profile; a contour-fit main seam; and a deep, riveted and sewn belt loop. Gallatin's interest in the Washington likeness perhaps originated with the presentation saddle made for Colonel Jesse Leavenworth, which also featured this motif. (Courtesy Dr. Georg Priestel Collection)

among western leather working artisans) was the introduction of applied incising, carving, tooling and stamping of the leather surface.

Often elaborate and finely detailed, hand-carved or incised pictorial embellishment appeared in human, animal and patriotic motifs on early holsters; as did full coverage in unusual, elongated vine and fern frond patterns. More familiar foliate, floral and border motifs dominated by the 1860s; while later examples typically featured a simpler, stamped or rolled border pattern, sometimes accompanied by a single, stamped rosette on the upper face of the pouch. These artistic applications set a precedent continued by western saddlers (and mimicked by eastern manufacturers) well into the twentieth century.[30]

In addition to such applied embellishment, the "California" holster also was distinguished by an extraordinary grace of form and line. This was particularly true of the open-topped variety, which, with its contoured main seam and recurved throat profile, presented a slim and remarkably handsome silhouette. Here the functional goals of capacity, carriage, protection and accessibility merged to produce a holster form that was both eminently useful and aesthetically pleasing. This convergence of functional simplicity and elegant form actually mirrored organic theories of design then current among such American philosophers as Ralph Waldo Emerson and Horatio Greenough,[31] and it established a benchmark in western holster manufacture that would influence production for several decades.

Contrary to the assertions of several writers,[32] there does not appear to have been a direct, antecedent influence in style between the military holster and the "California" pattern manufactured in the West for the civilian market. It was not until 1856 that the U. S. Ordnance Department tested its first experimental, flapped belt holster, and somewhat later that a regulation pattern was established.[33] Yet, the "California" holster actually appeared several

(opposite) "California" Pattern Holster for Colt Model 1849 Pocket Revolver. E. L. Gallatin, Denver, Colorado, 1860-1862. A fine Rocky Mountain interpretation of the graceful "California" style, this left-hand variation is semi-contour-fit and ornamented in a distinctive, incised motif incorporating open floral and vine elements. Constructed of medium-weight russet skirting leather, the holster features a triple-recurved throat profile, sewn and riveted belt loop, and sewn-in toe plug, and full buckskin lining. With the piece is a .31 caliber percussion, 1849 Colt Pocket revolver with small trigger guard and 6-inch barrel. (Courtesy R.M. Bachman Collection. Image courtesy Bill Manns)

"California" Pattern Holster for Colt Model 1851 Navy Revolver. Maker Unknown, 1855-1865. Yet another handsome example of the "California" style, this left-hand piece is fully buckskin-lined and nicely flower-carved over the pouch face. Made of medi- um-weight, dark russet leather, the holster incorporates the classic recurved throat, riveted and stitched belt loop, and contour-fit main seam with sewn-in toe plug typical of the style. Shrouded within is a .36 caliber percussion, Colt 1851 Navy revolver with carved ivory grip. (Unusual with this specimen is the use of the word "Saddler," instead of "Maker," in the center of the otherwise illegible cartouche on the belt loop.) (Courtesy R.M. Bachman Collection. Image courtesy Bill Manns)

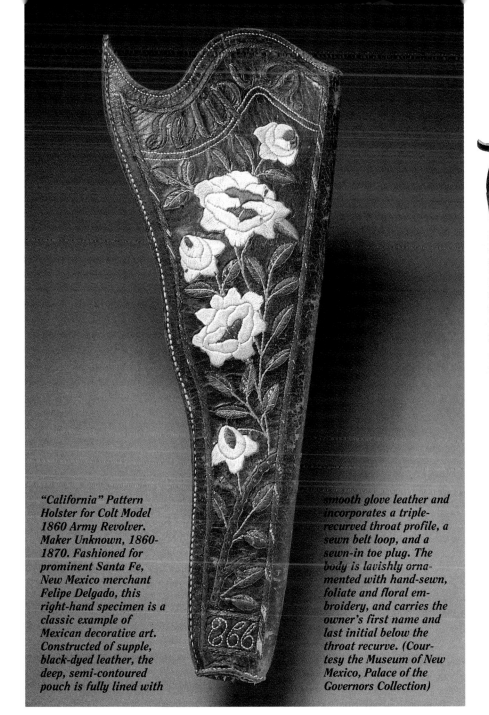

"California" Pattern Holster for Colt Model 1860 Army Revolver. Maker Unknown, 1860-1870. Fashioned for prominent Santa Fe, New Mexico merchant Felipe Delgado, this right-hand specimen is a classic example of Mexican decorative art. Constructed of supple, black-dyed leather, the deep, semi-contoured pouch is fully lined with smooth glove leather and incorporates a triple-recurved throat profile, a sewn belt loop, and a sewn-in toe plug. The body is lavishly ornamented with hand-sewn, foliate and floral embroidery, and carries the owner's first name and last initial below the throat recurve. (Courtesy the Museum of New Mexico, Palace of the Governors Collection)

"California" Pattern Holster for Colt Navy and Army Revolvers. Maker Unknown, 1860-1870. This variation of the "California" style holster is configured to accommodate either the Colt 1851 Navy or 1860 Army models. Constructed of black bridle-weight leather, the contoured, left-hand pouch has a sewn main seam running through the rounded toe and a fairly shallow, sewn belt loop. The unusual throat recurve completely shrouds the revolver's trigger area, but plunges at the leading edge of the body to fully expose the hammer – providing an adequately fast, yet safe drawing technique. A single, rolled borderline adorns the throat of the pouch. The holster carries a third variation, Colt Navy revolver with checkered ivory grips. (Courtesy Lacey and Virginia Gaddis Collection)

"California" Pattern Holster for Colt Model 1860 Army Conversion. Main & Winchester, San Francisco, California, 1860-1870. Product of the famed San Francisco saddlery, this left-hand holster was originally designed for the Colt Model 1860 Army percussion revolver with 8-inch barrel. Constructed of medium-weight russet skirting leather, the body features a triple-recurved throat profile, clearly exposing both the trigger and hammer. Finely carved floral motif over a stippled ground ornaments the pouch. The holster has been cut down to accommodate a .44 caliber, Richards Conversion of the Colt Model 1860 Army revolver with shortened barrel. (Courtesy Phil Spangenberger Collection)

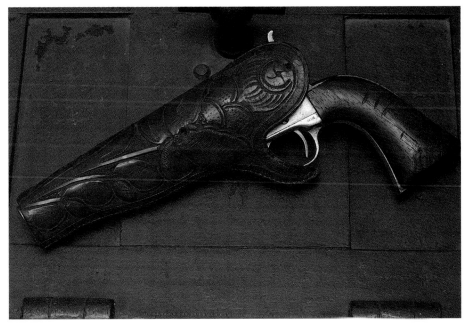

"California" Pattern Holster for Colt Model 1851 Navy Revolver. Possibly Gallatin & Gallup, Cheyenne, Wyoming Territory, 1867-1870. Carried by noted shootist James B. "Wild Bill" Hickok, this example typifies the late "California" pattern. The left-hand holster body is fabricated of medium-weight, dark russet skirting material with a simple, double-line border ornament and a full lining of smooth glove leather. The throat profile is triple-recurved with a deep recess over the hammer spur, while the main seam is semi-contoured and the toe closed with a sewn-in plug. With the holster is a .36 caliber percussion, Colt Navy revolver, fourth variation, with carved ivory grips, scroll engraving and backstrap inscription J.B. HICKOK 1869. (Courtesy Gene Autry Western Heritage Museum, Los Angeles)

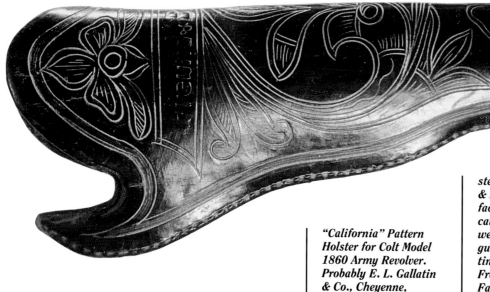

"California" Pattern Holster for Colt Model 1860 Army Revolver. Probably E. L. Gallatin & Co., Cheyenne, Wyoming Territory, 1870-1875. This open-topped "California" holster is marked "Freund & Br" across the upper face of the pouch, indicating its sale by the well-known Cheyenne gunsmithing and outfitting firm of F. W. Freund & Brother. Fabricated of dark russet skirting leather, the right-hand piece features graceful, incised-line floral decoration within a red-dyed borderline. (The white highlighting of the pattern is the result of salts leaching from the leather.) Typical of the pattern, this example has a riveted and sewn belt loop, a triple-recurved throat profile, semi-contoured main seam, and sewn-in toe plug. (Courtesy John E. Fox Collection)

"California" Pattern Holster for Colt Model 1851 Navy Revolver. Maker Unknown, 1865-1875. No doubt reflecting the tastes of its owner, this fancy "California" scabbard presents a marked departure from the usual embellishment of the pattern. A partially fringed buckskin panel, finished with a metal button and leather rosette, is sewn over the pouch face at the throat, while another full-fringed element is sewn along the semi-contoured main seam. Fabricated of medium-weight russet skirting leather, the left-hand piece is otherwise typical, having a double-recurved throat, narrow riveted belt loop, floral-carved ornament, and sewn-in toe plug. (Courtesy Richard Ellis Publications. Paul Goodwin, photographer)

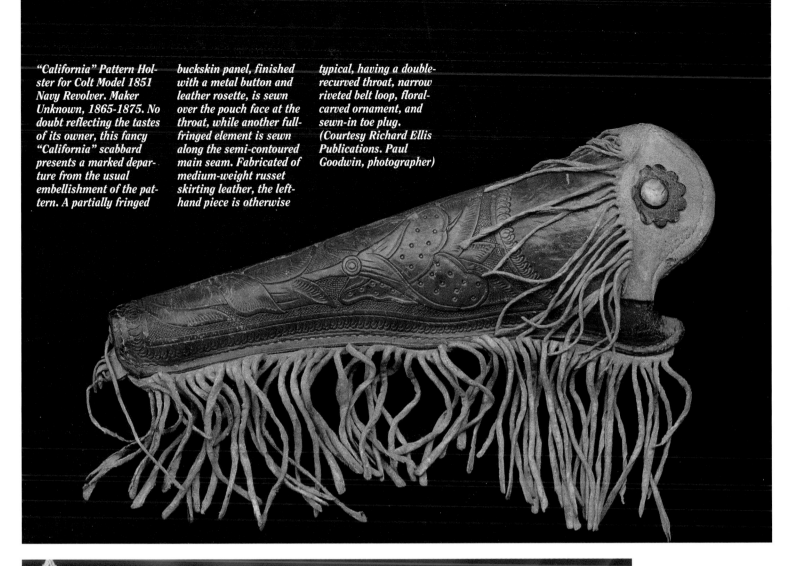

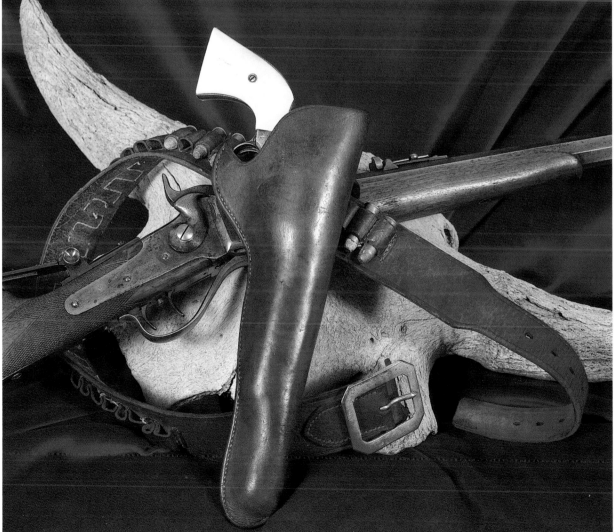

"California" Pattern Holster with Plain Cartridge Belt. S.C. Gallup & Co., Dodge City, Kansas, 1875-1878. In both its origin and design, this unadorned outfit characterizes the late frontier "California" rig. Fabricated of heavy skirting stock, the deep-bodied, right-hand holster incorporates a double throat recurve, riveted and sewn belt loop (carrying the maker's cartouch), and a semi-form-fit main seam that is stitched through the rounded toe. The plain, non-matching cartridge belt is probably of slightly later origin. The outfit carries a .45 caliber, Colt Single Action with full nickel finish, ivory grips and 7 1/2-inch barrel. (Courtesy R. M. Bachman Collection. Image courtesy Bill Munns)

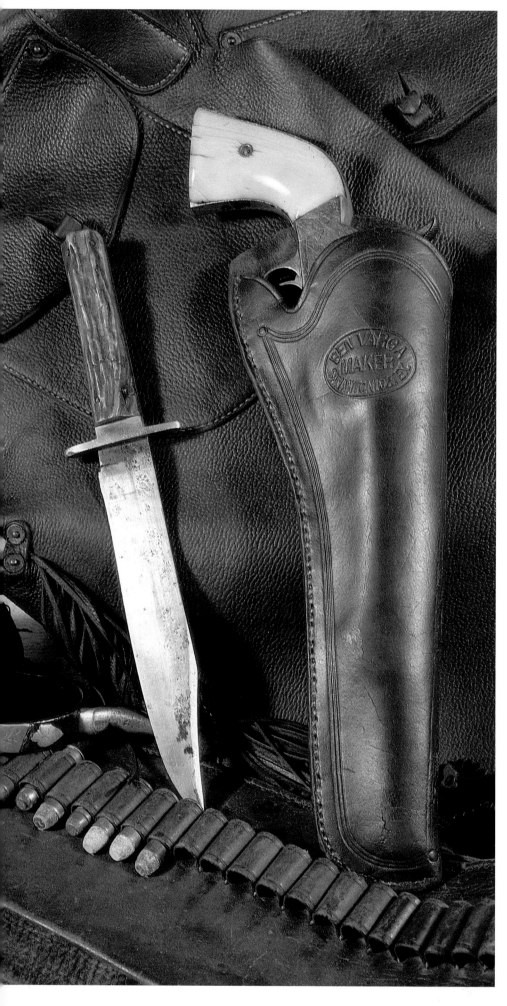

"California" Pattern Holster for Model 1875 Remington Army Revolver. Ben Varga, San Antonio, Texas, 1870-1880. This deep-bodied specimen retains the slender look of the classic "California" holster. Fabricated of dark russet skirting material, the right-hand piece incorporates a single throat recurve, a riveted and sewn belt loop deep enough for a wide cartridge belt, and a gently tapered main seam that is sewn through the toe. The pouch face is ornamented with a simple, rolled border line. The holster retains a .44 caliber, Model 1875 Remington Single Action Army revolver with ivory stocks, full nickel finish and 7 1/2-inch barrel. (Courtesy Joe Gish Collection. Image courtesy Bill Manns)

Posed in 1874, Texas buffalo hunter John Thomson Jones carries what is probably a Colt 1860 Army conversion in a "California" pattern holster with single recurved throat, semi-contoured main seam and rounded, sewn-through toe. His waist is girt with a civilian, "Prairie" pattern cartridge belt filled with .50/70 Govt. cartridges for the Sharps military conversion. (Image courtesy Panhandle-Plains Historical Museum, Canyon, Texas)

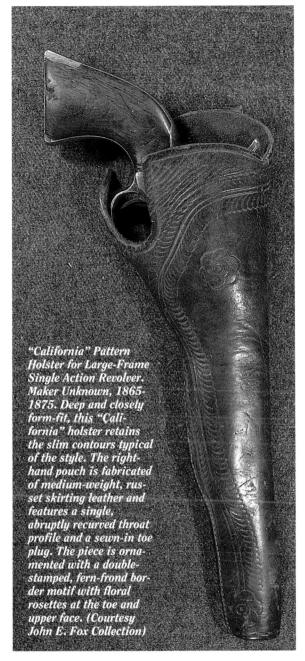

"California" Pattern Holster for Large-Frame Single Action Revolver. Maker Unknown, 1865-1875. Deep and closely form-fit, this "California" holster retains the slim contours typical of the style. The right-hand pouch is fabricated of medium-weight, russet skirting leather and features a single, abruptly recurved throat profile and a sewn-in toe plug. The piece is ornamented with a double-stamped, fern-frond border motif with floral rosettes at the toe and upper face. (Courtesy John E. Fox Collection)

"California" Pattern Holster for Smith & Wesson Model No. 3 Revolver. Maker Unknown, 1870-1880. This late example of the "California" style is contour-fit to the particular silhouette of its revolver and features an uncommon, arched throat profile. Constructed of black skirting-weight leather, the right-hand holster has a large, riveted belt loop and a sewn toe. With it is a .44 caliber, Smith & Wesson No. 3 Russian Model revolver. (Courtesy Private Collection)

Captured in a tintype of the mid-1870s, this youthful cowboy carries a Smith & Wesson American revolver in a transitional, or late "California," pattern belt holster with arched throat profile. The attached belt loop accommodates a relatively narrow, pistol cartridge belt with separate billets and a single-frame, horseshoe-shaped buckle. (Image courtesy Rick Bachman Collection)

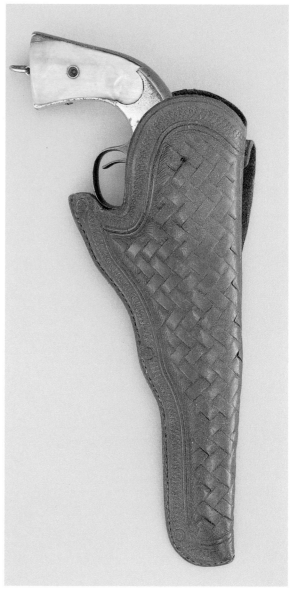

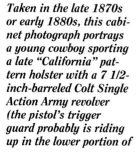

Taken in the late 1870s or early 1880s, this cabinet photograph portrays a young cowboy sporting a late "California" pattern holster with a 7 1/2-inch-barreled Colt Single Action Army revolver (the pistol's trigger guard probably is riding up in the lower portion of the throat recurve). The holster pouch appears to be lightly floral tooled, may incorporate a sewn-in toe plug, and has a back loop sufficient to mount on a single-thickness cartridge belt about three inches in width. (Image courtesy Herb Peck, Jr. Collection)

"California" Pattern Holster for Merwin Hulbert Army Revolver. Maker Unknown, 1885-1895. An early example of basket-stamped ornamentation, this right-hand specimen retains the graceful architecture of the "California" style. Fabricated of lightweight russet leather, the holster incorporates a deep, double-recurved throat profile, a riveted and sewn belt loop fit for a cartridge belt, and a semi-contoured main seam sewn through the rounded toe and reinforced with three iron rivets. A .44 caliber, Merwin Hulbert Army revolver with ivory stocks and 7-inch barrel fills the pouch. (Courtesy Phil Spangenberger Collection. Photo by Charlie Rathbun)

(opposite page) "California" Pattern Holster with Plain Cartridge Belt. Maker Unknown, 1875-1880. Fabricated of dark russet skirting stock, this latter-day interpretation of the West Coast holster incorporates a buckskin lining, triple throat recurve, semi-contoured main seam, open toe and delicately incised floral embellishment. The early pistol cartridge belt has slightly tapered ends and individually riveted cartridge loops. The rig is accompanied by a .44 caliber, Colt Single Action revolver with ivory stocking and a 7 1/2-inch barrel. (Courtesy George T. Jackson Collection. Image courtesy Bill Manns)

years prior to the military's initial adoption, and it seems to have evolved quite apart from the then nascent, martial pattern.

The generally shared characteristics of these two holster lines (deep, contour-fit bodies; riveted and sewn belt loops; and sewn-in toe plugs) may best be considered parallel developments dictated by the practical necessities of design and construction. In contrast, the typical dissimilarities between the military and "California" patterns (full-flapped versus usually open-topped design; consistent "left-hand" configuration versus either "right-" or "left-hand" design; straight versus typically recurved throat profiles; and lighter gauge bridle leather versus heavier skirting leather, respectively) appear more pertinent as differentiating factors and strongly suggest independent development of the indigenous western pattern. Further, the early and often flamboyant use of applied ornamentation on the "California" holster marked a distinct contrast with the unadorned military form.

During the late 1850s and early 1860s, the open-topped "California" pattern holster dispersed eastward, enjoying considerable popularity not only in Rocky Mountain mining camps, but in the Southwest and on the Great Plains as well. Examples were worn as far east as the Kansas-Missouri border during the Civil War, and famed saddler E. L. Gallatin of Denver became a prominent interpreter of the style early in the decade. By the mid-1870s, specimens fitted for the Smith & Wesson American and Colt Single Action

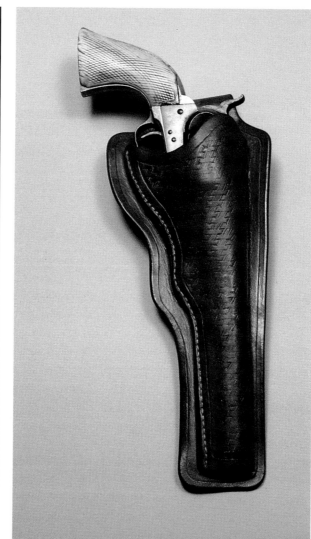

"California" Pattern Holster for Colt Single Action Army Revolver. Maker Unknown, 1890-1900. Probably made by an eastern leather goods manufacturer, this right-hand holster was intended for the commercial, mail order trade. Constructed of russet, bridle-weight leather, the semi-contoured main seam is sewn through the round toe and secured with a top rivet. The body is ornamented with a rolled border design having a stamped rosette at the upper corner. Such a holster was marketed through mail order firms like Montgomery Ward and Sears, Roebuck & Co. for as little as 35 cents. With the piece is a .45 caliber, Colt Single Action Army revolver with 7 1/2-inch barrel and ivory grips. (Courtesy R.M. Bachman Collection. Image courtesy Bill Manns)

In this circa 1880 studio photograph, Arizona pioneer Ed Schieffelin carries a pair of Smith & Wesson revolvers in custom-made, "California" pattern belt holsters fabricated of fair russet leather (note the molded pouch shapes and closely contoured main seams). The matching cartridge belt, fixed with arched billets, carries cartridges for the heavy barreled, Model 1874 Sharps sporting rifle. (Image courtesy Arizona Historical Society Library, Tucson)

Army revolvers appeared in limited numbers among plainsmen and cowboys. Period photographs and saddlery catalogs substantiate a continuing, albeit declining utilization of the "California" pistol scabbard into the 1890s.[34]

This handsome, West Coast holster pattern gradually was eclipsed during the late 1870s and early 1880s as a more practical form, better adapted to changes in arms technology and frontier usage, came into prominence. The popular acceptance of metallic cartridge ammunition, which led directly to the design and widespread adoption of cartridge belts, certainly hastened the "California" holster's decline from favor. Typically fitted with a loop too shallow to accommodate the bulkier cartridge belts then coming into use, it was supplanted by the simpler, one-piece "Mexican Loop" holster that was designed expressly for wear on belts of greater and varying dimension.[35]

Early "Mexican Loop" Pattern Holster with Plain Waist Belt. Makers Unknown, 1875-1880. A transitional form, the body of this right-hand holster retains the form-fit silhouette, deeply recurved throat profile, and sewn-in toe plug (now missing) typical of the "California" pattern. This is coupled in one-piece design with an unusual, three-quarter-length, flared skirt secured with a single, riveted loop. Constructed of light-weight russet skirting leather, the holster is ornamented with a rolled border design. The belt, with its early, rounded buckle, is made of light bridle leather, slightly tapered at the ends, and without cartridge loops. Accompanying the outfit is a .36 caliber percussion, Colt Model 1861 Navy revolver. (Courtesy Private Collection)

"MEXICAN LOOP" PATTERN HOLSTERS

The extensive utilization of cartridge belts among frontier civilians, which commenced in the late 1860s, strongly influenced the formulation of a new, more functional holster design. While no specific artisan can be credited with the creation of this purely indigenous western form, the "Mexican Loop"[36] pattern holster probably originated in northern Mexico or the American Southwest during the early to mid-1870s. The product of a rapid diffusion among frontier saddlers, this generic design was commonplace on the Great Plains from Texas to Canada within a decade.[37]

Featuring an ample and more flexible belt loop that could pass easily over the thicker and wider, cartridge-laden belts then in vogue, the "Mexican Loop" pattern was an ingeniously simple creation. Formed from a single piece of pattern-cut leather, the holster portion was folded over vertically and sewn along its main seam to create the body or pouch for the revolver. The full back panel (typically cut with two, four or six slits depending on length) was folded down horizontally, forming a spacious belt loop and contoured skirt *behind* the holster body. The pouch was then passed or "dropped" through the slits, creating one or more integral skirt loops that secured body and back skirt as a unit. In some instances (evidently more common among Montana and Texas makers than elsewhere) separate loops were riveted or sewn to the skirt to capture the holster's pouch.[38]

This versatile new design won immediate favor among westerners of all stripes. Arriving in Cheyenne, Wyoming Territory, around 1876, novice cowboy Edgar Bronson recalled that:

> Before leaving the train, I had prudently strapped to my waist a new (how distressingly new) Colt's six-shooter, that looked and felt a yard long....The rig I had taken so much time in selecting and felt so proud of [was] quickly consigned to the scrap heap...[My] pistol had to be stripped of its flap holster and rehabited in the then new decollete Olive [recurved throat, loop pattern] scabbard.[39]

In this 1896 outdoor photo, cowboy-songwriter D. J. O'Malley poses in classic western costume. His well-worn "Mexican Loop" pattern holster is mounted on a typical cartridge/money belt and houses the popular Colt Single Action Army revolver. Note the depth and flexibility of the belt loop/back skirt, which secures the pouch with two riveted loops. (Image courtesy John I. White Collection and Guy Logsdon)

"Mexican Loop" Pattern Holster for Colt Single Action Army Revolver. Maker Unknown, 1875-1885. An early example of the "Mexican Loop" pattern, the slender, form-fit body of this holster is reminiscent of the "California" silhouette style. The wide, rounded skirt has rolled border ornament and two integral loops securing the pouch. Constructed of russet skirting leather, both the skirt back and pouch interior are fully suede-lined. The right-hand holster body features a sewn main seam, deeply recurved throat profile, and matching border ornament with a single large rosette. Accompanying the holster is a .45 caliber, Colt Single Action Army revolver with 7 1/2-inch barrel. (Courtesy Bill Mackin Collection)

"Mexican Loop" Pattern Holster for Colt Model 1861 Navy Conversion. H. Keller, Corpus Christi, Texas, 1875-1880. Reminiscent of the "California" pattern, this early "Mexican Loop" holster presents a deep, relatively form-fit silhouette. Fabricated of light-weight russet skirting material, the right-hand pouch incorporates an unusual, abruptly recurved throat profile and a contoured main seam that is sewn through the rounded toe. The rather bulbous half-skirt secures the pouch with a single, integral loop. The body is ornamented with floral and frond motifs, while the skirt is plain edge-crimped. With the holster is a .38 caliber, Colt Model 1861 Navy conversion with 7 1/2-inch barrel and full nickel finish. (Courtesy Joe Gish Collection. Image courtesy Bill Manns)

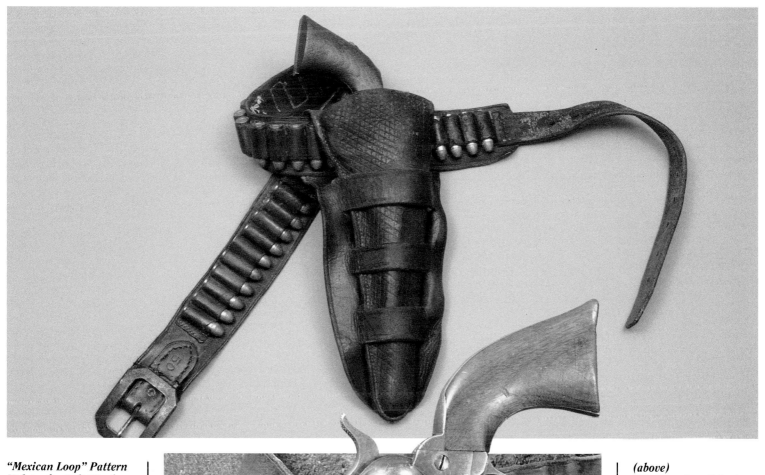

"Mexican Loop" Pattern Holster for Colt Single Action Army Revolver. G. H. & J. S. Collins, Omaha, Nebraska, 1876-1880. An early example of Collins brothers' gunleather, this left-hand specimen is fully suede-lined. Fashioned of medium-weight russet skirting material, the body incorporates a pleasing throat recurve, gently tapered main seam, and a sewn-in toe plug. The full-profile back skirt captures the pouch with two integral skirt loops of diamond pattern. A .45 caliber, Colt Single Action with 7 1/2-inch barrel accompanies the outfit. (Courtesy John E. Fox Collection)

(above) "Mexican Loop" Pattern Holster with Plain Cartridge Belt. Makers Unknown, 1875-1885. A somewhat rare variant, this deep, right-hand holster is secured to its skirt by three integral loops. Constructed of medium-weight, russet skirting leather, the body features an unusual, convex throat profile, incised, cross-hatched ornamentation, and a sewn main seam running through the toe. The belt, also of skirting leather, has sewn cartridge loops and billets. The rectangular "California" style buckle with clipped corners probably dates the belt somewhat later than the holster. With the set is a .45 caliber, Colt Single Action Army revolver with 7 1/2-inch barrel. (Courtesy Private Collection)

"Mexican Loop" Pattern Holster for Colt Single Action Army Revolver. Maker Unknown, 1875-1885. Secured with three integral skirt loops, the deep, tapered body of this right-hand specimen is fairly typical of early "Mexican Loop" production. Fashioned of medium-weight skirting stock, the piece has a deep throat recurve (over which the trigger guard has ridden for years), a sewn main seam running into the half-round toe, and an unusual, straight-sided back skirt. The holster carries a .44 caliber, Colt Single Action revolver with carved ivory stock and 7 1/2-inch barrel. (Courtesy George T. Jackson Collection. Image courtesy Bill Manns)

Photographed around 1885, Wild West cowboy Buck Taylor carries his Colt Single Action in a deep, triple-looped holster mounted on a "Mills" pattern cartridge belt. (Image courtesy Western History Collections, University of Oklahoma Library)

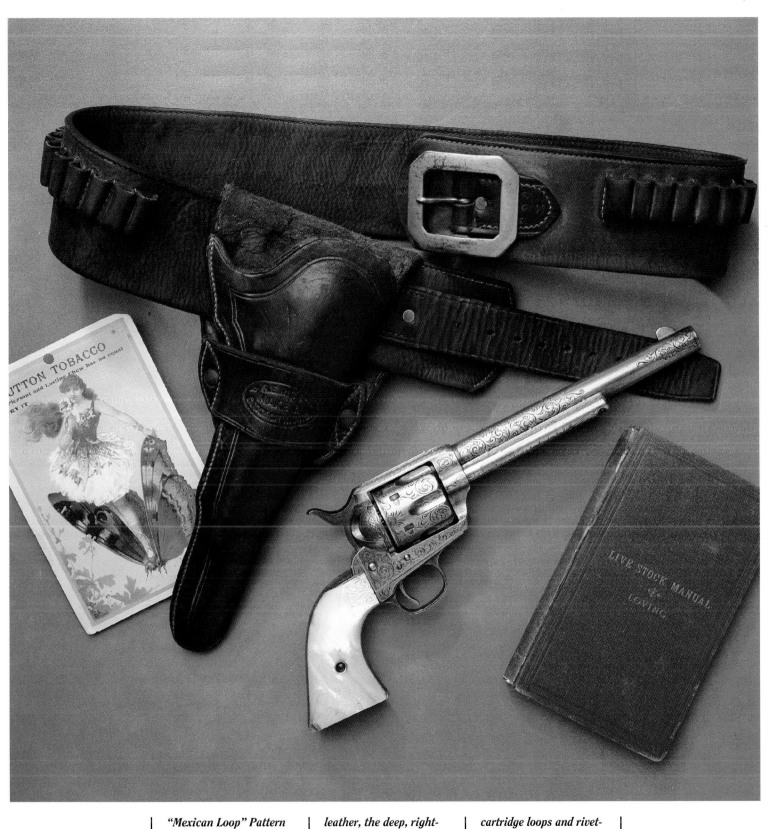

"Mexican Loop" Pattern Holster with Cartridge Money Belt. R. E. Rice, Dodge City, Kansas, 1878-1880. This matched rig, with provenance to one of the West's more notorious cattle towns, presents an early example of the "Mexican Loop" form. Constructed of medium-weight russet skirting leather, the deep, right-hand holster is secured to its truncated half-skirt with a single, riveted and sewn loop. The body incorporates a shallow throat recurve, contour-fit main seam sewn through the rounded toe, and clean borderline ornament. The cartridge money belt is of standard pattern with sewn cartridge loops and riveted and sewn billet and chape secured with a clip-cornered "California" buckle. Accompanying the outfit is a .45 caliber, Colt Single Action revolver with pearl grips, scroll engraving and 7 1/2-inch barrel. (Courtesy Gene Autry Western Heritage Museum, Los Angeles)

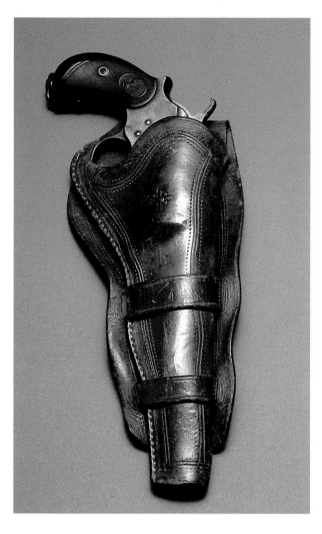

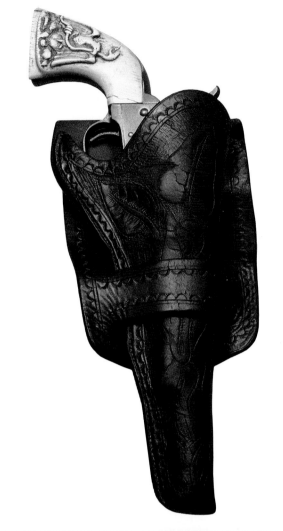

"Mexican Loop" Pattern Holster for Colt Single Action Army Revolver. Maker Unknown, 1880-1885. Presenting pleasing lines and embellishment, this one-piece holster embodies the work of a competent western saddler. Fabricated of dark russet skirting leather, the right-hand piece has a nicely-recurved throat profile, a contoured main seam with a slight "swell" below the skirt loop, and a sewn-in toe plug (now missing). While the latter characteristics typify northern plains holsters, the distinctive single-loop, half-skirt design is reminiscent of Texas makers like L. Frank of San Antonio and E. Tackabar of Fort Worth. The holster is decorated with a hand-carved foliate-and-vine motif over a stippled ground, all surrounded by a stamped border ornament on both pouch and skirt. (Courtesy Lacey and Virginia Gaddis Collection)

(above)
"Mexican Loop" Pattern Holster for Colt Single and Double Action Revolvers. Maker Unknown, 1880-1885. Characteristic of the "Cheyenne" variant popular in Montana and Wyoming, this right-hand holster features a sewn-in, "tear drop" toe plug and a swollen body profile between the integral skirt loops (designed to better retain the pouch.) Constructed of medium russet skirting leather, the piece has a gracefully recurved throat, sewn main seam, and incised-line border trim with a single small rosette. A .45 caliber, Colt Model 1878 Double Action Frontier revolver accompanies the piece. (Courtesy Private Collection)

(right)
"Mexican Loop" Pattern Holster for Colt Single Action Army Revolver. E. J. Kelly, Location Unknown, 1875-1885. Presenting a deep and gracefully tapered profile, this early "Mexican Loop" holster is suggestive of the late "California" pattern. Constructed of medium russet skirting leather, the right-hand pouch is secured to the full-profile back skirt by two integral loops and incorporates a recurved throat, semi-contoured main seam and sewn-in toe plug. Typical of the period, this specimen is ornamented with a single large rosette hand-stamped on the upper pouch face. The holster retains a .44 caliber, Colt Single Action Army revolver with 7 1/2-inch barrel. (Courtesy John E. Fox Collection)

(opposite page)
"Mexican Loop" Pattern Holster for Colt Single Action Army Revolver. Jos. Sullivan & Co., Ft. Benton, Montana Territory, 1880-1882. This left-hand specimen utilizes a contoured, three-quarter-length skirt with two narrow, integral loops. Fabricated of medium-weight russet skirting leather, the holster features a nicely recurved throat profile, semi-contour-fit main seam with open toe, and simple border tooling. Also made by Sullivan, the plain cartridge belt is fit for .32/20 ammunition. A .45 caliber, Colt Single Action revolver with ivory stocks and 7 1/2-inch barrel accompanies the outfit. (Courtesy R. M. Bachman Collection. Image courtesy Bill Manns)

Another western observer no doubt referred to the "Mexican Loop" style in describing some of the inhabitants of Muskogee, Indian Territory, in 1883: "At the station men appeared with big belts buckled around their waists full of cartridges, and forty-five calibre Colt six-shooters in holsters....Things began to look wild to me...."[40] By this time, certainly, the "Mexican Loop" holster was the predominant pattern on the rapidly diminishing frontier.

No doubt influenced by the antecedent "California" pattern, the earliest "Mexican Loop" holsters had bodies closely contoured to their respective weapons. The back skirts occasionally were quite broad and ill-defined, although by about 1880 most conformed fairly closely to the pouch silhouette. From the pattern's very inception, most of these holsters incorporated the recurved (i.e. decollete) throat profile introduced with the "California" design. But, unlike the West Coast form's typical, sewn-in toe plug, many "Mexican Loop" holsters were left open at the muzzle or had their sewn main seam extended through the toe. Throughout the heyday of their manufacture (circa 1880-1920), specimens of "right-hand" configuration appear to have outnumbered the "left-hand" variety in a ratio perhaps as high as forty-to-one.[41]

While a few of the early "Mexican Loop" holsters were fitted for percussion revolvers or metallic cartridge conversions, most accommodated the new generation of large-frame Colt, Remington or Smith & Wesson single-actions taking self-contained

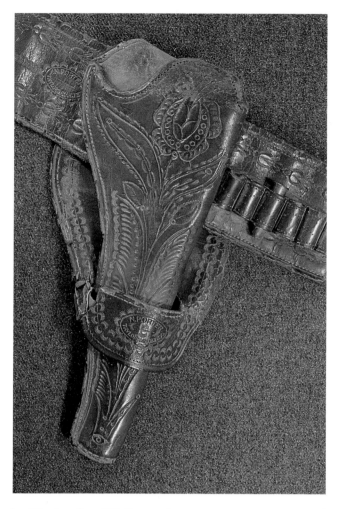

"Mexican Loop" Pattern Holster with Matching Cartridge Belt. N. Porter, Taylorsville, Texas, 1880-1885. This well-worn rig reflects Newton Porter's early production. Fabricated of medium russet leather, the right-hand holster is calfskin-lined and incorporates a recurved throat, tapered main seam, open toe, and full floral embellishment. The contour-cut back skirt is of two-thirds length and features a single, integral loop at the bottom. The outfit would accommodate a Colt Single Action Army revolver with 7 1/2-inch barrel. (Courtesy John E. Fox Collection)

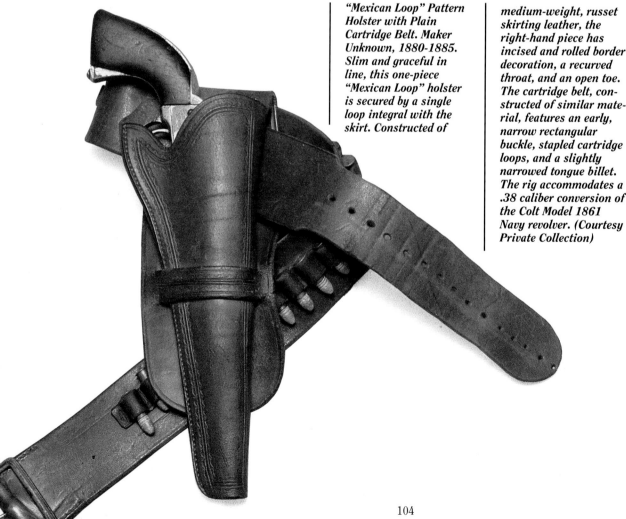

"Mexican Loop" Pattern Holster with Plain Cartridge Belt. Maker Unknown, 1880-1885. Slim and graceful in line, this one-piece "Mexican Loop" holster is secured by a single loop integral with the skirt. Constructed of medium-weight, russet skirting leather, the right-hand piece has incised and rolled border decoration, a recurved throat, and an open toe. The cartridge belt, constructed of similar material, features an early, narrow rectangular buckle, stapled cartridge loops, and a slightly narrowed tongue billet. The rig accommodates a .38 caliber conversion of the Colt Model 1861 Navy revolver. (Courtesy Private Collection)

(opposite) "Mexican Loop" Pattern Holster with Cartridge/ Money Belt. H. C. Heilig, Castroville, Texas, 1880-1885. Representative of a design popular in Texas, this deep-bodied example utilizes a short half-skirt with a single, integral loop retaining the pouch. Fabricated of medium-weight, dark russet skirting stock, the right-hand holster has a deep throat recurve and a semi-contour-fit main seam stitched through the toe. The pouch is ornamented with rolled borderlines and has a large floral rosette stamped on the upper face; the skirt loop is stamped with two "Texas" stars flanking the maker's cartouche. The piece holds a .45 caliber, Colt Single Action Army revolver with ivory stocks and 7 1/2-inch barrel. (Courtesy Jim Holley Collection. Image courtesy Bill Manns)

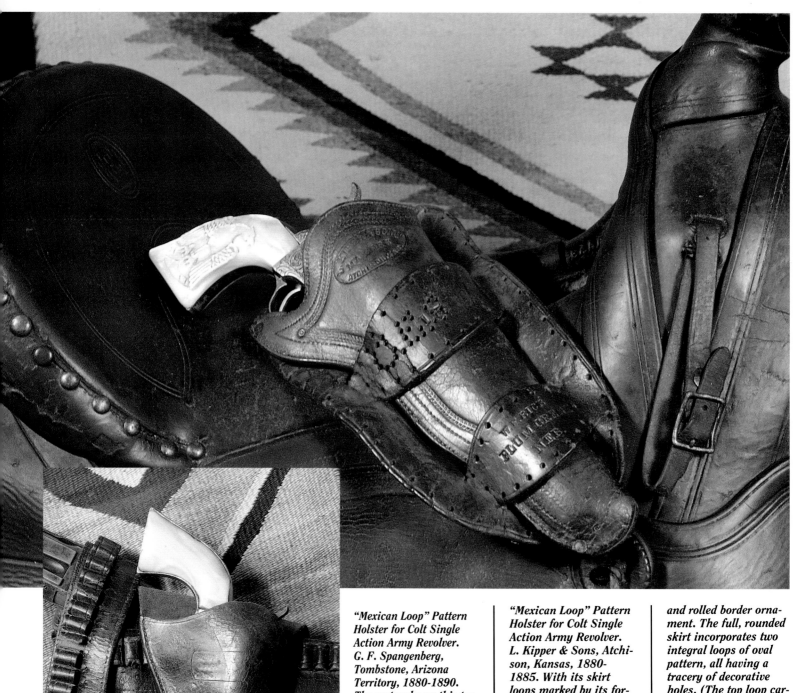

"Mexican Loop" Pattern Holster for Colt Single Action Army Revolver. G. F. Spangenberg, Tombstone, Arizona Territory, 1880-1890. The cartouche on this territorial piece carries the identification "Gunsmith" rather than the familiar "Maker". Fabricated of medium-weight, dark russet skirting stock, the right-hand pouch has a quite shallow throat recurve and a sewn main seam extending through the blunt toe. The pouch is secured to its broad, truncated half-skirt with a single integral loop. (Courtesy Brian Lebel Collection. Image courtesy Bill Manns)

"Mexican Loop" Pattern Holster for Colt Single Action Army Revolver. L. Kipper & Sons, Atchison, Kansas, 1880-1885. With its skirt loops marked by its former owners, this right-hand specimen truly evokes the history of the West. Fabricated of russet skirting leather, the holster body is lined with red flannel and features a shallow throat recurve, a curvilinear main seam reinforced with top and bottom rivets, and stitch marker and rolled border ornament. The full, rounded skirt incorporates two integral loops of oval pattern, all having a tracery of decorative holes. (The top loop carries initials, while the bottom loop is neatly stamped "W.F. RICE/ PLUM CREEK/NEB.") With the holster is a .45 caliber, Colt Single Action revolver with carved pearl grips and 7 1/2-inch barrel. (Courtesy Joe Gish Collection. Image courtesy Bill Manns)

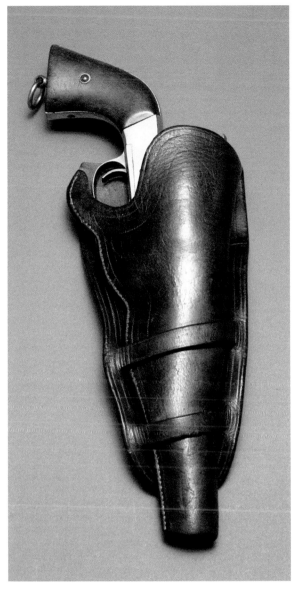

"Mexican Loop" Pattern Holster for Colt and Remington Army Revolvers. E. Goettlich, Miles City, Montana Territory, 1880-1885. Suggesting the earlier "California" style, this right-hand holster has a form-fit, contoured body and fairly deep, recurved throat profile. Constructed of heavy russet skirting leather, the pouch is secured to the skirt with two integral loops of unusual, canted design, and has a sewn main seam with open toe. All elements are finished with a faint, rolled border ornament. The holster carries a .44 caliber, Remington Model 1875 Single Action Army revolver. (Courtesy Phil Spangenberger Collection)

Posed at Scofield, Utah Territory, circa 1885, this buckskin-clad frontiersman carries his Colt Single Action in an early "Mexican Loop" pattern holster incorporating a slim body with a broad, truncated half-skirt and single, integral loop. Mounted on a narrow, pistol cartridge belt, the right-hand outfit is worn in cross-draw position with a hunting knife and sheath thrust beneath the skirt loop. (Image courtesy Brigham Young University Photo Archives, Provo, Utah)

"Mexican Loop" Pattern Holster for Colt Single Action Army Revolver. J. S. Collins, Cheyenne, Wyoming Territory, 1881-1886 . This right-hand specimen, with its parallel-edged pipe section extending nearly half the length of the pouch, presents an unusual interpretation of the "Cheyenne" holster variation. The holster body is fully lined with smooth buckskin and incorporates a recurved throat and main seam with a sewn-in toe plug of "tear drop" configuration. The three-quarter-length skirt secures the pouch with two integral loops. In lieu of the typical maker's cartouche, this holster is stamped with an unusual shield device carrying the maker's monogrammed initials beneath the town of origin. (Courtesy John E. Fox Collection)

ammunition in .44 or .45 caliber. As these weapons were at first most common in seven- to eight-inch barrel lengths, their attendant scabbards were comparatively long in the body and often secured with two or, in relatively rare instances, three skirt loops. Those large examples incorporating only a single retaining loop usually utilized a half- or three-quarter-length skirt that terminated well above the toe of the pouch.

By the late 1880s, as shorter-barreled revolvers came into vogue, the "Mexican Loop" holster took on a more compact and amorphous form typically having a full, contoured skirt with one or two loops. While earlier versions often were fabricated of relatively soft and pliable russet leather, by 1890 many western saddlers employed stiffer skirting material that better held its form and, perhaps, marginally increased the speed of the draw.[42]

Two regional interpretations of the "Mexican Loop" pattern holster were noteworthy for their distinctive characteristics. The first was the "Cheyenne" variation, formulated in that famed Wyoming cowtown between 1870 and 1880 by saddlers E. L. Gallatin, F. A. Meanea and, perhaps, J. S. Collins.

Popular throughout the northern plains country, the "Cheyenne" holster usually was distinguished by a noticeable swell or bulge in the pouch's main seam contour between the skirt loops. This contour was

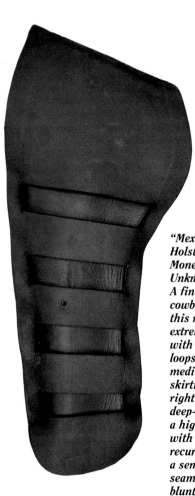

"Mexican Loop" Pattern Holster with Cartridge Money Belt. Maker Unknown, 1880-1890. A fine example of cowboy-era gunleather, this rig incorporates an extremely rare holster with four integral skirt loops. Fabricated of medium-weight russet skirting leather, the right-hand holster is deep-bodied and features a high throat profile with a fairly abrupt recurve over the trigger, a semi-contoured main seam sewn into the blunt toe, and a rolled

border element of tiny circles. The full profile back skirt is folded so as to cant the pistol grip forward. The accompanying cartridge/money belt is constructed in the usual fashion and features a lightly rolled border ornament of leaf motif and a rectangular, double-frame "California" pattern buckle. The outfit carries a .44 caliber, Smith & Wesson American revolver with full, 8-inch barrel. (Courtesy Robert W. Smith Collection)

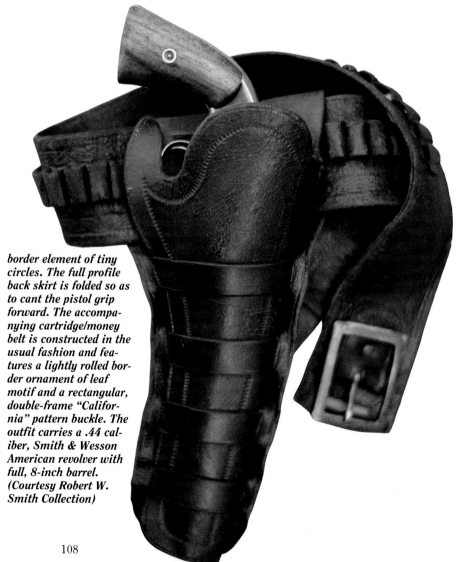

"Mexican Loop" Pattern Holster with Cartridge Money Belt. E. Goettlich, Miles City, Montana Territory, 1883-1885. Still in virtually new condition, this superb matched rig set a record price for western gunleather at auction in 1991. Constructed of medium-weight russet skirting material, the deep, right-hand holster incorporates a graceful throat recurve, semi-contour-fit main seam and sewn-in toe plug of "Cheyenne" pattern. The body is secured to the relatively broad back skirt with a separate, riveted loop at the mid-section and with an integral loop at the toe — a most unusual arrangement. Both the skirt loops and body are decorated with crimped border tooling, the latter with small corner rosettes. Of typical design, the combination belt is fabricated of pliable calfskin with sewn cartridge loops and sewn and riveted billets of light skirting leather; the piece secures with a clip-cornered "California" buckle. Accompanying the rig is a .44 caliber, Colt Single Action Army revolver with ivory grips and 7 1/2-inch barrel. (Courtesy Ken Bartlett Collection. Photo by William Manns.)

designed to "lock in" the pouch more securely, particularly when the revolver was drawn. Most specimens also incorporated a distinctive toe plug of "tear drop" configuration sewn in at the muzzle. Sometimes termed a "Cheyenne" plug, this feature was intended to better retain form in the lower pouch area and preclude snow from clogging the pistol barrel if the wearer hunkered in a drift.[43]

The other regional variation, the so-called "Texas Jockstrap" holster, appeared during the late 1890s among a few Lone Star saddlers, most notably H. A. Holtzer of Llano and S. D. Myres of Sweetwater. The salient feature of this design was a large, modified loop, or T-shaped "collar," patterned to secure the pistol pouch not only at each side, but at the bottom extremity as well (thus, the "Jockstrap" appellation). A separate element of the holster, this distinctive loop usually was fixed to the back skirt with rivets. In very rare instances, a full "pocket" was created by stitching

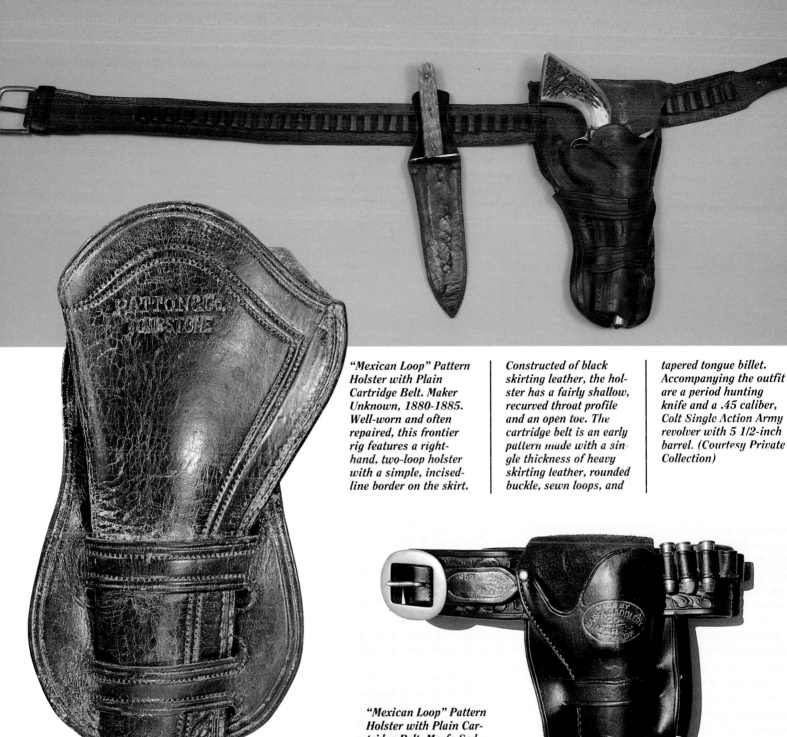

"Mexican Loop" Pattern Holster with Plain Cartridge Belt. Maker Unknown, 1880-1885. Well-worn and often repaired, this frontier rig features a right-hand, two-loop holster with a simple, incised-line border on the skirt.

Constructed of black skirting leather, the holster has a fairly shallow, recurved throat profile and an open toe. The cartridge belt is an early pattern made with a single thickness of heavy skirting leather, rounded buckle, sewn loops, and

tapered tongue billet. Accompanying the outfit are a period hunting knife and a .45 caliber, Colt Single Action Army revolver with 5 1/2-inch barrel. (Courtesy Private Collection)

"Mexican Loop" Pattern Holster for Colt Single Action Army Revolver. Patton & Co., Tombstone, Arizona Territory 1885-1895. This territorial piece is distinguished by some unusual design elements. Constructed of dark russet skirting leather, the left-hand holster pouch

has a fairly high — yet barely recurved — throat profile, while the contoured back skirt presents a singularly bulbous silhouette. The holster likely accommodates a 4 3/4 - or 5 1/2-inch-barreled Single Action Colt revolver. (Courtesy John E. Fox Collection)

"Mexican Loop" Pattern Holster with Plain Cartridge Belt. Marfa Saddlery, Marfa, Texas; Fred Mueller, Denver, Colorado, 1885-1895. This "pieced" outfit combines a plain but relatively rare, three-loop holster with a finely ornamented cartridge belt. Constructed of medium-weight, black skirting leather, the right-hand holster incorporates a fairly low throat recurve, a curvilinear main seam sewn into the toe and fixed with a top rivet, and a full-contoured skirt with integral loops securing the pouch. All

elements have an edge-crimped borderline. Made of substantial skirting material, the single-thickness cartridge belt is looped for .38 caliber pistol cartridges and features full floral carving and a

nickeled "California" buckle of oval pattern. The rig probably accommodated a Colt Single Action Army revolver with full 7 1/2-inch barrel. (Courtesy S.P. Stevens Collection)

"Mexican Loop" Pattern Holster with Cartridge Money Belt. Moran Bros., Miles City, Montana Territory, 1880-1890. This matched, territorial-era rig exhibits the craftsmanship that made Miles City saddlers famous. Fabricated of dark russet skirting leather, the right-hand holster incorporates an unusually narrow throat recurve at the trigger, a contoured main seam with straight "pipe" portion, and a sewn-in toe plug. The pouch is secured to the over-sized back skirt with a separate, riveted loop of comparatively wide proportion. All elements are edge-creased and the pouch and skirt loop feature a rolled, hash-mark border ornament. The combination belt is of typical material and construction except that it is stitched around all four sides. Riveted and sewn, the tongue billet and chape are joined by a typical, "California" pattern buckle. With the outfit is a .44 caliber, Colt Single Action revolver with 4 3/4-inch barrel. (Courtesy Joe Gish Collection. Image courtesy Bill Manns)

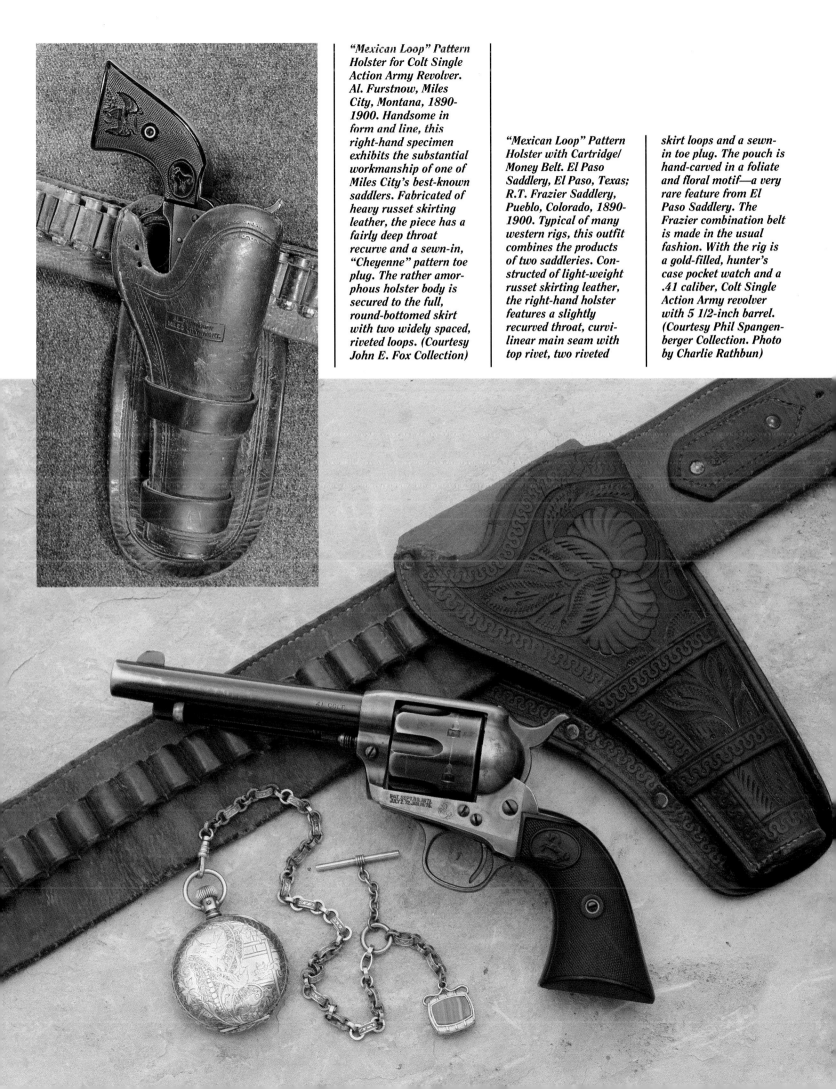

"Mexican Loop" Pattern Holster for Colt Single Action Army Revolver. Al. Furstnow, Miles City, Montana, 1890-1900. Handsome in form and line, this right-hand specimen exhibits the substantial workmanship of one of Miles City's best-known saddlers. Fabricated of heavy russet skirting leather, the piece has a fairly deep throat recurve and a sewn-in, "Cheyenne" pattern toe plug. The rather amorphous holster body is secured to the full, round-bottomed skirt with two widely spaced, riveted loops. (Courtesy John E. Fox Collection)

"Mexican Loop" Pattern Holster with Cartridge/Money Belt. El Paso Saddlery, El Paso, Texas; R.T. Frazier Saddlery, Pueblo, Colorado, 1890-1900. Typical of many western rigs, this outfit combines the products of two saddleries. Constructed of light-weight russet skirting leather, the right-hand holster features a slightly recurved throat, curvilinear main seam with top rivet, two riveted skirt loops and a sewn-in toe plug. The pouch is hand-carved in a foliate and floral motif—a very rare feature from El Paso Saddlery. The Frazier combination belt is made in the usual fashion. With the rig is a gold-filled, hunter's case pocket watch and a .41 caliber, Colt Single Action Army revolver with 5 1/2-inch barrel. (Courtesy Phil Spangenberger Collection. Photo by Charlie Rathbun)

Exhibiting a variety of "Mexican Loop" pattern holsters, these gents were photographed in Dodge City, Kansas, around 1885. From the left: a deep, three-loop variant; a typical double-loop design; and a wide, single-loop with truncated half-skirt. All are mounted on narrow, all-leather pistol cartridge belts with deringer pistols thrust beneath. (Image courtesy Herb Peck, Jr. Collection)

"Mexican Loop" Pattern Holster with Cartridge/Money Belt. Furstnow & Coggshall, Miles City, Montana, 1890-1895. This late, northern plains rig combines a relatively streamlined holster with a very wide combination belt. Fabricated of medium-weight russet skirting leather, the right-hand pouch features a typical throat recurve, a curvilinear main seam and a sewn-in toe plug. (Wear and stressing suggest that the weapon often was carried with the trigger guard riding up in the lower throat recurve.) The full, tapered skirt secures the pouch with two riveted loops. Constructed of pliable russet calfskin, the cartridge/money belt is a full 41/2-inches in width and retains the remnant of a small, scalloped and clip-cornered "California" buckle with nickeled finish. The outfit carries a .45 caliber, Colt Single Action Army revolver with 4 3/4-inch barrel and carved pearl grips. (Courtesy Robert W. Smith Collection)

In this circa 1895 cabinet photo, Buffalo Bill Wild West Show performer Alice McGowan strikes a pose with her considerable armament. She carries her ivory-stocked Colt Single Action in what appears to be a "Cheyenne" variant of the "Mexican Loop" pattern holster mounted on a wide cartridge/money belt. (Image courtesy Lee Silva Collection, the Greg Silva Memorial Old West Archives, San Pedro, California)

"Mexican Loop" Pattern Holster with Cartridge/Money Belt. E. L. Gallatin & Co., Cheyenne, Wyoming Territory, 1875-1880. An early example of the "Cheyenne" variant, this graceful holster is a virtual prototype of the form later popularized by Gallatin's understudy, F. A. Meanea. Fashioned of medium-weight skirting stock, the right-hand pouch is lined with red felt and incorporates the distinctive main seam swell and classic "tear drop" toe plug that hallmark this regional style. Two integral loops above and below the main seam bulge firmly secure the contour-fit body to its truncated back skirt. The piece is adorned with typical, rolled border ornament, and with rosettes and additional frond motifs at the corners. An ivory-stocked, .45 caliber, Colt Single Action Army revolver with 7 1/2-inch barrel accompanies the rig. (Courtesy Jim Holley Collection. Image courtesy Bill Manns)

a contoured facing leather over the front periphery of the skirt, completely shrouding the lower half of the holster body. While it never became widely popular, the "Jockstrap" variant was briefly copied beyond its area of origin by a few saddlers, including R. T. Frazier of Pueblo, Colorado, and Main & Winchester of San Francisco. Certainly, its chief practitioner during the twentieth century was S. D. Myres, who perpetuated the design from his El Paso, Texas, shop well into the 1940s.[44]

Continuing the tradition established with the "California" pattern, "Mexican Loop" holsters almost invariably featured some degree of applied embellishment. Earlier specimens generally carried on the late "California" treatment, having a relatively simple, tooled or stamped border element around the edge of the pouch and/or skirt with, perhaps, a single rosette motif on the upper pouch face. By the 1880s, full, hand-carved floral adornment reappeared among a few western saddlers; the work was often in motifs mirroring that applied to saddles. And, within another decade, leather embellishment truly came into its own with the advent of less costly machine stamping. By the turn of the century, "Mexican Loop" pattern holsters adorned with raised floral or basket-weave motifs in full coverage became prevalent. These later holsters often incorporated single, relatively wide skirt loops of scalloped, oval, circular or half-circle pattern on which the stamped motif also was applied.[45]

(opposite)
"Mexican Loop" Pattern Holster with Cartridge/Money Belt. Moran Bros., Miles City, Montana Territory, 1885-1890. With its sewn-in, "tear drop" toe plug and its slight main seam bulge below the single, riveted skirt loop, this right-hand holster is suggestive of the popular "Cheyenne" variant. Constructed of medium-weight russet skirting leather, the deep-bodied specimen sports a plunging throat recurve and a broad, uncontoured skirt. The holster body and separate skirt loop are decorated with a rolled border ornament. The unadorned combination belt is of typical design and material. A .45 caliber, Colt Single Action revolver with 7 1/2-inch barrel accompanies the outfit. (Courtesy Jim Holley Collection. Image courtesy Bill Manns)

Attired in a brand-new costume, this "studio" cowboy of circa 1890 wears a finely tooled, "Mexican Loop" holster of "Cheyenne" pattern (note the main seam swell between the two integral loops and the blunt toe profile with sewn-in plug). The holster appears to be suede or buckskin-lined, and is mounted on a combination cartridge/money belt sans ammunition. (Image courtesy The Wyoming State Museum, Cheyenne)

(opposite)
"Mexican Loop" Pattern Holster for Colt Model 1878 Frontier Revolver. Maker Unknown, 1880-1890. This stylish "Cheyenne" variant of the "Mexican Loop" pattern holster no doubt originated on the northern plains. Constructed of medium-weight russet skirting leather, its distinctive main seam swell between the skirt loops, and its sewn-in, "tear-drop" pattern toe plug are indicative of this regional interpretation. The right-hand pouch has a nicely recurved throat profile and is set off with rolled border ornament and a thonged concho. With the holster is a .45 caliber, Colt Model 1878 Double Action Frontier revolver with 7 1/2-inch barrel. (Courtesy Joe Gish Collection. Image courtesy Bill Manns)

"Mexican Loop" Pattern Holster with Cartridge Money Belt. F. A. Meanea Saddlery, Cheyenne, Wyoming. 1890-1900. This matched rig exhibits the craftsmanship of one of the West's master saddlers. The right-hand holster, constructed of heavy russet skirting leather, features a slight swelling of the body profile between the integral skirt loops (designed to keep the pouch from riding up when the revolver is drawn), and also has a "tear drop"-shaped, sewn-in toe plug — both traits typical of Wyoming and Montana-made holsters. The piece is gracefully-recurved at the throat and is deeply-stamped with a border pattern having small, stamped rosettes at the corners. The accompanying belt has a body of dark, supple leather with contrasting billets of skirting leather matching the holster. Constructed in the usual fashion, the belt has a nickeled "California" pattern buckle with clipped corners. (National Cowboy Hall of Fame Collection)

This jaunty, well-"heeled" cowpuncher of the 1880's is outfitted with the classic tools of his trade. He proudly displays his Model 1873 Winchester carbine, along with a Colt Single Action Army revolver with 7 1/2-inch barrel. His left-hand "Mexican Loop" holster is supported by a standard cartridge/money belt. The cross draw position of his gun rig was practical for a mounted cowboy. His chaps are of the popular shotgun style and the spurs are large roweled, drop shank design. (Photo courtesy Herb Peck, Jr.)

These cuts illustrate Frank Meanea's standard, "Cheyenne" variant of the "Mexican Loop" pattern holster from his No. 12 catalog of circa 1914 (border stamped and buckskin-lined or plain finish at $2.00 and $1.25 respectively).

"Mexican Loop" Pattern Holster for Colt Single Action Revolver. J.S. Collins & Co., Cheyenne, Wyoming Territory, 1886-1890. Elegant design and premium craftsmanship make this "Cheyenne" style holster a classic. With the holster is a matching Collins money belt. (Courtesy Arizona West Galleries. Image courtesy Bill Manns)

"Mexican Loop" Pattern Holster for Colt Single Action Army Revolver. F. A. Meanea Saddlery, Cheyenne, Wyoming, 1890-1900. Characteristic of northern plains design, this right-hand piece has a slight swell in the body contour between the two integral loops meant to "lock in" the pouch. Constructed of stiff russet skirting leather, the holster incorporates a shallow, recurved throat profile, sewn main seam, and Meanea's classic "tear drop," sewn-in toe plug (now missing.) The pouch is finely hand-carved in a beautiful floral motif. The holster carries a Colt Single Action Army revolver with ivory grips and a 5 1/2-inch barrel. (National Cowboy Hall of Fame Collection)

Hybrid "Mexican Loop" Pattern Holster for Colt Single Action Army Revolver. Al. Furstnow, Miles City, Montana, 1895-1905. Although military in appearance, this western holster in fact is a modification of a purely civilian product. Constructed of dark russet skirting leather, the right-hand piece incorporates a tapered, form-molded pouch with recurved throat and sewn-in toe plug, a wide, rounded back skirt, and two riveted retaining loops. The separate, sewn-on cover flap, which secures with a brass finial, no doubt represents a later addition, as it does not carry the rolled border lines that ornament the pouch and skirt. (Courtesy Richard Ellis Publications. Paul Goodwin, Photographer)

"Mexican Loop" Pattern Holster with Cartridge Money Belt. F. A. Meanea, Cheyenne, Wyoming Territory, 1885-1890. Still in virtually new condition, this handsome rig exhibits the classic attributes of the "Cheyenne" variant. Fabricated of medium-weight russet skirting material, the right-handed pouch incorporates a pleasing throat recurve, a partially welted main seam with the distinctive bulge between the integral skirt loops, and a sewn-in toe plug of "tear drop" configuration. The piece is ornamented with a multi-faceted, hand-stamped border decoration and accommodates a .44 caliber, Colt Single Action Army revolver with fine ivory grips and 7 1/2-inch barrel. The matching combination belt is a full four inches in width and of typical materials and construction. (Courtesy R.M. Bachman Collection. Image courtesy Bill Manns)

121

Posed in Cheyenne, Wyoming Territory, circa 1885, these fellows carry their Colt Single Action Army revolvers in buckskin-lined, "Mexican Loop" pattern holsters of "Cheyenne" style (note the main seam swells between the skirt loops and the sewn-in toe plugs). Combination cartridge/ money belts complete their rigs; the example at right is a particularly wide and supple variation. (Image courtesy Herb Peck, Jr. Collection)

"Mexican Loop" Pattern Holster for Colt Single Action Army Revolver. H. A. Holtzer, Llano, Texas, 1895-1905. An early example of the "Texas Jockstrap" variant, this specimen incorporates an applied facing element that is riveted and sewn to the contoured skirt, securing the lower half of the pouch at the muzzle and along both sides. Constructed of medium-weight, russet skirting stock, the right-hand pouch has been altered to a "Texas low-cut" throat profile with a leather hammer thong strap added for security. The wide collar or facing leather is stamped with a decorative pattern of interlocking circles and squares. (Courtesy John E. Fox Collection)

"Mexican Loop" Pattern Holster with Cartridge/ Money Belt. H. A. Holtzer, Llano, Texas, 1895-1905. This finely made "Jockstrap" interpretation of the "Mexican Loop" pattern holster utilizes an extremely deep, double-stitched facing collar to capture the body. Fashioned of medium-weight russet skirting leather, the right-hand pouch has a "low-cut," slightly recurved throat and a rounded, sewn-through toe. The facing leather, with its wrap-around toe element, is ornamented with tool stamping. With the outfit is a .45 caliber, Colt Single Action Army revolver with 5 1/2-inch barrel. (Courtesy Jim Holley Collection. Image courtesy Bill Manns)

(below)
"Mexican Loop" Pattern Holster for Colt Single Action Army Revolver. Maker Unknown, 1895-1905. This "Texas Jockstrap" variant employs a very wide, horizontal facing leather (with a comparatively narrow, vertical member) that is double-stitched to its broad back skirt to secure the pouch. Fabricated of light-weight russet skirting material, the right-hand pouch incorporates a shallow throat recurve and a barely contoured main seam that is sewn through the rounded toe. Both the body and the facing leather feature rolled border ornament. With the holster is a .45 caliber, Colt Single Action revolver with 4 3/4-inch barrel. (Courtesy Joe Gish Collection. Image courtesy Bill Manns)

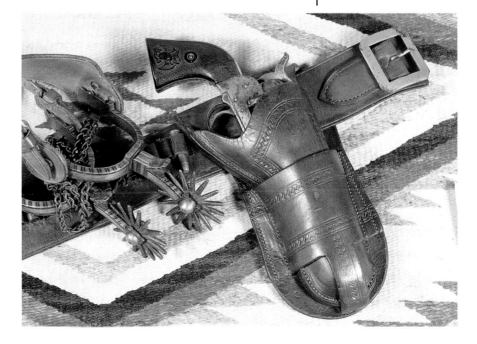

"Mexican Loop" Pattern Holster with Plain Cartridge Belt. The George Lawrence Company, Portland, Oregon, 1925-1930. Utilizing a deep, T-shaped collar to secure the pouch, this "Texas Jockstrap" variant parallels the style formulated by S.D. Myres. Fashioned of russet skirting leather, the right-hand holster features a relatively shallow throat recurve and a broad back skirt with full floral and foliate carving. The accompanying belt, also by Lawrence, incorporates woven-through cartridge loops and rolled border ornament. The rig holds a .45 caliber, Colt Single Action with stag grips and a 7 1/2-inch barrel. (Courtesy Jim Naramore Collection. Image courtesy Bill Manns)

"Mexican Loop" Pattern Holster for Colt Single Action Army Revolver. Possibly H. A. Holtzer, Llano, Texas, 1900-1910. An unusual variant of the "Mexican Loop" style, this "Texas Jockstrap" holster features a single, wide loop that also wraps around the toe, firmly securing the skirt to the body by means of numerous rivets. This right-hand example exhibits an extremely shallow recurve at the throat, and has a welted main seam sewn through the toe. (Courtesy Bill Macklin Collection)

"Mexican Loop" Pattern Holster for Colt Single Action Army Revolver. S.D. Myres, El Paso, Texas, 1920-1930. Constructed of medium-weight, russet skirting leather, this handsome "Texas Jockstrap" variation employs a separate, machine-riveted loop to secure the body and back skirt. Designed in a distinctive, elongated "T" pattern, the sloping cross member is nicely contoured into the extended vertical member that wraps over the toe. The left-hand holster body incorporates a canted belt loop fold that tips the pistol grip forward when mounted, and has a fairly shallow throat recurve with a welted and sewn main seam running through the closed toe. All elements feature hand-carved embellishment in a floral and oak leaf motif. The holster carries a .32 caliber, nickel-plated Colt Single Action Army revolver with pearl grips and 5 1/2 - inch barrel. (Courtesy Bill Mackin Collection)

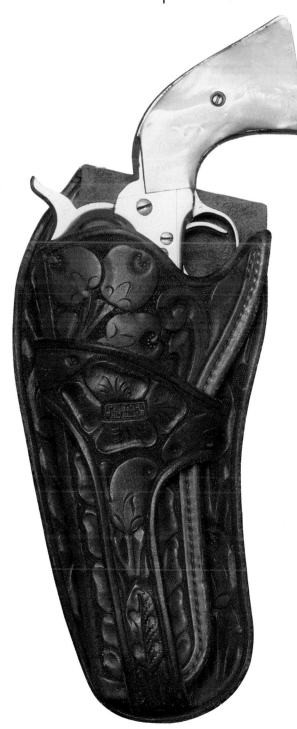

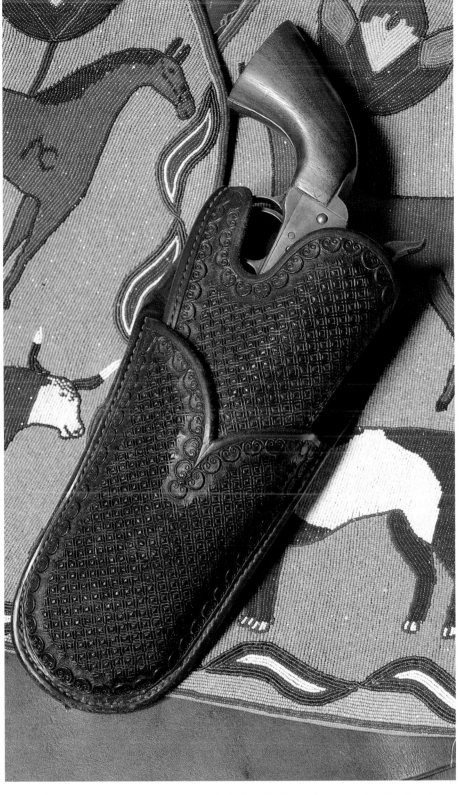

Semi-Modern Western Holster for Colt Single Action Army Revolver. Maker Unknown, 1940-1950. A very fine and most unusual interpretation of the "Mexican Loop" holster, this right-hand specimen is fabricated of heavy, dark russet skirting leather. A single, pattern-cut piece forms the holster body and belt loop/back skirt. The rather amorphous holster body, which has a recurved throat and sewn main seam running through the round toe, is captured in a full, V-throated pouch or pocket sewn on the face of the back skirt. Both elements are fully ornamented with a hand-cut, checkered-diamond pattern surrounded by a border of hand-stamped scallops. The holster is fitted for a Colt Single Action Army revolver with 5 1/2 inch barrel. (Courtesy Lacey and Virginia Gaddis Collection)

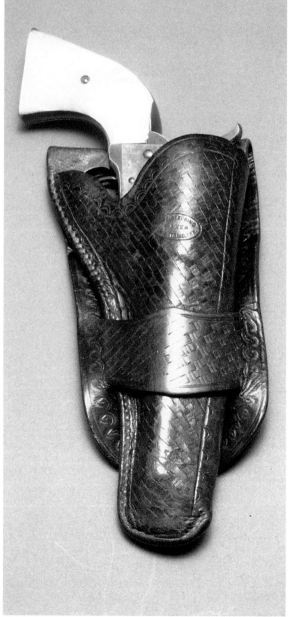

"Mexican Loop" Pattern Holster for Colt Single Action Army Revolver. Theodore Steubing, San Antonio, Texas, 1900-1910. Indicative of turn-of-the-century artistry, this right-hand specimen features stamped, basket-weave decoration and a single, fairly wide integral loop with a peaked profile. The pouch has a shallow throat recurve and a sewn main seam extending through the closed toe. Somewhat shorter than the body, the skirt has a rounded contour with rolled border ornament. The holster holds a .45 caliber, Colt Single Action Army revolver with pearl grips and 4 3/4-inch barrel. (Courtesy Phil Spangenberger Collection)

"Mexican Loop" Pattern Holster with Cartridge Money Belt. R. T. Frazier Saddlery, Pueblo, Colorado, 1905-1915. This matched rig epitomizes the quality and style of Frazier gunleather in the early twentieth century. The right-hand holster is something of a design departure, having a single, very wide, integral loop securing the body to the skirt; and having a canted belt loop fold that slants the revolver to the rear to better facilitate the draw. Constructed of dark russet skirting leather, the piece is embellished with a stamped, basket-weave pattern and large, carved floral rosette. The main seam and toe are finished with rawhide lacing. The belt, of black calfskin, is folded across the bottom and sewn along the top in customary fashion, and has sewn cartridge loops of black bridle-weight leather. The billets for the tongue and "California" style buckle are of russet skirting leather matching the holster. At the time of manufacture, this outfit sold at retail for $4.25. With the gunleather is a .44 caliber, Smith & Wesson Double Action Frontier revolver with pearl stocks. (Courtesy Bill Mackin Collection)

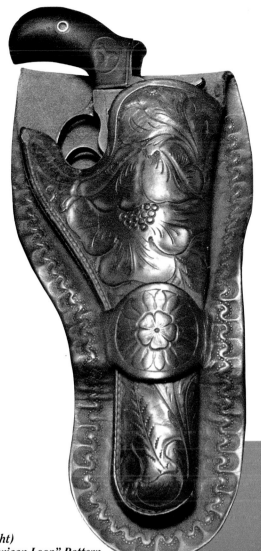

"Mexican Loop" Pattern Holster for Colt Model 1877 "Lightning" Revolver. T. Flynn Saddlery Co., Pueblo, Colorado, 1895-1905. A standard Flynn product well into the 1920s, this handsome, No. 3 pattern holster featured a floral-tooled body and a wide, border-stamped skirt with a stamped rosette on the single, circular-shaped integral loop. Constructed of "select California leather," the right-hand piece has a moderately deep recurved throat and a sewn main seam running through the toe and secured with a top staple. With the holster is a .38 caliber, Colt "Lightning" Double Action revolver with 6-inch barrel. (Courtesy Private Collection)

Not a few "Mexican Loop" holsters received more extensive, often garish embellishment. By the mid-1890s, some western saddlers, perhaps following the lead of their cowboy customers, offered holsters ornamented with thonged conchos on the upper body or skirt loops. Others brightened their products with applied fringing or a multitude of small, nickeled brass studs, or "spots," tracing the borders of the body and skirt elements. From south of the border, Mexican interpretations often featured finely applied embroidery in various plant fibers, or silken or metallic thread. Even a few Plains Indians adopted the "Mexican Loop" holster, usually adorning the form in full or partial coverage with vari-colored, lazy-stitch beadwork of geometric motif. And, somewhat prior to the the First World War, Anglo artisans commenced closing the holster's main seam with a contrasting lacing of rawhide thong (a practice later extended to all border elements).[46]

As previously alluded, many eastern and mid-western enterprises were not hesitant in appropriating the "Mexican Loop" pattern holster for their own product lines (some even copied the earlier "California" design). Perhaps as early as the mid-1880s, leather

(right)
"Mexican Loop" Pattern Holster for Colt Single Action Army Revolver. Charles Swope, Montrose, Colorado, 1890-1895. Brightened with nickeled "spots" and a pair of heart-shaped conchos, this right-hand, "Mexican Loop" holster probably was decorated by its cowboy owner rather than the maker. Constructed of medium-weight russet skirting material, the piece has a graceful throat recurve, contoured back skirt with two integral loops, and a curvilinear main seam sewn through the toe (with thong-laced repair at the top). The pouch features a rolled border ornament and a large floral rosette (now obscured by the upper concho). The holster retains a .45 caliber, Colt Single Action with 5 1/2-inch barrel. (Courtesy Phil Spangenberger Collection. Photo by Charlie Rathbun)

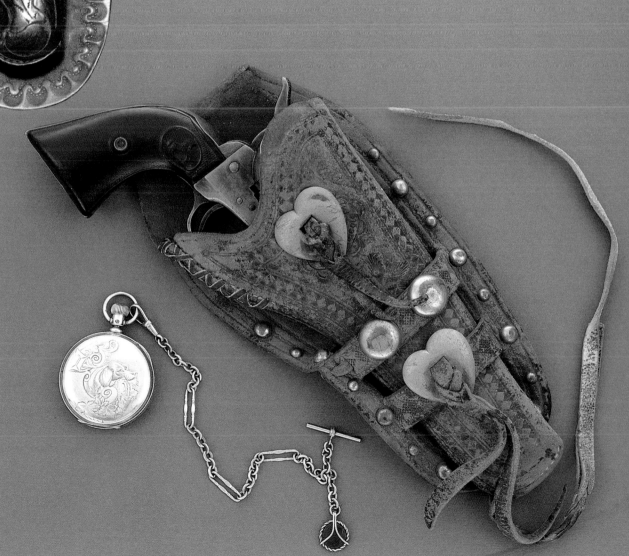

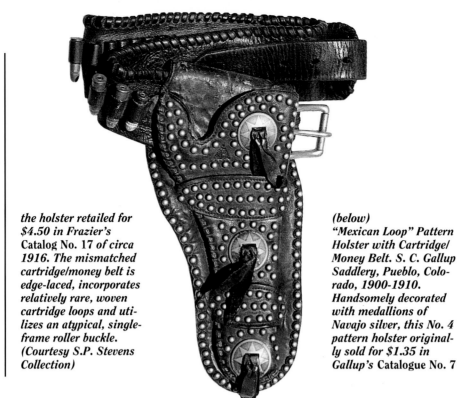

"*Mexican Loop*" *Pattern Holster with Cartridge/Money Belt. R.T. Frazier, Pueblo, Colorado, 1915-1925. Available with matching belt, chaps, cuffs and spur leathers, Frazier's showy, No. 205 holster features latigo-laced conchos and a profusion of nickeled "spots" tracing major elements. Constructed of black-dyed, medium skirting leather, the right-hand specimen has a recurved throat, edge-laced main seam extending through the rounded toe, and two integral skirt loops with a lined skirt back. Fit for a Colt Single Action with 7 1/2-inch barrel,* the holster retailed for $4.50 in Frazier's Catalog No. 17 of circa 1916. The mismatched cartridge/money belt is edge-laced, incorporates relatively rare, woven cartridge loops and utilizes an atypical, single-frame roller buckle. (Courtesy S.P. Stevens Collection)

(below) "*Mexican Loop*" *Pattern Holster with Cartridge/Money Belt. S. C. Gallup Saddlery, Pueblo, Colorado, 1900-1910. Handsomely decorated with medallions of Navajo silver, this No. 4 pattern holster originally sold for $1.35 in* Gallup's Catalogue No. 7 *of circa 1905. Fashioned of medium-weight russet skirting leather, the right-hand piece is full basket-stamped and incorporates a typical throat recurve, a sewn main seam extending through the round toe, and a single, integral loop of broad proportion. The accompanying combination belt is thong-laced and secures with a double-frame "California" pattern buckle. With the rig is a .45 caliber, Colt Single Action revolver with ivory stocking and 5 1/2-inch barrel. (Courtesy Douglas Deihl Collection. Image courtesy Bill Manns)*

"Mexican Loop" Pattern Holster for Colt Single Action Army Revolver. Maker Unknown, 1905-1915. Reflecting its twentieth century origin, this right-hand holster features machine-stamped, basket-weave ornament on its contoured body and oval-shaped loops. Constructed of dark russet skirting leather, the piece has a gracefully recurved throat profile, a main seam sewn through the toe, and a full silhouette skirt with two integral loops securing the pouch. (Courtesy Private Collection)

"Mexican Loop" Pattern Holster for Colt Single Action Army Revolver. Maker Unknown, 1905-1915. Suggestive of Colorado origin, this well-made, right-hand holster features the round loop and rawhide lacing favored by Denver and Pueblo manufacturers. Constructed of medium-weight russet skirting leather, the piece has a basket-stamped body with recurved throat and closed toe. The narrow skirt and single, integral loop are ornamented with border stamping and a plain, slotted concho. Accompanying the holster is a .45 caliber, Colt Bisley Model, Single Action revolver with a 4 3/4-inch barrel and pearl stocks. (Courtesy Phil Spangenberger Collection)

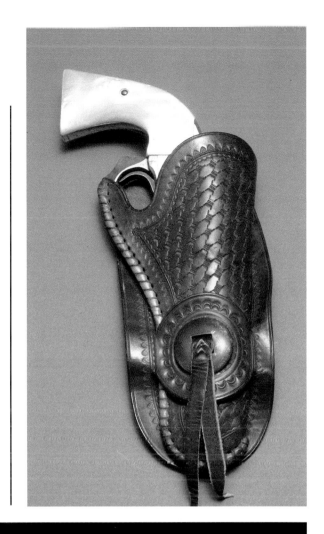

"Mexican Loop" Pattern Holster with Cartridge/ Money Belt. M. E. French Saddlery, Montrose, Colorado, 1900-1910. Typical of the era's better saddlers, this outfit combines quality leathers and meticulous construction. The one-piece holster, made of russet skirting leather, is secured with a single, integral loop of oval pattern. Ornamented with border stamping and floral carving on both the body and skirt, it features a graceful recurved throat, sewn main seam, and open toe. The accompanying cartridge/money belt, folded and sewn in the usual fashion, has sewn loops and billets of skirting leather with a square, clip-cornered "California" buckle. A .41 caliber, Colt Single Action Army revolver completes the outfit. (Courtesy Bill Mackin Collection)

"Mexican Loop" Pattern Holster with Two-Piece Cartridge Belt. Maker Unknown, 1910-1920. A superb example of Mexican leathercraft, this matched rig features extensive embroidery with yucca, or cactus fiber. Fashioned throughout of lightweight russet leather, the holster and back skirt are contour-cut, edge-laced, and secured with two riveted loops. The right-hand pouch has a straight throat profile and utilizes a snapped safety strap. The cartridge belt incorporates a double-billeted front panel with embroidered Mexican eagle motif, and loops of contrasting leather. The pouch face also features the Mexican eagle over an elongated, Grecian key motif. Accompanying the outfit is a .38 caliber, Colt Single Action revolver with 4 3/4-inch barrel. (Courtesy Jim Holley Collection. Image courtesy Bill Manns)

"Mexican Loop" Pattern Holster for Large-Frame Revolvers. Maker Unknown, 1905-1915. Constructed of medium-weight russet skirting leather, both pouch and skirt are contour-fit to the revolver and fully suede-lined. The body has a straight throat profile and a main seam braided through the closed toe. It is secured to the skirt with two riveted loops. The holster carries a Smith & Wesson First Model Schofield revolver. (Courtesy Private Collection)

Taken in 1906, this extremely rare photo shows a full-beaded, "Mexican Loop" pattern holster and matching beaded belt worn by Buffalo Bill Wild West Show performer Emma May Shaffer for toting her nickel-plated Colt Single Action. (Image courtesy Bill Manns)

"Mexican Loop" Pattern Holster with Matching Cartridge Belt. Eastern Sioux, 1900-1910. Although patterned on the lines of an Anglo rig, this fully beaded outfit clearly departs from the utilitarian norm. Fabricated of buckskin, the right-hand holster incorporates a scalloped throat profile, sewn-in toe plug and a broadly rounded skirt with a single integral loop. All elements are ornamented in floral applique beadwork within a roll-beaded border. The cartridge belt, made of buckskin with canvas backing, features geometric, lazy stitch beadwork within matching border treatment. The colorful rig carries a .41 caliber, Colt Single Action revolver with 5 1/2-inch barrel. (Courtesy Douglas Deihl Collection. Image courtesy Bill Manns)

goods manufacturers like the Smith-Worthington Company of Connecticut were producing the "Mexican Loop" form, while commercial supply houses such as Abercrombie & Fitch of New York and Hibbard, Spencer, Bartlett & Company of Chicago saw to its distribution. By the late 1890s, both Montgomery Ward and Sears, Roebuck & Company offered similar, comparatively inexpensive knock-offs. Many of these holsters were unmarked or stamped only with the monogrammed initials of the outfitting house. Some carried obscure trade names like "Olive" (also "Olive 5 in 1") and "Rival," while others bore recognized names such as "Diamond Brand" and "Moose Brand" (from the St. Louis firms of Shapleigh Hardware and Brauer Brothers Leather Goods, respectively).[47]

Although these non-indigenous, commercial versions of the "Mexican Loop" holster often were well made, the majority were fabricated of lighter, bridle-weight or "split" leathers that were inherently less durable than the western saddler's typical product of substantial skirting material. Most utilized holster bodies of a generalized contour so as to accommodate different makes and models of revolvers having similar size and proportion (thus, perhaps, the "Olive 5 in 1" moniker).

"Mexican Loop" Pattern Holster for Colt Model 1911 Automatic Pistol. R. T. Frazier Saddlery, Pueblo, Colorado, 1915-1920. Similar in design to Frazier's No. 9 (later No. 209) holster pattern, this right-hand piece incorporates a suede-lined, semi-contoured pouch with a deeply recurved throat profile, safety strap with snap closure, and thong-wrapped main seam extending through the toe. The fully contoured back skirt secures to the pouch with a single, riveted loop. The piece is lavishly decorated with three ornamented conchos and a tracery of 125 nickel-silver "spots." With the piece is a .45 caliber, Colt Model 1911 automatic pistol. (Courtesy Arizona West Galleries)

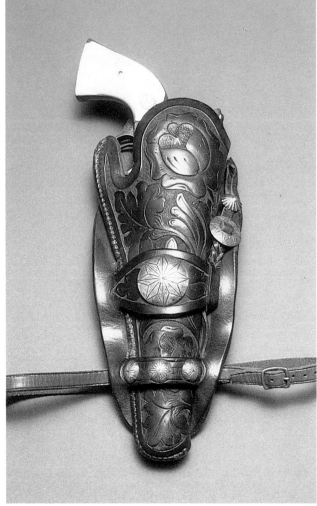

"Mexican Loop" Pattern Holster for Colt Single Action Army Revolver. Maker Unknown, 1910-1920. A classic example of leather craftsmanship, this piece combines graceful form and line with superb, hand-carved embellishment. Of right-hand design, the holster is constructed of heavy russet skirting leather with a meticulously applied, raised-carved floral motif on the body and upper skirt loop. Two integral loops secure the oval-patterned skirt to the body, which features a deeply-recurved throat and a rawhide-laced main seam extending through the toe. Engraved silver conchos adorn the piece; also present are a hammer thong and tie-down strap, both elements atypical of the historic western holster. (National Cowboy Hall of Fame Collection)

In addition to the use of lighter grades of leather, many of these "import" holsters were typified by the frequent use of top and/or bottom rivets reinforcing the main seam, and by fairly deep and abrupt throat recurves at the trigger area. In most instances, none but the poorest cowboy or unschooled tenderfoot invested in such material if the custom-quality gun-leather of a frontier saddler was available.

By 1890 the "Mexican Loop" holster had become the classic pattern of the late frontier era, the style most closely associated with cowboy culture and the "Wild West." Its widespread use in "Wild West" extravaganzas and early Hollywood films helped assure its place in the public mind as part of a burgeoning frontier legend. While this mythic role ultimately was distorted by the entertainment industry, the pattern nevertheless retained its popularity and utility among westerners well into the twentieth century. The "Mexican Loop" holster never faded entirely from use and, in recent decades, it has enjoyed a revival among frontier and gunfighter reenactment groups.

Straight from the outfitter's emporium to the photographer's studio, this trio of greenhorns from the late 1880s sports brand-new duds, chaps and gunleather. All carry Colt Single Action Army revolvers in "Mexican Loop" pattern holsters worn in crossdraw position. The gent at left has an oval-skirted, two-loop holster suggestive of the "Olive Patent" variant; the other two wear identical, three-loop holsters on combination cartridge/money belts. Both fellows at right have lifted their weapons for greater exposure; the pistol at center actually is reversed in the pouch. (Image courtesy The Kansas State Historical Society, Topeka)

"Mexican Loop" Pattern Holster for Large-Frame Revolvers. Maker Unknown, 1880-1885. Distinguished by its unusual, oval-patterned skirt, this example of the "Olive Patent" holster was marketed by western outfitters for more than twenty years. Fabricated of light russet skirting leather, the deep-bodied pouch is pigskin-lined and features a nice throat recurve and a curvilinear main seam sewn through the toe. The back skirt captures the pouch with two integral loops. (Image courtesy George T. Jackson)

(right)
"Mexican Loop" Pattern Holster with Cartridge/ Money Belt. Makers Unknown, 1880-1890. A commercial outfit, this rig features a rare, three-loop holster in combination with an early cartridge/money belt. The right-hand holster, constructed of russet bridle-weight leather, has a long, deep body with a shallow, recurved throat and sewn main seam extending through the toe. The body is secured to the close-fit- *ting skirt by a toe rivet and three riveted loops arranged in a canted spiral pattern. The belt, of supple bridle leather, is folded at the bottom and sewn along the top, with sewn-on cartridge loops and separate billets for the rectangular "California" buckle and tongue. A .44 caliber, Smith & Wesson Second Model American revolver with curved ivory grips accompanies the outfit. (Courtesy Private Collection)*

(left)
"Mexican Loop" Pattern Holster with Cartridge/ Money Belt. Makers Unknown, 1880-1890. This commercial rig incorporates a stylish, one-piece holster with a typical cartridge/money belt of the period. Constructed of lightweight russet skirting leather, the right-hand holster has two closely spaced, integral loops securing the pouch to the skirt. Patterned with a generalized profile to accept several of the different single action, *metallic cartridge revolvers then popular, the holster body features a deeply recurved throat, sewn main seam and toe, and delicate, rolled border ornament. The belt, somewhat unusual in being folded at the top and sewn along the bottom, has sewn cartridge loops and sewn and riveted billets with a nickel-plated, clip-cornered "California" style buckle. With the gunleather is a .44 caliber, Model 1875 Remington Army revolver. (Courtesy Private Collection)*

Probably photographed around 1905, this slack-jawed tenderfoot carries his Colt Single Action in a plain, commercially made "Mexican Loop" holster. The amorphous pouch has a barely contoured main seam fixed with a top rivet, and is secured by two, relatively wide skirt loops. A narrow belt, looped for pistol cartridges, completes his inexpensive rig. (Image courtesy Western History Department, Denver Public Library)

(right)
"Mexican Loop" Pattern Holster for Large-Frame Revolvers. Montgomery Ward & Co., Chicago, Illinois, 1915-1925. Richly embossed, this right-hand specimen is typical of commercial, mail order gunleather in the post-frontier period. Constructed of lightweight russet skirting material, the body incorporates an abrupt and deeply recurved throat profile, a semi-contoured main seam, and a sewn-in toe plug. The full, rounded skirt secures the pouch with a single, sewn-on loop of scalloped pattern. The skirt is border creased and stamped with acanthus leaves, while the loop features running deer. The pouch incorporates multiple border elements surrounding a diamond motif edged with foliate and frond elements. (Courtesy Bill Cleaver Collection)

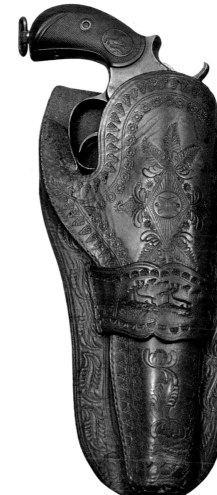

(above)
"Mexican Loop" Pattern Holster with Plain Cartridge Belt. Brauer Brothers, St. Louis, Missouri, 1895-1915. Although of commercial, Mid-western origin, this rig is well-made and serviceable. Constructed of medium-weight russet leather, the right-hand holster is of relatively amorphous contour and features a deep, abruptly recurved throat profile and a sewn main seam running through the rounded toe. The back skirt secures with two integral loops; the upper one carrying the firm's "Moosehead" logo. The plain cartridge belt is fabricated of lightweight russet leather with sewn loops and a double-frame brass buckle. With the outfit is a .38 caliber, Colt Bisley revolver with 4 3/4-inch barrel. (Courtesy A. P. Hays Collection. Image courtesy Bill Manns)

"Mexican Loop" Pattern Holster with Cartridge Money Belt. Hibbard, Spencer, Bartlett & Co., Chicago, Illinois; Knapp & Spencer Co., Sioux City, Iowa, 1890-1900. The combined product of two commercial supply houses, this rig features a graceful, somewhat form-fit holster of right-hand pattern. Constructed of light russet skirting leather, the body has a deeply recurved throat profile, a sewn main seam running through the toe, and neatly-rolled border trim that is repeated on the contoured, two-loop skirt. The belt, made of fairly substantial bridle-weight leather, is folded along the bottom edge and sewn along the top to form the interior pocket, and has riveted and sewn billets for the tongue and nickeled "California" style buckle. A .44 caliber, Merwin Hulbert Army Model revolver with ivory stocks completes the outfit. (Courtesy Private Collection)

(left)
"Mexican Loop" Pattern Holster for Large-Frame Revolvers. Montgomery Ward & Co., Chicago, Illinois, 1895-1905. A mere half-dollar (six cents extra if mailed) would fetch this "heavy and durable" specimen from Montgomery Ward's No. 57 catalog of 1895. Actually fabricated of "split" russet leather, the right-hand holster has a deep, rather amorphous body secured to its truncated half-skirt with two integral loops. The lower loop is stamped "44" and "7 1/2," indicating its intended capacity. Tongue-in-cheek, the catalog cautioned buyers: "Always forget to state caliber if you are in a hurry…then it will be necessary to write you for size." This piece holds a .44 caliber, Smith & Wesson American revolver with ivory stocks and 8-inch barrel. (Courtesy Jim Holley Collection. Image courtesy Bill Manns)

"Mexican Loop" Pattern Holster with Plain Cartridge Belt. Merwin & Bray Co., New York, New York, 1890-1900. Manufactured for an eastern supply house, this outfit represented an inexpensive option to the products of western saddleries. Constructed of medium-weight russet skirting leather, the left-hand holster features a relatively rare lining of red felt, a shallow recurve throat, three integral loops securing body to skirt, and an open toe. The single thickness, russet leather belt has a riveted "California" pattern buckle, slightly tapered tongue and rolled border ornament. Beneath the sewn cartridge loops is a stitched leather strip designed to prevent cartridges from slipping through loops. With the rig is a .45 caliber, Smith & Wesson Second Model Schofield revolver with 7-inch barrel. (Courtesy Bill Mackin Collection)

"Mexican Loop" Pattern Holster with Cartridge/Money Belt. R.T. Frazier Saddlery, Pueblo, Colorado, 1910-1920. A mixed outfit, this rig combines Frazier products of contrasting leathers and finishes. The left-hand holster is constructed of oak tanned, russet skirting leather and features integral, two-loop design with recurved throat, floral-carved body, and rawhide-laced main seam and toe. The piece is patterned and folded so that it hangs in a raked attitude, slanting to the rear for a faster draw. The belt is constructed of soft, chrome-tanned calfskin with sewn-on cartridge loops and billets of tan skirting leather. (National Cowboy Hall of Fame Collection)

"Mexican Loop" Pattern Holster with Cartridge Money Belt. F. A. Meanea Saddlery, Cheyenne, Wyoming, 1890-1900. A classic cowboy outfit, this matched rig illustrates the quality that made the Meanea shop famous. The right-hand holster, constructed of dark russet skirting leather, is a popular, two-loop pattern with a pleasing recurve at the throat and typical, border stamping on the body. Unlike most examples, this piece has a sewn toe in lieu of the "tear drop," or "Cheyenne," toe plug characteristic of the Meanea line. The 3 1/2-inch wide belt, of supple bridle leather, is folded along the bottom and sewn across the top in typical fashion. The cartridge loops and billets are of russet skirting leather; while the nickle-plated, clip-cornered "California" buckle is complimented with nickeled-brass "spots" ornamenting the belt. A .45 caliber, Colt Single Action Army revolver with 7 1/2-inch barrel accompanies the rig. (Courtesy Bill Mackin Collection)

Striking a studio pose around 1895, this gent wears a floral-stamped, "Mexican Loop" pattern holster for a Colt Single Action Army revolver. The pouch has a relatively deep throat recurve and secures to the three-quarter-length skirt with a single, riveted loop. (Image courtesy Amon Carter Museum, Fort Worth, Texas)

"Mexican Loop" Pattern Holster for Colt Single Action Army Revolver. S. C. Gallup Saddlery, Pueblo, Colorado, 1900-1910. The plain version of this No. 2 pattern belt holster retailed for a mere $2.00 in Gallup's Catalog No. 7 of circa 1905. Constructed of russet skirting material, the right-hand pouch is fully suede-lined and incorporates a pleasing throat recurve and a tapering main seam sewn through the rounded toe. The full-profile skirt secures the pouch with two integral loops of oval pattern, each carrying the maker's cartouche. Body and loops are hand-carved in an elongated floral motif and all elements are set off with rolled borderlines. A .45 caliber, Colt Single Action revolver with carved ivory grips and 7 1/2-inch barrel accompanies the piece. (Courtesy Joe Gish Collection. Image courtesy Bill Manns)

"Mexican Loop" Pattern Holster with Plain Cartridge Belt. Maker Unknown, 1905-1915. Incorporating a variety of ornamental touches, this showy rig probably was intended for a "Wild West" performer. The right-hand holster features a shallow throat recurve with an applied panel of fringing extending over the body and set off with a thong-laced concho. The holster's main seam, double integral loops and back skirt are all thong-wrapped at the edges. Also thong-wrapped, the cartridge belt is partially decorated with nickeled "spots" and secured with a "California" pattern buckle; holes are punched through each cartridge loop, perhaps to reveal the additional color of the brass cases. The outfit is accompanied by a .45 caliber, Colt Single Army revolver with a 7 1/2-inch barrel, carved ivory grips and scroll-engraved, nickel-plated finish. (Courtesy Richard Ellis Publications. Paul Goodwin, Photographer)

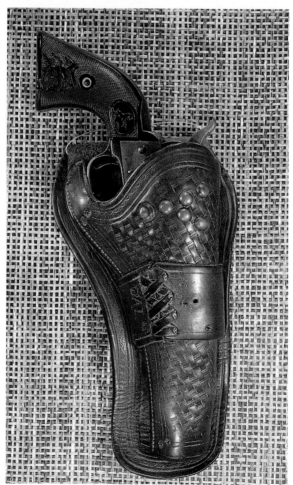

"Mexican Loop" Pattern Holster for Colt Single Action Army Revolver. E. Goettlich, Helena, Montana, 1905-1915. Reflecting turn-of-the-century changes in style and design, this right-hand holster represents a departure from Goettlich's earlier, Miles City production. Constructed of stiff russet skirting leather, the specimen features a rather amorphous pouch which is secured to the contoured skirt with a single, riveted loop that is rawhide-laced on the face seam. The pouch is ornamented with basket-weave stamping and creased border elements. The applied "spots" in "lazy Y" motif probably were added by the owner. The holster holds a .45 caliber, Colt Single Action Army revolver with 5 1/2-inch barrel. (Courtesy R.M. Bachman Collection)

"Mexican Loop" Pattern Holster with Matching Cartridge Belt. Arizona Saddlery Co., Prescott, Arizona, 1915-1925. Constructed of heavy russet skirting leather, this handsome outfit captures the zenith of quality and artistry in early twentieth century gunleather. The left-hand holster body, secured to its fairly wide, rounded skirt with two riveted loops, has a pleasing recurved throat profile and graceful sewn main seam that runs smoothly through the toe. The wide, single-thickness belt has sewn cartridge loops and separate, riveted and sewn billets for the tongue and nickle-plated, clip-cornered "California" style buckle. Both elements are ornamented with finely executed hand-carving in a foliate and floral motif. (Courtesy Private Collection)

"Mexican Loop" Pattern Holster with Cartridge/ Money Belt. Al. Furst-now, Miles City, Montana, 1915-1920. Finely carved in a floral motif, this specimen is fabricated of heavy skirting leather and incorporates a nice throat recurve, a thong-wrapped main seam, sewn-in toe plug and a wide, tooled skirt with double, riveted loops. The piece is designed for a Colt Single Action revolver with 7 1/2-inch barrel. (Courtesy Ron Soodalter Collection. Image courtesy Bill Manns)

"Mexican Loop" Pattern Holster with Cartridge/ Money Belt. Frank Olzer, Gillette,Wyoming, 1905-1915. Worn by "Wild West" performer, rodeo contestant and peace officer George Gardner, this matched rig is *accompanied by the owner's trophy bronc belt won in 1919. The right-hand holster body is fabricated of medium-weight russet skirting leather and features a pleasing throat recurve, slightly contoured main* *seam, sewn-in toe plug and floral tooling. The broad back skirt is basket-stamped and secures with a single, riveted loop of circular pattern having a stamped rosette. The combination belt is of typical configu-* *ration, set off with an attractive, rounded frame buckle. With the outfit is a .45 caliber, Colt Single Action Army revolver with 4 3/4-inch barrel. (Courtesy Gene Autry Western Heritage Museum, Los Angeles)*

WORLDS CHAMPION
BEST ALL ROUND COWBOY
GLENDIVE ROUNDUP 1919
Won by
Geo. T. Gardner

"Mexican Loop" Pattern Holster for Colt Single Action Army Revolver. C. P. Shipley Saddlery, Kansas City, Missouri, 1915-1925. Similar in design to the No. 107 pattern in Shipley's Catalog No. 23, this right-hand specimen presents a clean, well-finished look. Fabricated of medium-weight russet skirting material, the holster body has a deeply recurved throat profile, a tightly thong-wrapped main seam and a full, open toe. The pouch is secured to the broad, rounded back skirt by two integral loops, the bottom one stamped with a petal-patterned rosette. Both the body and skirt are finished with a stamped border ornament. The piece holds a .45 caliber, Colt Single Action revolver with ivory grips and 4 3/4-inch barrel. (Courtesy Joe Gish Collection. Image courtesy Bill Manns)

(left)
"Mexican Loop" Pattern Holster for Colt Single Action Army Revolver. C. P. Shipley, Kansas City, Missouri, 1915-1925. Exhibiting early twentieth century design and embellishment, this outfit's right-hand holster was offered for $3.00 in Shipley's 1923 mail order catalog. Constructed of light-weight russet skirting leather, the No. 108 holster incorporates a relatively shallow throat recurve and a slightly contoured main seam that is sewn through the rounded toe. The pouch is secured to the skirt with a single, wide, half-circle loop. Both elements are basket-stamped and the skirt loop features a circular ornament with stamped floral motif. The holster is fitted for a Colt Single Action Army revolver with 5 1/2-inch barrel. (Courtesy John E. Fox Collection)

"Mexican Loop" Pattern Holster for Colt Single Action Army Revolver. Bob Meldrum, Rawlins, Wyoming, 1916-1921. This right-hand holster was made by saddler, lawman and convicted felon Bob Meldrum while serving time at the Wyoming State Penitentiary. Constructed of substantial russet skirting leather, the piece incorporates a full, contoured skirt with two integral loops of different width. The rather amorphous body has a typical throat recurve, sewn main seam running through the toe and stamped, basket-weave decoration with a cloverleaf rosette at the muzzle. Accompanying the holster is a .32 caliber, Colt Single Action Army revolver with full nickel finish, pearl grips and 5 1/2-inch barrel. (Courtesy Bill Mackin Collection)

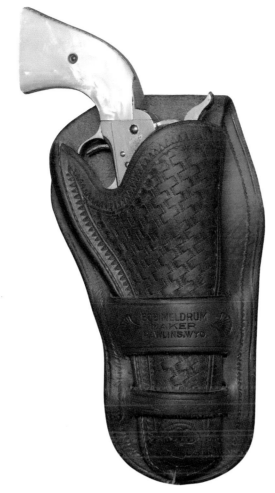

(above)
"Mexican Loop" Pattern Holster for Colt Single Action Army Revolver. L. H. Hatch, Pinedale, Wyoming, 1925-1935. A late example of the classic cowboy holster, this right-hand piece features two unusual elements: sewn cartridge loops on the upper body, and a riveted tie-down strap with clip closure. The body is finely hand-tooled with a floral motif over stippled ground, while the skirt has a rolled, "sun burst" border ornament. Constructed of heavy russet skirting leather, the holster pouch has a relatively deep recurved throat and a rawhide-laced main seam running into the closed toe. The skirt, with two widely-spaced integral loops, narrows at the top to form a slim belt loop. (Courtesy Lacey and Virginia Gaddis Collection)

"Mexican Loop" Pattern Holster for Colt Single Action Army Revolver. Kingsville Lumber Co., Kingsville, Texas, 1925-1940. Carrying the famed "Running W" brand, this No. 23 pattern holster retailed for $3.00 in the firm's Catalog No. 23. Fabri-cated of medium-weight, dark russet skirting leather, the full-lined, right-hand pouch has a low-cut, slightly arched throat and a tapered main seam running through the toe. The full-profile back skirt retains the pouch with a single, double-riveted loop of circular pattern. The piece is ornamented with basket-weave and border stamping; it carries a .45 caliber, Colt Single Action revolver with ivory grips, nickel finish and 4 3/4-inch barrel. (Courtesy Joe Gish Collection. Image courtesy Bill Manns)

THE "BRIDGEPORT RIG"

Although the "Mexican Loop" holster was the mainstay of pistol-packing westerners from the 1880s onward, a few attempts were made during the era to further simplify the means of carriage and increase the speed with which the sidearm could be brought into action. Chief among these efforts was the so-called "Bridgeport Rig," an intriguing device designed to suspend the revolver from a waist or cartridge belt without the encumbrance of a full leather holster. This rare and unusual gun accoutrement was patented in January of 1882 by Louis S. Flatau, a resident of Pittsburg, Texas, and sheriff of surrounding Camp County.[48]

Patent drawing of L. S. Flatau's Pistol and Carbine Holder, which formulated the design of the so-called "Bridgeport Rig." (Image courtesy Oklahoma State University Library)

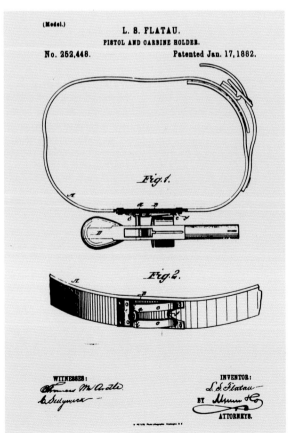

Posed around 1890, "Wild West" showman Jose "Mexican Joe" Barrea wears a double "Bridgeport Rig" carrying a Colt Single Action Army and a European double action revolver. The pronged "pistol carriers" are riveted on a military pattern waist belt with a cast plate carrying the Mexican national motif. (Image courtesy Jean E. King Collection)

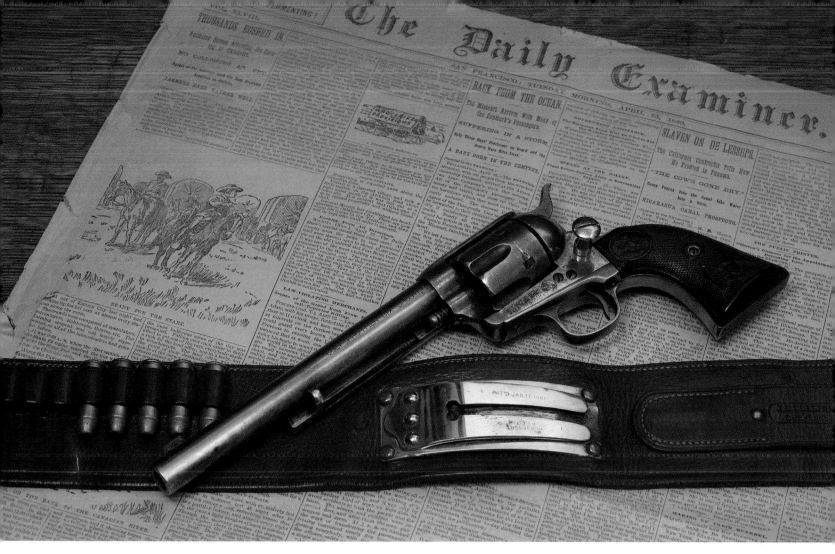

Flatau's "Pistol Holder" with Cartridge/Money Belt. Bridgeport Gun Implement Co., Bridgeport, Connecticut; J. S. Collins Saddlery, Cheyenne, Wyoming Territory, 1883-1885. Commonly referred to as a "Bridgeport Rig," this rare gun accoutrement was patented in 1882 by Louis S. Flatau, sheriff of Camp County, Texas. Designed to securely carry the revolver and yet facilitate a truly fast draw, the device was manufactured for the civilian market in very limited numbers. The "holder" utilized a slotted plate of spring steel riveted to a back plate, which, in turn, was riveted to the belt. The revolver was suspended from the "holder" by a special, button-headed hammer screw inserted in the slot. (Courtesy Bill Mackin Collection)

Flatau's "Pistol Holder" with Military Waist Belt. Bridgeport Gun Implement Co., Bridgeport, Connecticut. Rock Island Arsenal, Illinois, 1882-1883. Mounted on an 1874 Pattern Waist Belt of black bridle leather with US plate, this

"Bridgeport" device typifies the military version trialed in 1883. Five hundred units were issued from the San Antonio Arsenal, most to troopers of the Eighth and Tenth Cavalry Regiments. (Courtesy Scott Meadows Collection)

The Flatau device consisted of a two-pronged, slotted clip of spring steel riveted to a slightly arched, rectangular back plate. This unit, in turn, was riveted to the belt in either a "right-" or "left-hand" position. The intended revolver was suspended from the "holder" by means of a special, modified hammer screw having an enlarged, button-shaped head and an extended shaft that protruded about three-quarters of an inch beyond the frame. The leading edge of the "holder's" back plate was slightly dished to facilitate the insertion of the screw head beneath the prongs, while a rounded seat at the junction of the prongs (the rear of the slot) allowed the weapon to rest on the shaft of the hammer screw in a muzzle-down atti-

tude. The pistol could be extricated very swiftly simply by thrusting it forward from the slot, or it could be swivelled upward in the seated position and fired "from the hip."[49]

Flatau's original concept, described in the patent specifications as a "PISTOL AND CARBINE HOLDER," envisioned the carriage of either type of weapon with the device mounted on a belt or saddle. Flatau may well have targeted military contracts with this dual-purpose concept; in fact, he approached the army within a few months of receiving his patent. As noted in the discussion of experimental military holsters, the U. S. Army trialed 500 Flautau "pistol holders" among infantry and cavalry units in the Southwest during 1883. These were fabricated by the Bridgeport Gun Implement Company of Bridgeport, Connecticut, supplied to the army by Hartley and Graham of New York City, and assembled on belts at Rock Island Arsenal. (To the writer's knowledge, fixture of the device to saddles for the carriage of shoulder arms was never attempted.) The military found the "holders" unsuitable because the revolver was afforded no protection from moisture and dirt, was insufficiently secure in carriage, and was prone to tangling in clothing and equipment. Some of the rejected army rigs no doubt entered the civilian market as surplus in later years (they may, in fact, have constituted the only commercial supply).[50]

While the Flatau device was dismissed in military circles, it did enjoy limited acceptance among a few frontier civilians, particularly peace officers and other "professional" gunmen who appreciated its speed of access. As described in a reminiscence, one of these was former Texas Ranger James B. Gillett, who evidently employed a double "Bridgeport Rig" while serving as chief of police in El Paso, Texas, during the early 1880s:

In this series of contemporary photographs, author-collector Phil Spangenberger demonstrates the use of a reproduction "Bridgeport Rig" and modified Colt Single Action for swivel, hip shooting. The revolver could also be thrust forward, cocked, levelled and fired free of the device. (Images courtesy Guns & Ammo magazine)

Photographed around 1905, Deputy Sheriff W. I. Smith of Las Animas County, Colorado, utilizes the rare "Bridgeport Rig" to carry his Smith & Wesson Model 1903, .32 Hand Ejector revolver. The device is riveted on a plain leather cartridge belt in "right-hand" draw position. (Image courtesy Alex Gibson and Charles Worman)

I had always worn a pistol in a belt holster, and I was used to drawing fast from that position....A little later, I put on a belt which carried two Colts without holster....I could swing the gun muzzles up or down, and they were out of the way and at the same time ready for instant use. I could shoot the pistols — though I never had to — without drawing them, just as one shoots out of an open-toed swivel holster.[51]

Period photographs and scattered references indicate that the "Bridgeport Rig" was used by some lawmen into the early twentieth century.[52]

While it was something of a novelty item, the Bridgeport Gun Implement Company may have continued commercial manufacture of the Flatau "pistol holder" into the 1890s, marketing it to western saddlers through various outfitting and supply houses. Produced in very limited quantities, "Bridgeport Rigs" were always an extremely scarce item. Today, there probably are as many fraudulent copies as legitimate specimens; collectors of western gunleather should move cautiously in attempting to acquire such a piece.

Hip Pocket Holster for Medium-Frame Revolvers. Maker Unknown, 1890-1900. Similar in design to the G.W. Browne patent of 1884, this substantial specimen employs a folded and thickly welted sheath of rectangular pattern with a stitched-in pistol contour. Constructed of heavy black bridle leather, the lower panel features a small pouch (about the size for business cards) with six cartridge loops sewn on its face. The holster body is open-toed, has an abrupt, double throat recurve, and is fully suede-lined. A narrow loop is riveted at the top of the panel for securing with a waist belt. (Courtesy Bill Mackin Collection)

Patent drawing of G. W. Browne's Pocket Holster, which formulated the initial design of the hip pocket, panel-type holster with sewn-in pistol profile. (Image courtesy Oklahoma State University Library)

(opposite) "Skeleton" Pattern Shoulder Holster for Large-Frame Revolvers. Al. Furstnow, Miles City, Montana, 1900-1910. Still in very fine condition, this variation of the "Sheriff's Lightning Spring Shoulder Holster" is relatively unusual — and rare — in this left-hand configuration. Constructed in typical fashion, the rig holds a .45 caliber, Colt Single Action revolver with 7 1/2-inch barrel and ivory stocking. (Courtesy R.M. Bachman Collection. Image courtesy Bill Manns)

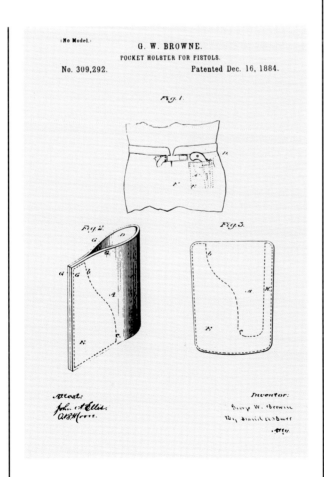

(No Model.)

G. W. BROWNE.

POCKET HOLSTER FOR PISTOLS.

No. 309,292.

Patented Dec. 16, 1884.

Fig. 1.

Fig. 2.

Fig. 3.

Attest:
John A. Ellis
O. S. H[...]

Inventor:
George W. Browne
By David [...]buff
Atty.

Hip Pocket Holster for Medium-Frame Revolvers. Shapleigh Hardware, St. Louis, Missouri, 1900-1910. A virtual copy of O.M. Hanscom's 1885 patent design, this hip pocket holster utilizes a contoured half-pouch sewn on a double-layer back panel. Constructed throughout of smooth bridle leather, the original russet material has been stained black and the throat profile has been altered to a deep and relatively wide recurve. With the holster is a .38 caliber, Belgian "Boxer" revolver. (Courtesy Bill Mackin Collection)

HIP POCKET AND SHOULDER HOLSTERS

By the mid-1880s, civilization was gaining a secure foothold throughout the West, and sedentary townsfolk — and their newspaper editors — cast an increasingly jaundiced eye on those who went openly "packing iron." Many towns passed ordinances proscribing the carrying of firearms, and Texas was among the first to institute a statewide ban. In July of 1887, the *Tascosa Pioneer* observed: "The new pistol law is in operation, and the man who carries too much gun...is in danger of losing both some of his role and some of his liberty."[53] Many latter-day frontier types, seeking to avoid such civic censure while still "going heeled," adopted less conspicuous gunleather elements. The hip pocket holster and the shoulder holster, both designed to carry one's pistol concealed beneath a coat, were the most common, standardized forms utilized.[54]

The hip pocket holster came into use during the mid-1880s, largely in concert with the proliferation of inexpensive, small-frame revolvers now characterized as "suicide specials." In addition to concealment, its basic object was to maintain the pistol within the pocket in a safe and consistently retrievable position. The first known patentee, G. W. Browne of New York City, provided the rationale for this unusual gunleather element:

> In carrying pistols in the pocket difficulty is oftentimes experienced in getting hold of the weapon and in withdrawing it, because of its settling down into an inclined position within the pocket and because of its engagement with the flexible lining...in the act of its removal.[55]

The distinguishing feature of such holsters, then, was an external configuration that conformed to the typical dimension and shape of the pocket.

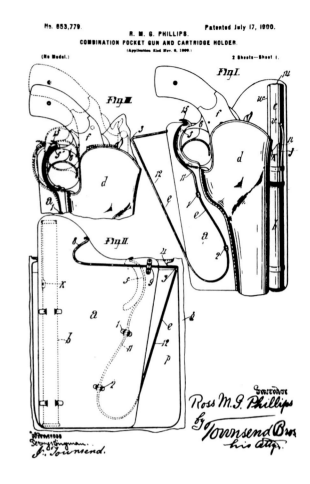

J. A. E. ANDERSON.
PISTOL POCKET.

No. 468,556.   Patented Feb. 9, 1892.

FIG. 1.

FIG. 2.

FIG. 3.

FIG. 4.

Patent drawing of J.A.E. Anderson's Pistol Pocket, which introduced a spring-loaded, trigger guard keeper to hip pocket holster design. (Image courtesy Oklahoma State University Library)

(right)
Patent drawing of R.M.G. Phillips' Combination Pocket Gun And Cartridge Holder, which pushed hip pocket holster design beyond practicality. (Image courtesy Oklahoma State University Library)

Hip Pocket Holster for Small-Frame Revolver. Maker Unknown, 1900-1910. Designed by R.M.G. Phillips, this hip pocket pattern holster incorporates his patented trigger guard retainer and auxiliary magazine tube. Constructed of light-weight, russet bridle leather, the half-pouch is sewn to a double-layered back panel and features a radically recurved throat and open toe. The back panel also is recurved at the top for easier acquisition of the pistol. A .32 caliber, Colt New Pocket revolver with pearl grips accompanies the holster. (Courtesy Bill Mackin Collection)

No. 653,779.   Patented July 17, 1900.
R. M. G. PHILLIPS.
COMBINATION POCKET GUN AND CARTRIDGE HOLDER.
(Application filed Nov. 6, 1899.)
(No Model.)   2 Sheets—Sheet 1.

Fig. I.

Fig. II.

Fig. III.

Ross M.G. Phillips
by Townsend Bros
his atty.

Witnesses:
Seryg Brygman.
J. Townsend.

Between Browne's 1884 patent and that of R. M. G. Phillips in 1900, the hip pocket holster underwent a progressively more sophisticated evolution. The earliest and simplest versions consisted of a folded and sewn leather sheath of rectangular pattern with a stitched-in profile of the intended weapon. More common variations, such as that patented by O. M. Hanscom in 1885, utilized a half-pouch sewn on a leather back panel proportioned to the pocket. J. A. E. Anderson's 1892 patent introduced a spring-loaded keeper at the trigger guard to better retain the revolver; while the Phillips version of 1900 incorporated a similar, spring-loaded security shroud over the trigger guard in combination with an attached, tubular magazine for additional cartridges! Differing from these panel-type designs was J. W. Townsend's 1906 patent, which employed a regular, contoured holster body that could be clipped to the top edge of the pocket and buttoned to the trousers.[56]

While they were not an indigenous western form, hip pocket holsters no doubt enjoyed some use in the region during the late nineteenth and early twentieth centuries, perhaps most among bankers and other businessmen. Only a few native saddlers appear to have manufactured the form at any time. Of those surveyed, H. H. Heiser, Victor Marden and Padgitt Brothers produced variations of the half-pouch, rectangular back panel pattern; while S. D. Myres offered a button-on, contoured body design similar to the later Townsend patent. The H. H. Heiser firm was the most prolific western manufacturer, offering as many

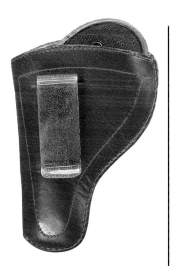

Hip or Vest Pocket Holster for Remington Double Deringer. Maker Unknown, 1910-1915. Utilizing a spring clip for secure carriage, this diminutive piece is fully lined with billiard table felt. The amorphous pouch is made of red calfskin and features an arched throat and recurved main seam sewn through the toe. The holster holds a .41 caliber, Type Two Remington Double Deringer with 3-inch, superposed barrels. (Courtesy R. M. Bachman Collection. Image courtesy Bill Manns)

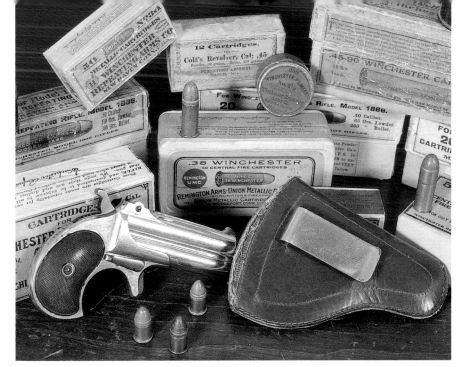

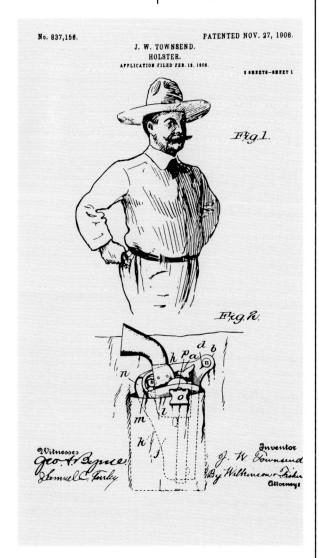

Patent drawing of J. W. Townsend's [Hip Pocket] Holster, which formulated the contoured pouch design with clip and button fixtures. (Image courtesy Oklahoma State University Library)

as four styles that ranged in price from $1.25 to $3.00 depending on leather weight and embellishment.[57] Still, the hip pocket holster was a marginal form in the West, probably because it was necessarily too small to accommodate the large-frame revolvers traditionally favored in the region.

The shoulder holster, fitted for large-caliber handguns and easily concealed beneath a coat, proved far more practical and popular with westerners of the late frontier era. Peace officers, gunfighters and the sporting set (who often were indistinguishable), found such rigs beneficial in carrying sufficient firepower while avoiding undue attention. Although they may have been foreshadowed by the so-called "gambler's vest" of the ante-bellum period (which incorporated sewn-in pistol pouches of light glove leather), available evidence suggests that true shoulder holsters probably were an indigenous western creation that came into use during the late 1870s. These were characterized by an ovoid pattern shoulder loop that allowed a comfortable "hang" for the pistol holster when worn beneath the arm in a vertical position.[58]

The earliest and most common type of shoulder holster employed in the West was the so-called "Texas" pattern, perhaps popularized — though certainly not invented — by notorious Texas shootist Ben Thompson. This generic form, which evidently appeared somewhat prior to 1880, typically incorporated a contoured half-pouch of pliable, bridle-weight leather sewn (and sometimes riveted) to a heavier leather back panel. Two contoured tabs extending from the top of the back panel were stitched or thong-laced to the shoulder loop, which varied from 1 3/4 to 2 1/2 inches in width. A narrower chest or cross-shoulder strap of leather or linen was fixed to the lower reaches of the shoulder harness at front and back to further secure the holster (it typically was not secured at the toe).[59]

While "Texas" pattern shoulder holsters apparently were produced relatively widely, such deep and full-bodied rigs were inherently difficult to draw from

Hip Pocket Holster for Medium-Frame Revolvers. Maker Unknown, 1910-1920. Reminiscent of J.W. Townsend's 1906 pattern, this specimen employs a spring clip for attachment to the pocket edge or waist band of the trousers. Fabricated of russet bridle leather, the amorphous pouch has a straight throat, an edge-laced main seam running through the toe, full suede lining and machine-stamped embellishment. (Courtesy Phil Spangenberger Collection)

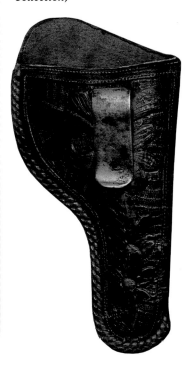

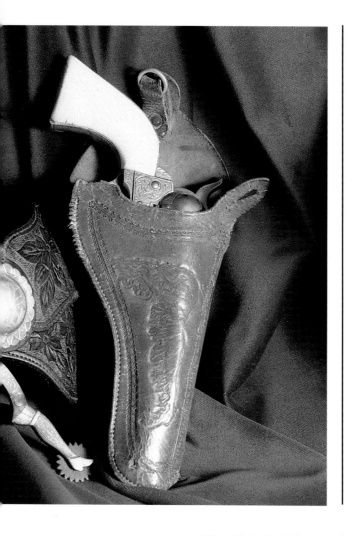

"Suspender" Pattern Holster for Medium-Sized Revolvers. Maker Unknown, 1910-1920. A cousin of the hip pocket pattern, this commercial piece was designed to be worn inside the trousers with the two, "button-holed" ears (the left ear now missing) folded over the waist band and fixed to the suspender buttons, while the brass ring at the top of the back panel fastened into the suspender cast off. Constructed of medium-weight russet bridle leather, the semi-contoured, right-hand pouch is machine-embossed with an unusual, Art Nouveau female figure surrounded by a rolled border element. The holster carries a .44 Caliber Colt Single Action revolver with 4 3/4-inch Barrel and ivory stock (Courtesy Bill Cleaver Collection. Image courtesy Bill Manns)

when speed was of the essence. With the pistol fully seated in the pouch, it often required both hands to extricate the weapon while holding the holster body down in its usual position. Moreover, the pistol had to be lifted vertically several inches before it could be drawn laterally to "clear leather," a challenging maneuver when working under one's coat and armpit! To overcome these constraints, not a few wearers evidently carried the pistol partially withdrawn (the trigger guard riding up in the lower throat recurve) when trouble appeared imminent.[60]

The so-called "Skeleton" or "Clip Spring" pattern shoulder holster, which apparently evolved during the late 1890s, represented a remarkable improvement in terms of the "fast draw." In place of the familiar leather holster pouch, this innovative design utilized a plain back panel of stiff leather that was generally contoured to the silhouette of the intended revolver and sewn to the shoulder loop at its upper edges. The upper face of the back panel was fixed with a riveted, rawhide or leather-covered metal clip spring of semi-circular configuration, while the lower extremity was mounted with a shallow, sewn-on "toe boot" of leather. The revolver, secured at the cylinder and muzzle, respectively, did not have to be drawn upward to "clear leather," but simply pulled free in a swift lateral motion. Some variations, such as that made by H. H. Heiser, incorporated an abbreviated leather flap over the pistol's hammer and upper cylinder to preclude clothing snags and protect the weapon from corrosive perspiration.[61]

"Gambler's Vest" for Single-Shot Percussion Pistols and Dirk. Maker Unknown, 1835-1845. A possible precursor of the true shoulder holster, this unusual rig carried a brace of pistols concealed beneath the wearer's arms and coat. Constructed of white linen, the two piece vest is over-sewn with panels of red morocco leather that are joined at the back with a double, strap-and-buckle arrangement. Each panel is mounted with sewn-on, contoured half-pouch holsters having slightly arched throat profiles and sewn-in toe plugs. (Courtesy Norm Flayderman Collection)

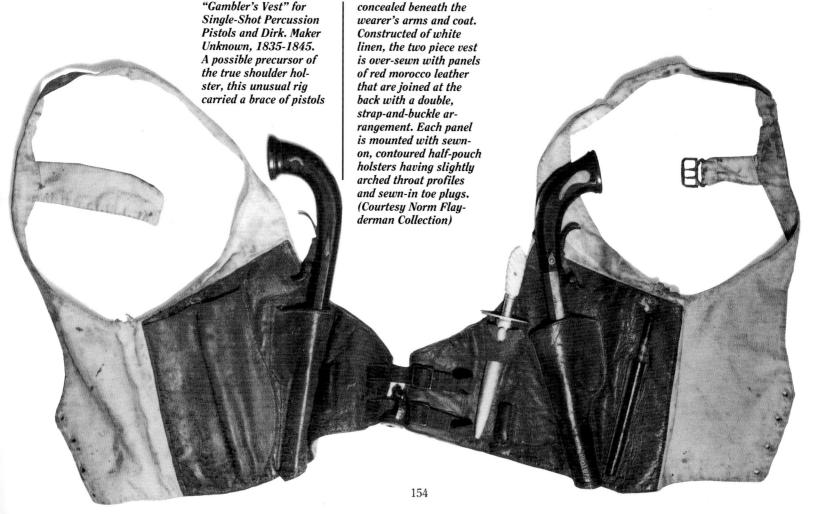

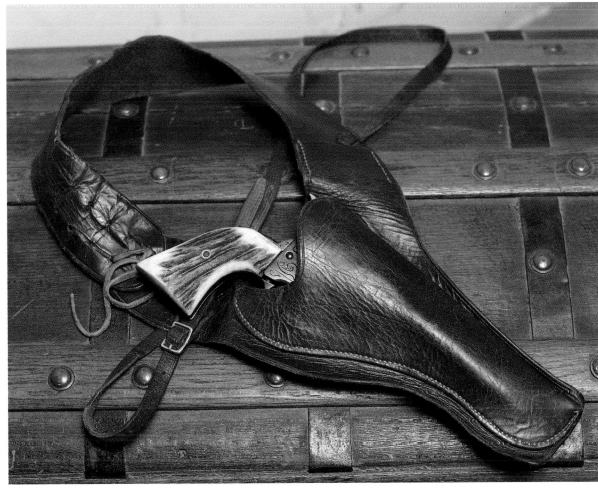

(right)
"Texas" Pattern Shoulder Holster. Maker Unknown, 1890-1900. Designed for concealment beneath a coat, this "Texas" style shoulder holster was probably the earliest type worn by westerners on both sides of the law. Constructed of medium-weight russet bridle leather, the piece has a wide shoulder strap and a narrow "belt" that buckled around the chest to secure the rig. The "half-pouch" holster body is sewn to the back skirt, and features a recurved throat profile and main seam sewn through the toe and secured with a top rivet. With the rig is a .38 caliber, Colt Single Action Army revolver. (Courtesy Bill Mackin Collection)

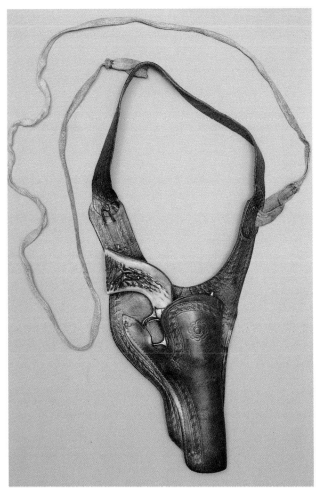

(left)
"Texas" Pattern Shoulder Holster. Maker Unknown, 1890-1900. The product of a commercial manufacturer, this specimen is fabricated of light-weight, split leathers and incorporates typical, "half-pouch" design. The back panel, shoulder strap and body feature rolled border tooling, while stamped rosettes ornament the pouch face. A .44 caliber, Colt Single Action Army revolver with 4 3/4-inch barrel and stag grips accompanies the outfit, which still retains its linen, cross-shoulder strap. (Courtesy Private Collection)

(right)
"Texas" Pattern Shoulder Holster. Maker Unknown, 1900-1910. This well-worn example boasts a rolled border ornament on all elements. Constructed of light russet leather, the piece has a medium-width shoulder strap secured by thongs that can be adjusted for fit. The "half-pouch" holster body is sewn and riveted to the skirt, and features a deeply-recurved throat at the trigger guard area and an open toe. Accompanying the rig is a .38 caliber, Colt Model 1877 Lightning Double Action revolver. (Courtesy Phil Spangenberger Collection)

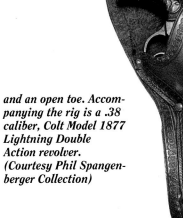

"Skeleton" Pattern Shoulder Holster. H. H. Heiser, Denver, Colorado, 1910-1920. Claimed as an invention of the Heiser firm, their No. 126 Safety-Spring Shoulder Holster actually was a knock-off of the original Zimmerman/Furstnow design with the addition of a flap leather over the grip and hammer area of the pistol. Fabricated of medium-weight, russet leather, the rig is otherwise of typical design and accommodates a .38 caliber, Colt Lightning Double Action revolver with 6-inch barrel. (Courtesy John E. Fox Collection)

Patent drawing of E.D. Zimmerman's Pistol Holder, which formulated the design of the so-called "Skeleton" pattern shoulder holster. Note the use of a facing shroud of leather along the leading edge of the holster — a feature replaced by a separate, sewn-on "toe-boot" in commercial production. (Image courtesy Oklahoma State University Library)

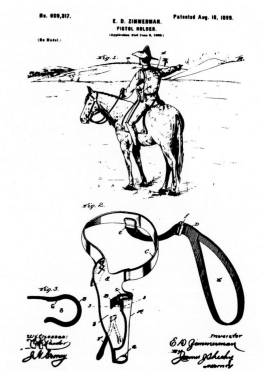

"Skeleton" Pattern Shoulder Holster. Al. Furstnow Saddlery, Miles City, Montana, 1895-1905. Designed for both concealment and a fast draw, this "Skeleton" pattern was popularized by Furstnow, who advertised his "Sheriff's Lightning Spring Shoulder Holster" as "...Absolutely the fastest action holster on the market today." Constructed of two sewn layers of russet skirting leather, the contoured back panel incorporates a riveted, rawhide-covered spring clip that secures the revolver's cylinder, and a lower "boot" with sewn-in toe plug that retains the muzzle. The medium-width shoulder strap, made of russet bridle leather, is sewn between the back panel layers and utilizes thong closure adjustable for fit. Both elements feature a simple rolled ornament. The rig holds a .45 caliber, Colt Single Action Army revolver with 7 1/2-inch barrel and carved pearl grips. (Courtesy Bill Mackin Collection)

While the precise derivation of the "Skeleton" pattern shoulder holster remains unclear, its origin on the northern plains seems relatively certain. What appears to be the prototype patent was awarded to E. D. Zimmerman of Alzada, Montana, in August of 1898. His patent specifications included:

...a shallow pocket at [the] lower end to seat the muzzle of a pistol....[and]...a U-shaped spring, preferably a strip of resilient metal.... to clamp the revolving cylinder of a pistol when the same is placed in the holder, so as to effectually prevent casual displacement of the pistol and yet permit of the same being readily withdrawn in a lateral direction when desired.[62]

Other sources suggest that saddler Al. Furstnow of Miles City, Montana, may have designed this rig. His custom "Sheriff's Lightning Spring Shoulder

Late Frontier Shoulder Holsters. At lower left, a "Skeleton" pattern by Charles Coggshall Saddlery, Miles City, Montana, circa 1905. At upper right, a basket-stamped "Texas" pattern by Lon Bradbury Saddlery, Grand Junction, Colorado, circa 1910. (Courtesy Joe Gish Collection. Image courtesy Bill Manns)

Holster," which incorporated the salient features of the Zimmerman patent, certainly popularized the form well into the 1900s. Furstnow established his own shop in Miles City in 1884; as he and Zimmerman were located only 135 miles apart in Custer County, the two actually may have collaborated in the design and initial fabrication of this intriguing gunleather element.[63]

A survey of early twentieth century trade catalogs suggests that the "Texas" pattern shoulder holster enjoyed the widest production among western saddlers. Between 1900 and 1930, such well-known artisans as Duhamel, Flynn, Frazier, Gallup, Garcia, Hamley, Heiser, Marden, Myres, Padgitt Brothers and Shipley offered the form, which generally ranged in price from $1.50 to $3.50. In contrast, the "Skeleton" pattern was favored most by a few northern plains craftsmen like Furstnow, Meanea and Miles City

In this contemporary photo, author-collector Phil Spangenberger wears an historic, "Skeleton" pattern shoulder holster made expressly for the .32 caliber, Chicago Firearms "Protector" palm pistol. This extremely rare, late 1890s rig is from the collection of William R. Williamson. (Image courtesy Guns & Ammo magazine)

Saddlery; although some of the more prolific manufacturers, such as Frazier, Heiser, Myres and Shipley, also included it in their product lines. Evidently considered something of a specialty item, "Skeleton" pattern shoulder holsters ranged in price from $2.50 to $5.00 over the years surveyed.[64]

Today quite scarce, both the "Texas" and "Skeleton" pattern shoulder holsters were gradually supplanted during the early twentieth century by the so-called "Half-Breed" pattern. This design utilized the spring clip retainer and semi-closed toe of the "Skeleton" variation in combination with a full leather pouch, or contoured facing shroud, that was left open along the main seam to facilitate an easy draw. Evidently patented in 1911 by F. R. Lewis of Reno, Nevada, the "Half-Breed" design was the prototype of most modern, law enforcement shoulder holsters. While it may have maintained the pattern's traditionally western orientation, the "Half-Breed" shoulder holster clearly fell beyond the historic frontier period in its appearance and use.[65]

"Skeleton" Pattern Shoulder Holster. Maker Unknown, 1905-1915. Although unmarked, this handsome "Skeleton" rig obviously was the product of a skilled saddlery. Patterned on the Furstnow design, it incorporates the leather-covered spring clip and muzzle "boot" with toe plug on a contoured back panel of russet skirting leather with rawhide-laced trim. The adjustable shoulder strap is lined with smooth glove leather. The narrow retaining strap was designed to run under the right arm and back to the top of the shoulder strap. All elements are ornamented with rolled border tooling. The holster retains a .45 caliber, Colt Model 1878 Frontier Double Action revolver. (Courtesy Private Collection)

"Half-Breed" Pattern Shoulder Holster for Colt Single Action Army Revolver. Maker Unknown, 1915-1925. Very likely the product of a western saddlery, this specimen is fabricated of medium-weight skirting stock with full chamois lining and basket-stamped and border-tooled ornament on the pouch face. Fitted with a spring steel band to retain the revolver's cylinder, the folded holster is thong-laced at the toe and sewn closed along the arched top line, while a snap-fastened security strap passes above the trigger guard. The missing shoulder harness was sewn along the back main seam opening for a vertical hang. A .44 caliber, Colt Single Action with 5 1/2 inch barrel and carved ivory grips accompanies the piece. (Courtesy Donald Bates Collection)

Clip-Spring "Wrist Holster" for Remington Double Deringer. S. D. Myres, El Paso, Texas, 1920-1930. Another variation of "hideaway" gunleather, this unusual specimen utilizes the clip-spring element common in "Skeleton" pattern shoulder holsters. The retaining clip is leather-covered and riveted to the wide wrist band, which secures with two buckled straps that are riveted to and woven through the band. With the "holster" is a .41 caliber, Remington Double Deringer with full nickel finish and pearl grips. (Courtesy John E. Fox Collection)

Flapped Shoulder Holster. Maker Unknown, 1905-1915. No doubt of Mexican origin, this handsome piece is fabricated of medium-weight, russet skirting leather and features a pattern-cut cover flap integral with the slim, contour-fit holster body. Both elements are fully lined with red morocco leather. Ornamented with circular and border tooling, the flap is inset with a panel of sueded leather and secures with a harness buckle at the toe. The holster has an adjustable, cross-torso strap and secures to the belt with a short, riveted loop. A .44 caliber, Merwin Hulbert revolver with 7-inch barrel and pearl grips accompanies the rig. (Courtesy Private Collection)

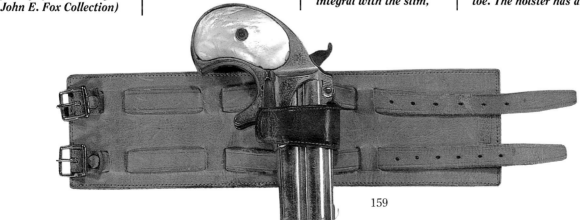

159

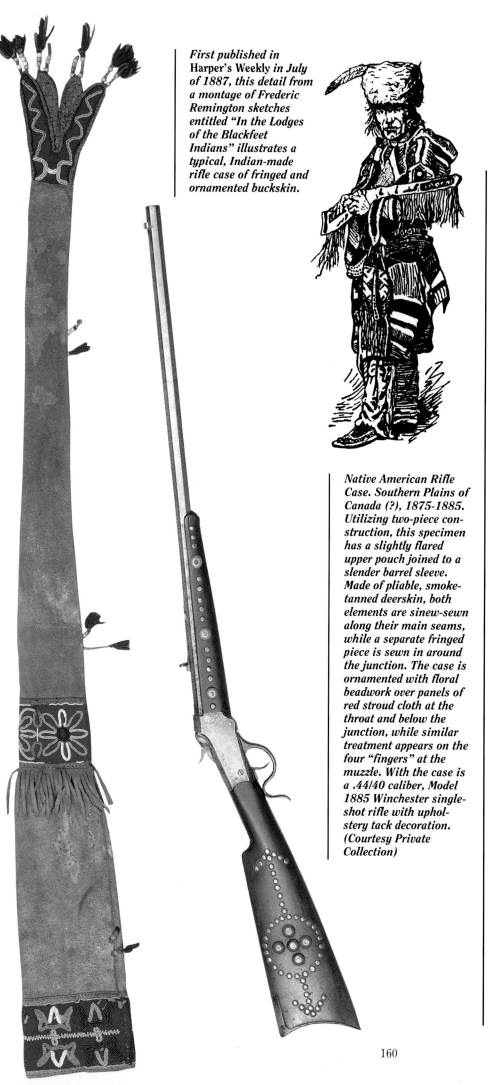

First published in Harper's Weekly in July of 1887, this detail from a montage of Frederic Remington sketches entitled "In the Lodges of the Blackfeet Indians" illustrates a typical, Indian-made rifle case of fringed and ornamented buckskin.

Native American Rifle Case. Southern Plains of Canada (?), 1875-1885. Utilizing two-piece construction, this specimen has a slightly flared upper pouch joined to a slender barrel sleeve. Made of pliable, smoke-tanned deerskin, both elements are sinew-sewn along their main seams, while a separate fringed piece is sewn in around the junction. The case is ornamented with floral beadwork over panels of red stroud cloth at the throat and below the junction, while similar treatment appears on the four "fingers" at the muzzle. With the case is a .44/40 caliber, Model 1885 Winchester single-shot rifle with upholstery tack decoration. (Courtesy Private Collection)

CASES, LOOPS AND SCABBARDS

Longarms, too, were an essential part of civilian material culture on the frontier. Whether it was a heavy Hawken rifle of the ante-bellum period or a handy Winchester carbine of the 1890s, shoulder arms were as important to westering civilians as were their counterparts to those in the military.[66] And the prevalence of horseback travel over the region's great expanses, coupled with the often harsh environment, dictated that these weapons, too, were accompanied by a variety of gunleather fit for their carriage and protection. In the main, these elements appear to have been indigenous to the West, developed by frontier denizens as a practical response to such challenging conditions.

The earliest form of gunleather utilized in the West for longarms was the full-length rifle case, which evidently appeared during the 1830s among such Northern Plains tribes as the Blackfeet, Crow and Sioux. Intended more for the protection of the weapon than for its carriage, these cases were semi-contour fit and shrouded the respective gun from muzzle to butt. Similar in materials and construction to contemporary Indian bow cases, they were fabricated of supple, brain-tanned deer or elkskin; sinew-sewn along the main seam; and decorated with applied fringing, quillwork, beadwork and colored cloth. Many Anglo trappers, traders and frontiersmen of the ante-bellum era no doubt found these distinctive, Indian-made cases attractive and useful in preserving their trusty plains rifles from the elements.[67]

Some early examples of native American rifle cases — usually designed for muzzle-loading guns — incorporated bodies of two-piece construction, having a narrow barrel sleeve sewn to a funnel-shaped pouch that flared outward to the throat from just below the lock and trigger guard area. The much more common pattern — ideal for later, lever action shoulder arms — was of one-piece construction, having a straight fold line along the top with a gradually widening, slightly curvilinear main seam running to the throat along the bottom. Some of these cases were fixed with lightweight rawhide or buckskin shoulder straps, but they would not have safely carried a rifle of appreciable weight if slung from the saddle pommel. Variations expressly made for Anglos sometimes incorporated buttoned flaps to close the throat and, except for applied fringing, were usually unadorned. The form was made on various reservations well into the 1900s and was a common parade element in later years.[68]

Native American Rifle Case. Crow Reservation, Montana, 1890-1900. Both practical and attractive, this rifle case is made of soft, brain-tanned deerskin and ornamented with red stroud cloth and beaded panels of geometric design. The separate element of long fringing is sinew-sewn into the case's main seam. The throat, instead of being fringed, is cut at intervals to form a series of rectangular "flaps." Accompanying the case is a .44/40 caliber, Model 1873 Winchester rifle decorated in Indian fashion with brass upholstery tacks. (National Cowboy Hall of Fame Collection)

Entitled "Aiding a Comrade," this oil painting by Frederic Remington depicts the common use of saddle-mounted, "horn loops" for the carriage of longarms on horseback among cowboys in the West. (Image courtesy The Museum of Fine Arts, Houston; the Hogg Brothers Collection, gift of Miss Ima Hogg)

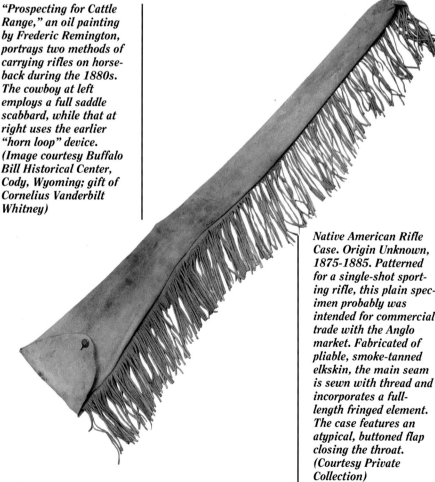

"Prospecting for Cattle Range," an oil painting by Frederic Remington, portrays two methods of carrying rifles on horseback during the 1880s. The cowboy at left employs a full saddle scabbard, while that at right uses the earlier "horn loop" device. (Image courtesy Buffalo Bill Historical Center, Cody, Wyoming; gift of Cornelius Vanderbilt Whitney)

Native American Rifle Case. Origin Unknown, 1875-1885. Patterned for a single-shot sporting rifle, this plain specimen probably was intended for commercial trade with the Anglo market. Fabricated of pliable, smoke-tanned elkskin, the main seam is sewn with thread and incorporates a full-length fringed element. The case features an atypical, buttoned flap closing the throat. (Courtesy Private Collection)

While the soft buckskin rifle case provided excellent protection for its intended weapon, it did not afford an adequate means of carriage; shoulder arms of substantial weight still had to be carried balanced across the saddle pommel in the fashion typical of frontier plainsmen. Among civilians in the West, the first means of securing longarms on horseback — aside from the familiar shoulder sling of military derivation — was the so-called "horn loop," an abbreviated leather sleeve that attached to the saddle horn and through which the rifle slipped in a muzzle-down attitude. Perhaps suggesting its area of origin, some period accounts refer to the item as a "California horn loop."[69]

Usually fabricated of skirting-weight material, this simple, often "home-made" contrivance consisted of a panel about 10 to 12 inches square with rounded corners. This was folded diagonally to create a roughly triangular sleeve, and both layers were pierced at the open apex with a "hole-and-slit" sufficient to pass over the crown of the saddle horn and hang about its neck. When so mounted, the "horn loop" could be rotated 360 degrees, carrying the rifle vertically on either the near or off side, or horizontally across the pommel. Some specimens probably were stitched around the upper apex to keep the sleeve from opening inadvertently. More sophisticated versions, perhaps inspired by the military, consisted of a longer, contoured and folded sleeve sewn along its main seam and fixed with a riveted strap that buckled about

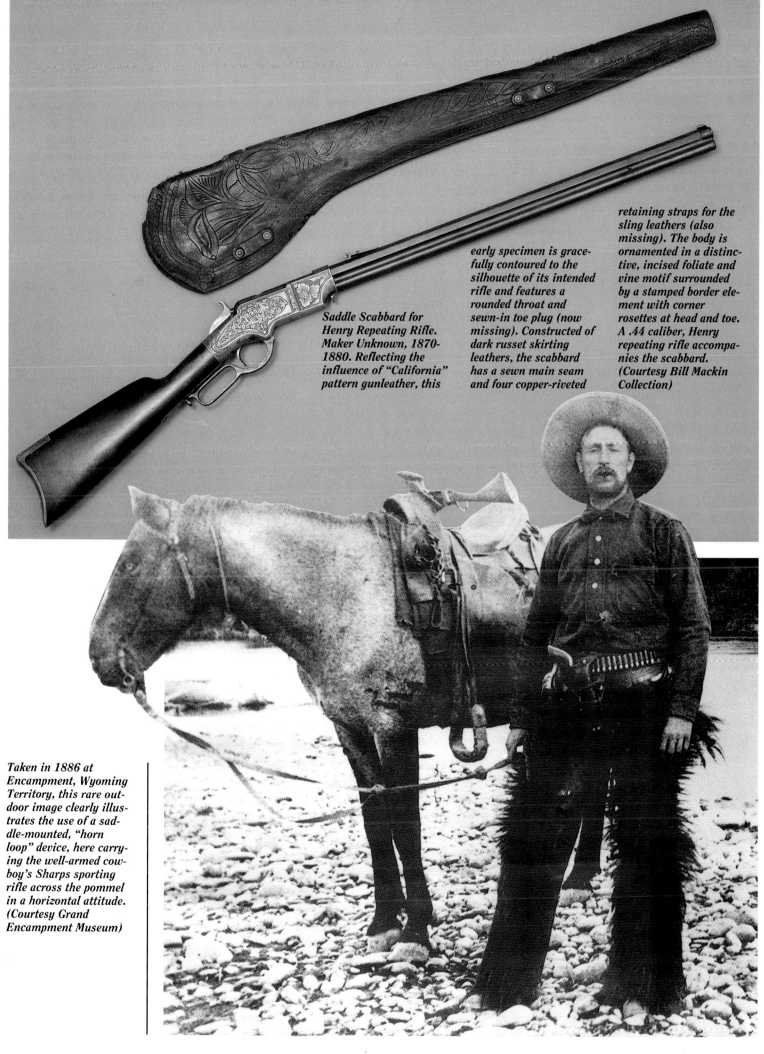

Saddle Scabbard for Henry Repeating Rifle. Maker Unknown, 1870-1880. Reflecting the influence of "California" pattern gunleather, this early specimen is gracefully contoured to the silhouette of its intended rifle and features a rounded throat and sewn-in toe plug (now missing). Constructed of dark russet skirting leathers, the scabbard has a sewn main seam and four copper-riveted *retaining straps for the sling leathers (also missing). The body is ornamented in a distinctive, incised foliate and vine motif surrounded by a stamped border element with corner rosettes at head and toe. A .44 caliber, Henry repeating rifle accompanies the scabbard. (Courtesy Bill Mackin Collection)*

Taken in 1886 at Encampment, Wyoming Territory, this rare outdoor image clearly illustrates the use of a saddle-mounted, "horn loop" device, here carrying the well-armed cowboy's Sharps sporting rifle across the pommel in a horizontal attitude. (Courtesy Grand Encampment Museum)

Saddle Scabbard for Lever Action Rifle.. Maker Unknown, 1870-1880. An intriguing "field" creation, this light carbine scabbard might have been fabricated by a scout or buffalo hunter (the workmanship certainly is not of Indian quality). Constructed of raw buffalo hide with the hair left intact on the interior, the piece is roughly pattern-cut and closed at the main seam with thong lacing. The upper body is double-slit on either side to secure a short, rawhide pommel strap. The scabbard holds a .44 caliber, Model 1866 Winchester Rifle(National Cowboy Hall of Fame Collection)

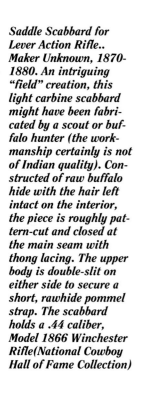

Outfitted with complete equipage, this Montana cowboy posed in 1887. He carries his Smith & Wesson revolver in a late, "California" pattern holster and utilizes a full saddle scabbard for his Winchester rifle. Note that the extremity of the scabbard is secured with an unusual, billet-and-ring attachment sewn into the main seam. (Image courtesy the Library of Congress)

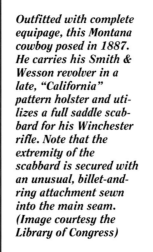

Saddle Scabbard for Lever Action Repeating Rifles. F.A. Meanea, Cheyenne, Wyoming Territory, 1885-1890. Made by one of the West's best-known saddleries, this substantial piece is patterned to accommodate different models of Winchester, Whitney or Marlin repeating rifles. Constructed of heavy russet skirting leather, the scabbard has an arched throat profile and gently tapered main seam that is sewn through the bluntly rounded toe and finished with a top rivet. Two brass rings are riveted into the main seam to secure the sling leathers; the remaining leather is fixed with a nickeled brass, roller-type buckle. A continuous, rolled border ornament traces the periphery of both sides of the piece. With the scabbard is a Model 1873 Winchester rifle. (Courtesy Bill Mackin Collection)

Saddle Scabbard for Henry Repeating Rifle. Maker Unknown, 1875-1885. Reminiscent of the "California" pattern holster, this rifle scabbard is closely form-fit to the contours of its weapon. Constructed of medium-weight russet skirting leather, the piece features a gracefully curved throat and main seam, with rolled border ornament and a large rosette stamped on the upper body. Heavily worn, the original sewn-in toe plug has been covered with a leather muzzle cap, while the sewn main seam has been reinforced with numerous upholstery tacks. The sling leathers are secured to the scabbard body by copper-riveted straps and fixed with square, single-frame brass buckles. With the scabbard is a .44 caliber, Henry repeating rifle. (Courtesy Private Collection)

Saddle Scabbard for Model 1876 Winchester Rifle. Padgitt Brothers, Fort Worth, Texas, 1877-1880. Contour-fit to its large rifle, this substantial scabbard is constructed of heavy black skirting leather with a sewn main seam extending through the rounded toe. The piece is ornamented with linear border tooling and a stamped rosette motif below the curved throat. Copper-riveted straps retain the sling leathers, which have unusual, double-frame buckles of stamped alloy metal. Accompanying the scabbard is a .45/75 caliber, Model 1876 Winchester rifle, third variation, with half-octagon barrel. (Courtesy Private Collection)

Saddle Scabbard for Single-Shot Sporting Rifles. Maker Unknown, 1890-1900. Presenting a gracefully tapered silhouette, this rifle scabbard was designed to accommodate the various Sharps, Remington, or Winchester single-shot sporting rifles then in vogue. Constructed of medium-weight russet leather, the piece has an abruptly rounded throat profile, rolled border decoration of linear and diamond motif, and a sewn main seam running through the closed toe and reinforced with a top rivet. The sling leathers, fixed with small brass buckles, are secured to the scabbard body by closely-spaced straps with iron rivets. With the piece is a .40/70 caliber, Remington No. 1 Rolling Block Sporting rifle. (Courtesy Private Collection)

the saddle horn.[70] Such a variation evidently was adopted by the Northwest Mounted Police of Canada for carriage of the Model 1876 Winchester carbine.

The origin of the "horn loop" remains obscure; no examples are found in available saddler's catalogs, and no historic specimens of civilian provenance are known to the writer. The form probably appeared well prior to the Civil War. Its use may have been alluded to in an 1840 Indian fight recounted by Texan James Wilson Nichols: "After fireing [sic] my rifle I was unable to reload it, and I consigned it to the holder at the horn of my saddle...."[71] Certainly, by the late 1860s, the "horn loop" was commonplace over most of the West and it remained in vogue well into the 1880s (Frederic Remington depicted the device in a number of his illustrations and paintings). But, while it afforded fairly secure carriage and easy accessibility, the "horn loop" provided little protection for the shoulder arm. (It probably was used most commonly on the open plains, where the rifle was free from entanglements in brushy thickets.) Both it and the rifle case were supplanted by another gunleather element that combined all the attributes desired on the frontier.

The true saddle scabbard answered most westerners' requirements for the convenient carriage and adequate protection of their shoulder arms. Utilizing a nearly full-length sheath of durable skirting leather fixed with adjustable sling straps, this practical item could be attached to the pommel and rear rigging on either side of the saddle, riding beneath the stirrup and sweat leathers in a canted attitude that typically carried the weapon butt forward. Like the "Mexican

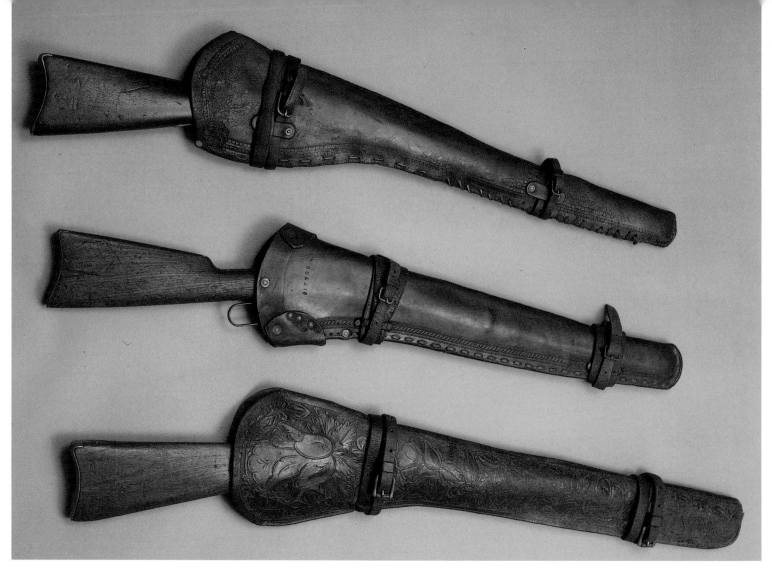

Loop" holster, the saddle scabbard apparently was a generic frontier innovation that appeared among western saddlers during the early 1870s. Coincident with the availabilty of handier, breech-loading and repeating longarms, the form proliferated over the West during the succeeding decade.[72]

The provenance of the saddle scabbard remains uncertain, but early references to its use seem to appear most frequently among Texans. Taking a herd north in 1879, novice cowboy Baylis Fletcher remembered that "I had brought no pistol, my only weapon being a Winchester carbine, which hung in a leather scabbard from my saddle horn."[73] Reginald Aldridge, an Englishman who ranched in the Texas Panhandle during the late 1880s, also remarked on employing a saddle scabbard:

I have now a Sharp's hammerless carbine, .400 cal., which I can carry in a leather scabbard attached to my saddle, and passing under the right leg....[It is] handy to carry [in this manner] when one is not going out purposely for game, but wishes to be able to have a shot if any should accidentally come in the way.[74]

Whatever its precise origin, photographic evidence clearly substantiates the widespread popularity of the saddle scabbard among civilians in the West by the mid-1880s (at least a decade prior to the army's adoption of the form).

(top)
Saddle Scabbard for Model 1873 Winchester Carbine. J. K. Polk, Sweetwater, Texas, 1880-1890. Made and used on the Texas frontier, this scabbard features a frond motif, rolled border ornament with large corner rosette. Constructed of medium-weight russet skirting leather, the piece has a curved throat profile and a contoured main seam sewn through the toe and secured with a top rivet (crude repairs with rawhide and shoe lacing are now evident). The sling leathers, fixed with single-frame iron buckles, are secured with copper-riveted straps to the scabbard body. The piece is paired with a .44/40 caliber, Model 1873 Winchester carbine, third variation, with full nickel finish. (Courtesy Private Collection)

(center)
Saddle Scabbard for Lever Action Carbines. Maker Unknown, 1890-1900. Designed to accommodate any of the Marlin or Winchester carbines then popular, this scabbard is less contoured in silhouette than earlier patterns. Constructed of heavy russet skirting leather, the piece features an arched throat profile and a nearly straight main seam with rolled border ornament (both elements reinforced in later years with a copper-riveted collar and rawhide lacing). The sling leathers, with their brass buckles, probably are not original equipment. With the scabbard is a .38/40 caliber, Model 1892 Winchester carbine. (Courtesy Private Collection)

(bottom)
Saddle Scabbard for Lever Action Carbines. Maker Unknown, 1900-1910. Probably marketed by an eastern sporting goods house, this scabbard is relatively uncontoured in form and quite roomy, so as to hold a wide array of varying firearm makes and models. Constructed of heavy russet bridle leather, the piece features machine-stamped, full-floral ornament with rounded throat profile and fairly straight main seam sewn through the toe. The sling leathers, secured to the scabbard by iron and copper-riveted straps, are closed with single-frame brass roller buckles. A .30/40 Krag caliber, Model 1895 Winchester carbine accompanies the piece. (Courtesy Private Collection)

Saddle Scabbard for Single-Shot Sporting Rifles. Maker Unknown, 1890-1900. Slim and pleasing in profile, this example suggests a latent "California" influence in its design and embellishment. Constructed of heavy russet skirting leather, the scabbard's rounded throat curves gracefully into the tapered main seam, while a sewn-in, "Cheyenne" pattern toe plug closes the muzzle. The piece is ornamented with a hand-carved, foliate and floral motif over stippled ground, the field enclosed with a lightly rolled border element. Suggesting the scabbard's later origin, small patent rivets are employed to secure the main seam and the straps retaining the sling leathers. Accompanying this specimen is a .38/55 caliber, Model 1885 Winchester rifle with medium-weight barrel. (Courtesy Bill Mackin Collection)

Photographed in 1887, Texas Ranger Ira Aten carries his deluxe, lever action Winchester rifle in a full saddle scabbard with arched throat profile and riveted retaining straps for the sling leathers. (Image courtesy Western History Collections, University of Oklahoma Library)

Saddle Scabbard for Lever Action Repeating Rifles. Maker Unknown, 1885-1895. Presenting a graceful, curvilinear silhouette, this scabbard is patterned to carry different repeaters of similar design and proportion. Constructed of heavy russet skirting leather, the piece has rounded throat and toe profiles joined by a slightly contoured, rawhide-laced main seam. The body is ornamented with a deep, hand-carved floral motif surrounded by a rolled, sawtooth border. The scabbard holds a .44/40 caliber, Model 1873 Winchester rifle, third variation. (Courtesy Bill Mackin Collection)

Usually fabricated of medium or heavy-weight russet skirting leather, saddle scabbards were pattern-cut to the general contours of the intended rifle or carbine, folded over, and sewn or rawhide-laced along the main seam. They typically shrouded the weapon from the muzzle up to or above the comb area of the butt stock; those made for carbines were about 32 inches in length, while rifle scabbards normally ranged from 35 to 37 inches. The two sling or mounting leathers generally were fixed with double-frame bridle, or single-frame roller, buckles for adjustment on the saddle, and usually were secured to the faces of the scabbard body by four riveted retaining straps. In rare instances, a pair of circular metal rings were stitched into the scabbard's main seam to retain the sling leathers.[75]

Saddle scabbard design somewhat paralleled the general evolution of contemporary pistol holsters. The earliest examples, circa 1870-1885, usually incorporated relatively slim, contoured bodies reminiscent of the late, "California" silhouette pattern. These scabbards had close-fitting, gracefully curvilinear profiles through the throat and main seam, and sometimes featured a blunt muzzle configuration with a sewn-in toe plug.

During the late 1880s and the 1890s, a roomier and more generalized design came into vogue. Intended to accommodate different longarms of similar pattern and proportion, these later scabbards were typified by straight or slightly arched throat profiles, tapering main seams of more amorphous contour, and rounded, sewn-through toes that sometimes were fixed with bottom rivets. While varying in style from maker to maker, such scabbards mirrored similar design trends evident in "Mexican Loop" holsters of the same time period.[76]

Given their larger surfaces, carbine and rifle scabbards usually were more sparingly ornamented than contemporary pistol holsters. From the pattern's inception, however, a simple, stamped or rolled border decoration around the periphery of the scabbard was nearly universal. During the 1870s and early 1880s, while a few specimens were fully carved in the elongated floral and vine motif of "California" style, the great majority were only border stamped and occasionally incorporated a single, large floral rosette centered on the upper body. With the advent of machine-stamped embellishment in the mid-1890s, more elaborate, floral, waffle and basket-weave patterns in full or partial coverage became readily available. But saddle scabbards finished in this manner remained comparatively scarce because such applications often doubled the cost.[77]

From the 1880s onward, saddle scabbards, too, were copied by eastern manufacturers and marketed in the West by mail order and outfitting houses. (Some of the smaller frontier saddlers evidently retailed such jobber merchandise, often stamping it with their own maker's cartouche.) While generally serviceable, this imported, often mass-produced gunleather usually undercut the price of better-made western products. A few of the larger frontier saddleries competed by offering scabbards in either heavy or light-weight skirting stock, typically varying the price by one dollar. But, whatever its origin or quality, the saddle scabbard was employed throughout the West, and it has maintained its utility in the region's back country to the present day.[78]

This cut from the 1890 catalog of San Antonio's L. Frank Saddlery illustrates a utilitarian line of gunleather, including saddle scabbards for both carbines and rifles.

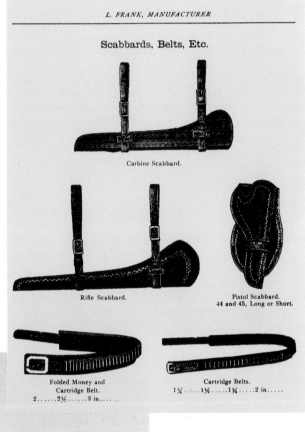

L. FRANK, MANUFACTURER

Scabbards, Belts, Etc.

Carbine Scabbard.

Rifle Scabbard.

Pistol Scabbard.
44 and 45, Long or Short.

Folded Money and
Cartridge Belt.
2......2½......3 in......

Cartridge Belts.
1¼.....1½.....1¾.....2 in.....

Photographed in 1916, 101 Ranch showman Tex Cooper carries his rifle in a full saddle scabbard ornamented with floral stamping, edge lacing and a thong-laced concho below the throat. (Image courtesy National Cowboy Hall of Fame and Western Heritage Center)

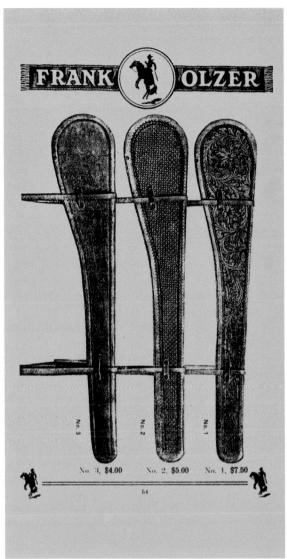

FRANK OLZER

No. 3, $4.00   No. 2, $5.00   No. 1, $7.50

54

Saddle Scabbard for
Lever Action Repeating
Carbines. W. H. Clay,
Brownsville, Texas,
1910-1915. This inter-
esting specimen incor-
porates three snap-
flapped cartridge
pouches sewn on each
face of the body, each
accommodating five
rounds of ammunition.
Fabricated of dark rus-
set skirting leather, the
scabbard features a
round throat profile, a
nearly straight main
seam sewn through the
toe, and four riveted
straps for the sling
leathers. The scabbard is
finished with stamped
border and waffle
pattern ornament. A
.30/30 caliber, Model
1894 Winchester
carbine accompanies the
piece. (Courtesy Joe
Gish Collection. Image
courtesy Bill Manns)

Frank Olzer's Arizona
Saddlery catalog of circa
1905 preferred rifle
scabbards with edge
tooling, waffle stamping
or floral carving to suit
the status — or pocket-
book — of any buyer.

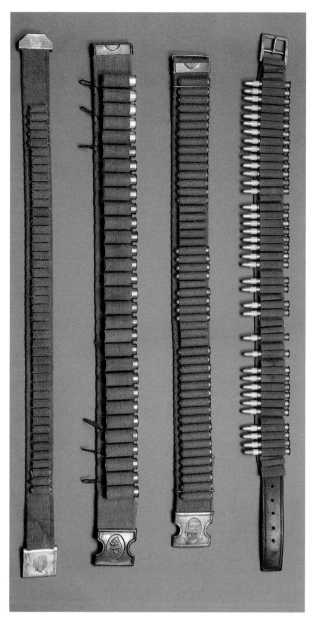

(right)
Model 1876 "Prairie" Cartridge Belt. Watervliet Arsenal, New York, 1876-1881. The so-called "Prairie Belt" was popular in both military and civilian circles because the cloth material eliminated the problem of verdigris formation common with brass cartridges stored in leather loop belts. Representing adoption by a civilian hunter, this example holds .45/100 Sharps Straight rifle cartridges popular in the buffalo harvest. (Courtesy Private Collection)

CARTRIDGE BELTS

As observed heretofore, the basic perfection of self-contained metallic cartridges during the 1860s had a marked influence on the development of western gunleather. The cartridge belt certainly was the most obvious innovation to spring from this technological advance. While its exact origins remain somewhat unclear, this practical gunleather element probably derived from the field improvisations of former Civil War soldiers who ventured west after the conflict. Given the often great distances and time intervals between sources of ammunition supply, and the potential need to rapidly reload one's weapons in the midst of a sustained shooting affray, a belt carrying 35 to 45 cartridges ready at hand proved to be a remarkably useful accoutrement on the far reaches of the frontier.[79]

(left)
"Mills" Pattern Cartridge Belt. Gilbert Loom Company(?), Worcester, Massachusetts, 1881-1886. Marketed by the Winchester Repeating Arms Company of New Haven, Connecticut, this belt features the scarce "Bear's Head" plate of nickeled-brass. Constructed of tan cotton webbing on the "Mills" pattern, the narrow belt incorporates 45 integrally-woven loops for the popular .44/40 Winchester cartridge (widely used in both revolvers and rifles.) (Courtesy Bill Mackin Collection)

(left center)
"Mills" Pattern Shotshell Belt. T. C. Orndorff, Worcester, Massachusetts, 1885-1895. Manufactured for the civilian market, this specimen features the classic "H" pattern, "Dog's Head" belt plate of stamped and gilded brass. Constructed of loomed cotton webbing, the belt has 30 shell loops woven into the body. It is fitted with game hooks suspended from grommetted holes on the lower edge of the belt. This example accommodates full brass shells for a 12 bore shotgun. (Courtesy Private Collection)

(right center)
"Mills" Pattern Cartridge Belt. T. C. Orndorff, Worcester, Massachusetts, 1887-1890. Developed by then Major Anson Mills, the woven cartridge belt with classic "H" plate closure first appeared in 1880. This example has the 1887 style, stamped "H" pattern belt plate with U.S. marking. The belt, of tan webbing, has 50 loops to accommodate either of the standard .45/70 Government cartridges for rifle or carbine. (Courtesy Private Collection)

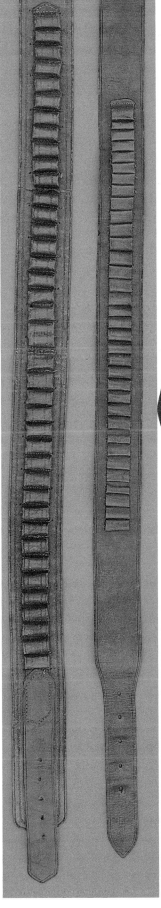

Plain Cartridge Belt.
Maker Unknown, 1890-
1900. Fixed for .44 cal-
iber ammunition, this
single-thickness belt fea-
tures a fancy, double-
frame buckle with scal-
loped edges and nickeled
finish. The loops and
tongue billet are sewn
on, while the buckle
chape is also triple-rivet-
ed. All leather elements
are edge-creased.
(Courtesy Phil Spangen-
berger Collection. Photo
by Charlie Rathbun)

Plain Cartridge Belt.
Maker Unknown, 1875-
1885. This single-thick-
ness belt is fabricated of
medium-weight russet
skirting leather with
sewn loops for .44 cali-
ber cartridges. Of early
pattern, it utilizes an
integral, tapered tongue
and a separate, riveted
and sewn chape with the
clip-cornered, nickel-
plated "California"
buckle. (Courtesy Phil
Spangenberger Collec-
tion. Photo by Charlie
Rathbun)

Probably photographed
in the late 1870s or
early 1880s, this
stalwart cowboy wears
his Colt Single Action
Army revolver in cross-
draw position. His
"Mexican Loop" pattern
holster is mounted on a
single-thickness, all-
leather belt which
appears to have woven-
in cartridge loops for
pistol ammunition.
(Image courtesy
Western History
Department, Denver
Public Library)

By the late 1860s, waist belts fixed with multiple loops, or "thimbles," for rifle and carbine cartridges were becoming fairly commonplace among civilians in the West. In particular, such belts found a ready market with the hundreds of buffalo hunters who converged on the central and southern plains during the early 1870s. Similar rigging adapted for pistol cartridges evidently appeared almost simultaneously, providing the catalyst for the development of the "Mexican Loop" pattern holster. Certainly, by 1875, cartridge belts were a well-established article of gun-leather among western saddlers and their colorful clientele.

During the early years of cartridge belt manufacture, there was a considerable interchange and sharing of attributes between civilian and non-regulation, military varieties. While most civilian or saddler-made belts were fabricated entirely of leather, some incorporated loops or bodies of canvas to preclude the formation of verdigris coincident with the use of copper and brass cartridge cases. This treatment often was utilized in field-made military belts as well, and it ultimately was standardized in the army's 1876 "Prairie" pattern cartridge belt. The regulation "Prairie" belt, in turn, found many devotees — and copyists — among frontier civilians because of its relative freedom from verdigris, its generally substantial construction, and its ready accommodation of long-cased rifle cartridges.[80]

Although originally conceived for military service, the "Mills" patent cartridge belt also was popular with civilians in the West. Almost from its inception in the early 1880s, this all-textile pattern was manufactured for the civilian market, first by Gilbert Loom Company and then by the Mills-Orndorff firm, both of Worcester, Massachusetts. The belts were sold through various outfitting houses, ranging from Abercrombie & Fitch in New York City, to N. Curry & Brother in San Francisco. In 1884 the latter firm offered "Mills" belts at $1.50 each, noting that:

(below)
Hunter's Cartridge Belt. Maker Unknown, 1885-1895. Lightweight yet serviceable, this specimen combines a tightly woven body of course wool with leather elements of russet bridle material. Three flapped pouches with small finial closures (now missing) are sewn on the body face, between which are 14 sewn loops containing .50/70 Sharps rifle cartridges. The belt secures with a double-tongued billet that engages a double chape fixed with single-frame bridle buckles. (Courtesy Private Collection)

Photographed around 1895, John Slaughter (former sheriff of Cochise County, Arizona) wears a "Mills" pattern shotshell belt carrying 12 gauge loads for his Model 1887 Winchester shotgun. The "Mexican Loop" pattern holster appears to be an inexpensive, commercial product with unusual, concave throat profile. (Image courtesy National Cowboy Hall of Fame and Western Heritage Center)

(above)
Plain Shotshell Belt. Maker Unknown, 1880-1890. Fabricated of medium-weight, dark brown bridle leather, the body of this sportsman's belt is 2 1/4 inches in width with an integral, tapered tongue and sewn chape with japanned roller buckle. Eleven, slightly narrower loops for 12 gauge shells are sewn on the left face of the body, leaving ample space for a game bag or hunting knife sheath. All elements feature straight crimp and stitch marker borderlines. (Courtesy Private Collection)

The loops are woven in and form part of the fabric of the Belt, so that they cannot be torn off, and are of such accurate form...[that] the cartridge cannot drop out. Handsome and durable buckles are furnished, so formed that the wearer may adjust the length of the Belt to his person without sewing or cutting....[81]

Various frontier types, particularly sport hunters, were quick to adopt the commercial versions of this very functional belt design.

Somewhat lighter in weight and more resistent to wear and moisture than all-leather cartridge belts, the commercial "Mills" pattern belt was manufactured in a variety of styles and loop sizes for rifle, pistol and shotgun ammunition. The latter variation often was fitted with a series of hooks along the lower edge for carrying game in the field and sometimes incorporated leather shoulder straps or "braces." Most of these belts secured with "Mills" patent, rectangular or "H" pattern closure plates of stamped and gilded brass, featuring the familiar "Dog's Head" motif. Others utilized narrower, rectangular plates with nickel finish, such as the very scarce "Bear's Head" variation marketed by Winchester Repeating Arms Company between 1881 and 1885 and later sold by Bannerman's of New York City. (Mill's-type, "H" pattern plates with Remington, Sharps Old Reliable, Winchester, Wells Fargo and Texas Ranger logos are spurious productions and bereft of any historic provenance.)[82]

While ammunition belts of canvas or woven cotton webbing had their place in the West, most frontier saddlers relied on quality skirting leather in fabricating their cartridge belts. It has been suggested that the use of "California Oak tanned" leathers eliminated the formation of verdigris, but any survey of existing belts holding copper or brass cartridges belies this theory. In the main, western saddlers simply ignored the verdigris problem and, for the remainder of the nineteenth century and beyond, concentrated their efforts on the production of all-leather cartridge belts.[83]

The earliest, saddler-made cartridge belts possessed bodies of single-thickness, russet leather and ranged from 1 1/2 to 3 inches in width. Both ends of the belt usually tapered to form the tongue billet and the chape, which retained a relatively small, single- or double-frame buckle of iron or brass (even harness and roller buckles sometimes were employed). By the early 1880s, this pattern was being replaced by belts with separate, sewn and/or riveted billets fitted for the classic, double-frame "California" buckle having clipped corners and nickel-plated finish.

Cartridge loops on either style of belt usually were sewn, wired or riveted in place from a single strip of leather, on most examples often numbering as many as the body could accommodate between its tongue and buckle billets. More meticulous artisans or shops sometimes wove the leather strip through a series of slits cut into the belt body, creating much more durable cartridge loops. The Denver Manufacturing Company, for example, offered a belt in its 1883 cata-

Photographed around 1884 in his cowboy garb, future President Theodore Roosevelt wears a "Mexican Loop" holster suspended on a "Mills" patent, rifle cartridge belt. The belt is secured with the rare, Winchester "Bear's Head" closure plate of nickeled brass. (Image courtesy The State Historical Society of North Dakota)

173

These early-twentieth-century Arizona Rangers carry their ammunition in extremely wide leather belts. The man at left wears a combination cartridge/money belt about 3 1/2 inches in width with two rows of loops for either pistol or rifle ammunition (note the wide "hang" of the belt loop on the "Mexican Loop" pattern holster). The officer at right wears a single-thickness belt of about 5 1/2 inches width with two tiers of loops for rifle and pistol cartridges (note that the holster's belt loop is especially configured to accommodate this belt). (Image courtesy Arizona Historical Society Library, Tucson)

(opposite)
Cartridge/Money Belt with "Mexican Loop" Pattern Holster.
J. S. Collins, Cheyenne, Wyoming Territory and J. S. Collins & Company, Cheyenne, 1881-1885 and 1886-1890. This matched outfit joins an extremely wide, combination cartridge/money belt with a nice, "Cheyenne" variant holster. Fabricated of soft russet leather, the folded belt is a full five inches in width and is faced with two tiers of cartridge loops for rifle and pistol ammunition. Sewn along the top and both ends, the body is mounted with riveted and sewn billets of skirting leather and secured by a rectangular, double-frame buckle of nickeled iron. The buckle billet or chape is stamped "45/30/30," indicating loops sized for .45 Colt pistol and .30-30 Wesson rifle cartridges (.30-30 Winchester rounds, as illustrated here, were not available until 1895). The "Cheyenne" variant holster, with its contoured main seam and sewn-in toe plug, is typical of Collins' styling and workmanship. (Courtesy Joe Gish Collection. Image courtesy Bill Manns)

Cartridge/Money Belt. Maker Unknown, 1885-1895. Originally machine-stitched, the body, tongue billet and chape of this specimen have been resecured with rawhide lacing. The cartridge loops, formed from a strip of skirting leather, are woven through a series of slots on the belt face and secured with studs of nickeled brass. Mounted with a "California" pattern buckle, the belt accommodates 23 rounds of .44/40 ammunition for revolver, carbine or rifle. (Courtesy Private Collection)

Photographed in the early 1890s, a pair of Montana bear hunters display their equipage. The man at left wears a commercial, "Mills" patent belt with "H" pattern, "Dog's Head" closure plate and integrally woven loops for rifle cartridges. The gent on the right wears a relatively wide, combination cartridge/money belt of leather with typical, "California" pattern buckle having clipped corners. (Image courtesy Montana Historical Society, Helena)

Plain Cartridge Belt. Maker Unknown, 1875-1885. Fabricated of heavy skirting leather, this specimen incorporates markedly narrowed tongue and buckle billets that are integral with the body. The left end of the belt is fixed with an auxiliary strap for mounting a shallow-looped holster over the face of the cartridges. Both the strap and belt secure with iron roller buckles. The piece accommodates 42 rounds of .44/40 Winchester ammunition. (Courtesy Private Collection)

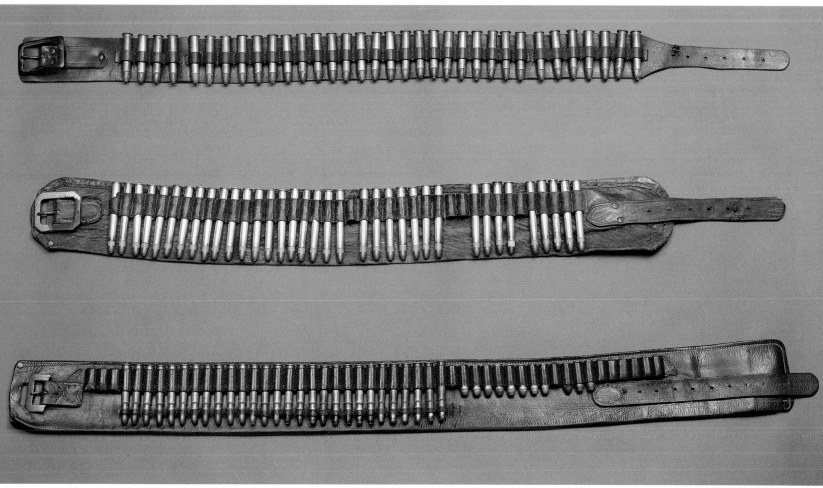

(top)
Plain Cartridge Belt. Maker Unknown, 1890-1900. An inexpensive, mail order product, this belt is constructed of a single thickness of russet bridle leather. The body has an integral, tapered tongue and a machine-rolled border ornament. The cartridge loops are sewn on, while the buckle billet is riveted and holds a rectangular brass buckle with recessed center bar. The belt is loaded with .40/70 Sharps Necked rifle cartridges. (All courtesy Private Collection)

(center)
Cartridge/Money Belt. Newton & Andrews (?), El Paso, Texas, 1885-1890. Crudely-finished and often-repaired, this well-worn belt still retains traces of unscraped cow hair on various elements. The body, designed for long-cased rifle cartridges, is an unusual 4 1/4 inches in width and is folded and sewn in typical fashion to form the interior pocket (the seam has been over-wrapped, sewn, and riveted in a later repair). The sewn-on belt loops, and the buckle and tongue billets, are made of medium skirting leather (the latter element, carrying the Newton & Andrews mark on the reverse tip, is reinforced with rivets). The belt is fitted with a nickel-plated, clip-cornered "California" buckle and carries the powerful .40/90 Sharps Straight rifle cartridge.

(bottom)
Cartridge/Money Belt. Shelton-Payne Arms Co., El Paso, Texas, 1905-1915. This substantial belt, designed to accommodate both rifle and revolver cartridges, features thin, laced-through loops retaining the noses of the necked-down, smokeless rifle cartridges. Constructed of supple russet leather, the 3 3/4-inch-wide body is folded along the bottom and sewn closed along top and side; the seam is reinforced with two rivets. The main cartridge loops and separate tongue and buckle billets are sewn. Part of the small, square "California" buckle remains. This belt pattern was popular among the Mexican bandits and revolutionaries of the period and sometimes was worn in bandoleer fashion. The piece carries .35 Winchester rifle and .44 Winchester revolver cartridges.

log in which: "The cartridge pockets are laced in with a band of leather, one in. wide, so arranged that the belt can neither rip or wear out....it is the most durable belt made." In the late 1890s, some belts appeared with a fairly deep spacing strip of leather stitched beneath the loops to evenly seat the cartridges and keep rimless rounds from slipping through entirely.[84]

The unique western contribution to such gunleather design was the combination, cartridge/money belt, a pattern prevalent on the waning frontier between 1880 and 1900. Simple, pouch-type money belts had been common in the West for decades among miners, gamblers and overland travelers; with the widespread adoption of looped cartridge belts during the 1870s, it was natural that a combination of these practical forms soon evolved. Writing of an encounter with a Miles City, Montana Territory, dancehall girl in 1883, cowboy "Teddy Blue" Abbott alluded to the use of such a belt: "...she told me she had a room back there and invited me to go....But there was a dark hall...and as we started along it I remembered that I had seven hundred dollars on me, in my six-shooter belt."[85]

Constructed of supple calfskin or "chaparejo" leather, the body of the cartridge/money belt was fixed with loops along its upper face, folded in half along its bottom length, and sewn around the top seam and one or both ends to create an elongated, internal pocket. Coins, currency or documents were inserted into the buckle end of the belt through the

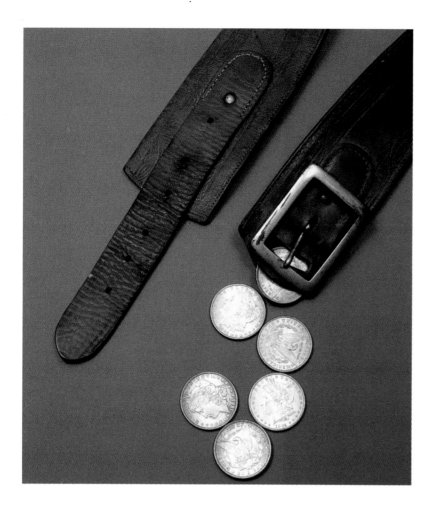

because the softer body leather did not take the tooling as readily as stiffer skirting material. On these belts, the maker's cartouche, as well as numbers indicating belt or cartridge size, usually were stamped on the heavier tongue and buckle billets. Around the turn of the century, single-thickness cartridge belts retailed from $1.50 to $2.00, while combination belts went from $2.50 to $5.00, depending on width. The cost differential for ornamentation on the former belt pattern generally was one dollar or less.[87]

Whether of plain or combination design, saddler-made cartridge belts almost invariably were utilized in conjunction with a pistol holster of some pattern. Few of these outfits, however, actually were "made to match" by their manufacturers. The catalogs of numerous western saddlers clearly indicate that, even in the early twentieth century, the majority of cartridge belts and holsters were designed and priced as separate articles and subsequently "pieced" together. Still, those outfits bearing identical maker's marks on both elements — or exhibiting similar style, workmanship and the consistent wear of long association when unmarked — may be considered to constitute a "matched rig" by today's students and collectors.[88]

Taken as a whole, historic western gunleather intended for the civilian market was remarkable for both its diversity and its versatility. Although eastern and mid-western leather goods manufacturers played a role in the civilian trade, it was the legion of individual western saddlers, working in intimate contact with their clientele, that established the benchmarks for quality and design. Most of their products embodied a consistent attention to practicality and functionalism, while still revealing the subtleties of individual artisanship in style, design and ornament. In this regard, indigenous western gunleather certainly was imbued with greater "character" than either its commercial or military counterparts during the nineteenth century.

unsewn opening, or if closed, through a vertical slot cut through both body layers at the outer periphery of the buckle. The valuables were then "locked in" by passing the tongue billet through the slot from back to front and engaging the buckle.

Such combination belts typically utilized separate billet leathers with the "California" pattern buckle and ranged from three to four inches in width. The wider examples sometimes incorporated double rows or tiers of cartridge loops for carrying both pistol and rifle (or carbine) ammunition. Particularly popular in cowboy culture, the cartridge/money belt commonly was employed in late western rigs utilizing the "Mexican Loop" pattern holster.[86]

Between 1870 and 1900, most saddler-made cartridge belts of single-thickness skirting leather were ornamented with only a simple, stamped or rolled border line along the upper and lower edges of the face. Some were offered with nickeled "spots" or fuller, machine-stamped coverage in floral or waffle motifs during the early 1900s, but full-carved belts were a relative rarity at any time. Combination cartridge/money belts were rarely even edge or border-stamped

This cut from an H. H. Heiser catalog presents the full particulars on cartridge/money belt construction and use. Such combination gunleather was very popular in the West for holster carriage between 1880 and 1900.

Combination Cartridge and Money Belt

No. 66—Made of the best quality of chrome-tanned chaparejo leather, which is very soft and tough and not affected by perspiration. Folded part is 2½ inches wide and cut long enough to entirely encircle the body. This belt has but one seam at the top, which is stitched with heavy flax thread. The Belt has 30 cartridge loops ⅞ of an inch wide. A billet 1½ inches wide by 9 inches long buckles into a nickel California belt buckle after passing thru both pieces of the folded leather, thus closing the opening. Money cannot be taken out of belt unless this billet is withdrawn from the buckle, and, as the entire belt forms one large pouch, it can readily be seen that considerable money can be carried in a most convenient manner............$5.00

No. 68—This is exactly the same Belt as shown in the above cut and described under No. 66, but is made three inches wide in a first-class manner...............$5.50

In ordering belts always give the waist measure and caliber of cartridge.

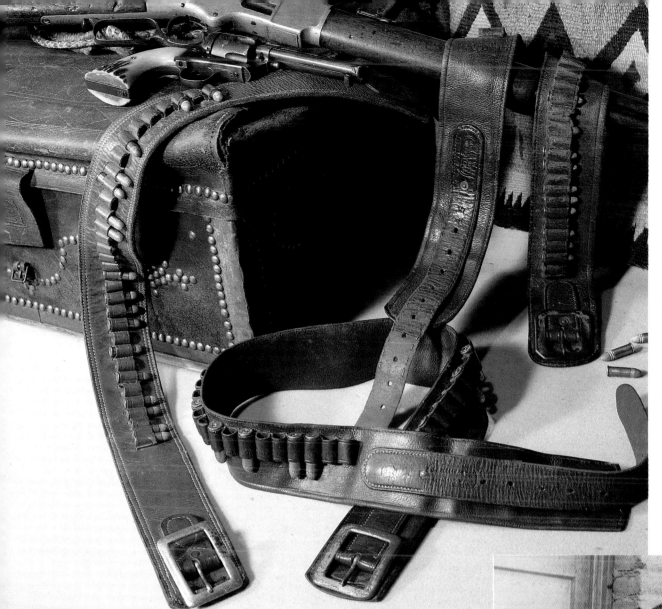

Striking a bellicose pose at Naco, Sonora, Mexico, in 1915, this Constitutionalist soldier is encumbered with some 200 rounds of ammunition for his Mauser rifle. Two "Mills" pattern bandoleers of woven cotton drape his shoulders, while a pair of leather cartridge belts span his mid-section. Carrying a Colt Single Action revolver, a third cartridge belt with flap-covered pockets for additional rifle ammo girds the gentleman's hips. (Image courtesy Lawrence Jones Collection)

(left)
Cartridge/Money Belt. Maker Unknown, 1890-1900. Atypical of the usual, folded pattern, this belt uses two layers of leather to form the interior pocket. Constructed of medium-weight skirting material, the body is double sewn on three edges, leaving access at the buckle end. Separate tongue and buckle billets of skirting leather are riveted and sewn to the body, and utilize a rectangular, nickel-plated "California" buckle with recessed center bar. The belt has a lightly rolled, geometric border ornament and carries .38 Long revolver cartridges. (Courtesy Private Collection)

(top right)
Cartridge/Money Belt. Moran Brothers, Miles City, Montana, 1885-1895. A typical example of the pattern, this belt has a 2 3/4-inch-wide body slotted at the buckle for access to the interior pocket. Constructed of pliable, pebble-grained russet leather, the belt is folded along the bottom and sewn around the top and end seams. The separate billets for tongue and buckle are both sewn and riveted. The rectangular buckle is classic "California" style, with center bar, clipped corners, and nickel-plated finish. The belt carries .38 Long rim fire cartridges. (Courtesy Private Collection)

(bottom right)
Cartridge/Money Belt. J.S. Collins & Co., Cheyenne, Wyoming, 1885-1890. Manufactured by one of the West's great saddlers, this combination belt joins fine materials and superior craftsmanship. Constructed of supple, russet leather, the 3-inch-wide body is folded and sewn along the ends and top to create the interior pocket. Made of skirting leather, the relatively narrow row of cartridge loops is sewn high on the body. The tongue and buckle billets, also of skirting material, are riveted and sewn, and utilize a nickel-plated iron center bar buckle. (Courtesy R.M. Bachman collection. William Manns photo)

179

THE HOUSE OF HEISER

Between 1880 and 1920, many of the West's best-known saddlery companies crafted quality gunleather as a sideline to their regular production. Only a few, however, drew on their own and their customers' experience to formulate superior gunleather elements as a specialty line. The indisputable leader among the more innovative shops was the H. H. Heiser Saddlery of Denver, Colorado. Unlike nearly all its competitors, the Heiser firm made an intentional transition from general saddler to gunleather specialist in the decades around the turn of the century. While in no way minimizing its saddle business, this diversification may have helped the company avoid the many shop mergers and outright failures prompted by the advent of automobile transportation and the later onset of the Great Depression.

The Heiser enterprise was founded by Hermann H. Heiser, a native of Altenburg, Saxony, who immigrated to the United States in the late 1840s. Trained in his native land as a harness and saddler maker, Heiser supposedly moved west in late 1850s and established himself at Denver, Colorado, the center of a bustling commercial district and a ready market for gunleather. It was there that Heiser no doubt fashioned his first pistol holsters. Seeking more lucrative opportunities, he evidently purchased the Gallup & Gallatin shop in 1874, where he soon gained a reputation for quality saddlery and custom-crafted gunleather. By 1878 his business had grown to such an extent that Heiser felt compelled to register his "Triple H" trademark with the state. High-grade, custom-made holsters, cartridge belts and saddle scabbards by then were a regular part of his larger product line.[89]

Heiser's attention to the gunleather business was perhaps best illustrated in the firm's later trade literature. By about 1910, seven years after the founder's death, the company was publishing and distributing mail order catalogs devoted exclusively to gunleather. These included historical (and obviously promotional) sketches of the company's innovation and gradual specialization in the trade. Catalog No. 19 of circa 1924, quoted on the following two pages, was typical.

A half-seat stock saddle by H.H. Heiser Saddlery Company, circa 1885. (Image courtesy Bill Manns)

Heiser catalog from 1898. (Courtesy George Pitman)

Mr. Hermann H. Heiser, founder of the H. H. Heiser Saddlery Company of Denver, circa 1900. (Image courtesy Western History Department, Denver Public Library)

Belt Holster for Large-Frame Revolvers. H.H. Heiser Saddlery, Denver, Colorado, 1925-1935. This No. 415 Fancy Design Spotted Holster sold for $6.00 in the firm's No. 20 catalog of circa 1928. Of one-piece design, the right-hand holster is fabricated of "heavy California skirting leather" with a fully lined pouch and "solid nickel ornaments." The piece incorporates the "Quick Draw" belt loop design over an integral, contoured skirt that is riveted to the back of the body. Accompanying the holster is a .45 caliber, Colt Single Action revolver with 7 1/2-inch barrel and stag grips. (Courtesy Ron Soodalter Collection. Image courtesy Bill Manns)

"Mexican Loop" Pattern Holster for Colt Single Action Army Revolver. H. H. Heiser Saddlery, Denver, Colorado, 1900-1910. The form and design of this right-hand piece clearly indicate that it is a No. 122 Hand Basket Stamped Revolver Holster as illustrated in Heiser's No. 14 catalog. Made of "heavy California skirting leather with unlined pouch," the holster incorporates a shallow throat recurve, sewn main seam extending through the toe with top and bottom rivets, and a full back skirt secured with two integral loops. The body is fully decorated with rolled border tooling and basket-weave stamping, while the upper skirt loop carries the early Heiser cartouche. The holster accommodates a Colt Single Action .45 with a 7 1/2-inch barrel. (Courtesy Arizona West Galleries. Image courtesy Bill Manns)

Since the spring of 1858 when the firm that is now soliciting your patronage began their career, experience has been the teacher.... Mr. Hermann H. Heiser, who came from the East, knew but very little of the exacting demands that were made by gunmen, sheriffs and the pioneer trail blazers...in regard to their pistol holsters as well as cartridge belts and other equipment.... [H]e was surprised to learn that ninety percent of the population of this primitive section had to depend upon weapons for defense and the ability to draw them quickly from holsters and scabbards in order to protect both lives and property.

The suggestions made by patrons from time to time in regard to holsters, belts, etc., were carefully noted so that these details could be used in recommendations to others...,and it was also then that Hermann H. Heiser reached the conclusion that all goods of this character should be made up to special order if every customer was to be satisfied, since nearly everyone had their own peculiar way of handling a gun, some shooting from the hip, others at full arms length, some were right handed, others left handed, [etc.]....

"Mexican Loop" Pattern Holster. H. H. Heiser Saddlery, Denver, Colorado, 1900-1910. This Heiser No. 133 Revolver Holster features the narrow "quick draw belt loop that avoids interference of the Holster in the grasping of the revolver grip...." Constructed of heavy California skirting leather, the right-hand piece is finished plain with gracefully recurved throat, sewn main seam and toe with top and bottom rivets, and contoured skirt with two integral loops. The upper loop carries the early Heiser cartouche. (Courtesy Bill Mackin Collection)

"Mexican Loop" Pattern Holster. H. H. Heiser Saddlery, Denver, Colorado, 1905-1915. This Heiser No. 200 Bull's-Head Design is constructed of medium-weight, oak-tanned russet leather in plain finish. The pouch has a fairly deep, recurved throat profile and a main seam sewn through the toe and reinforced with a top rivet. A single integral loop of circular design secures the body to the ample skirt and is adorned with the bull's head stamp. The item sold for $1.00 prior to the First World War. (Courtesy Bill Mackin Collection)

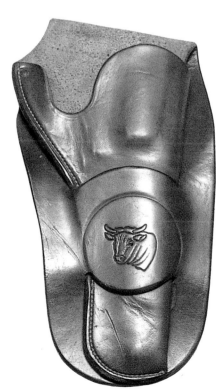

While the manufacture of these holsters and scabbards...was carried on in a small way and was of a purely local nature, the reputation of the pioneer Hermann H. Heiser as a maker of "Real Western Stuff" began to spread.... Occasional orders from distant points gradually developed...until our sales of today are represented by shipments to all parts of the world, in addition to which a large modern factory employing upwards of thirty skilled mechanics is largely engaged in the manufacture of this OUR HOBBY AND CHOSEN SPECIALITY.[90]

"Mexican Loop" Pattern Holster for Colt Single Action Army Revolver. H. H. Heiser Saddlery, Denver, Colorado, 1905-1915. Another example of the Bull's-Head Design, this right-hand piece is fabricated of heavy, black-dyed skirting leather, a special order variant. The No. 100 pattern, with deep throat recurve and single top rivet, sold for $1.50 during the period. Later production, cited as the No. 407 Round Loop Belt Holster, retailed for $3.25 during the 1920s. (Courtesy Arizona West Galleries. William Manns, photo)

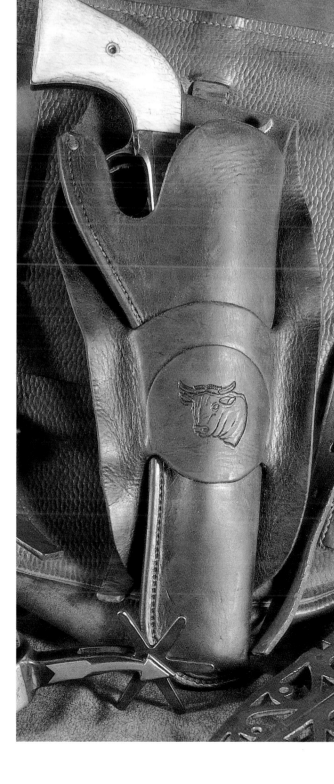

"Mexican Loop" Pattern Holster with Matching Cartridge Belt. H. H. Heiser Saddlery, Denver, Colorado, 1915-1920. This handsome rig joins the No. 710 Loop Style Holster with the No. 72 Calfskin-Lined Cartridge Belt, both made of "finest Oak Tanned California skirting leather." The right-hand holster, "...originated by one of the most expert gun men in the West," features a plain skirt with two integral loops and narrow, "Quick Draw" belt loop. The holster body is "full Mexican hand carved" with deeply recurved throat, open toe, and sewn main seam with top and bottom rivets. The matching belt is also hand-tooled in floral motif and has sewn cartridge loops and separate billets for the tongue and brass, single-frame roller buckle. In 1920 the outfit retailed for $12.50, transportation charges prepaid by Heiser. (Courtesy National Cowboy Hall of Fame Collection)

"Mexican Loop" Pattern Holster. H. H. Heiser Saddlery, Denver, Colorado, 1910-1915. Incorporating integral, scalloped skirt loops, Heiser's No. 120 Loop-Style holster retailed for $2.50 in the firm's No. 14 catalog. Fabricated of California skirting leather, this specimen features a calfskin lining, nicely recurved throat, sewn main seam with top and bottom rivets, and a generous back skirt. Accompanying the holster is a cartridge/money belt made by Bools & Butler of Reno, Nevada, and a Colt Single Action with carved ivory grips and 5 1/2-inch barrel. (Courtesy Joe Gish Collection. Image courtesy Bill Manns)

"Mexican Loop" Pattern Holster for Single and Double Action Revolvers. H. H. Heiser Saddlery, Denver, Colorado, 1915-1925. Heiser's No. 190 Original Design Revolver Holster introduced a shortened, half-length back skirt secured with an integral, thong-laced loop. Made of heavy russet skirting leather, this right-hand example lacks the standard calfskin lining. The pouch incorpo-

rates a deep and relatively wide throat recurve, and has an amorphous main seam contour sewn through the rounded toe and secured with top and bottom rivets. Priced at $2.00 during the period, this piece holds a .45 caliber, Colt Single Action Army revolver with 7 1/2-inch barrel. (Courtesy Arizona West Galleries. William Manns, photo)

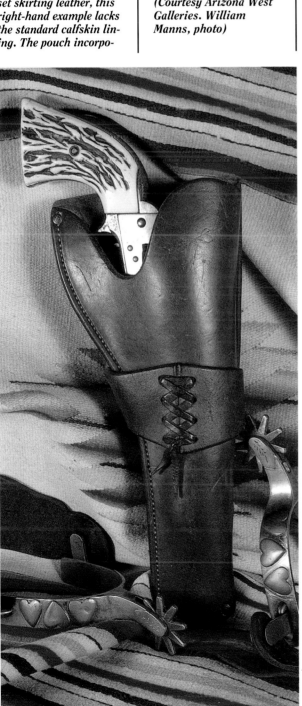

(below, left) "Mexican Loop" Pattern Holster. H.H. Heiser Saddlery, Denver, Colorado, 1915-1925. Heiser's No. 410 Loop Style Holster is constructed of dark russet

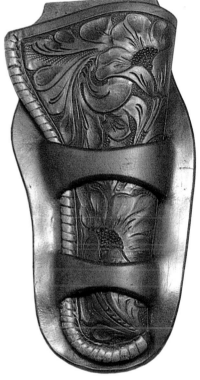

"California skirting leather." The top and bottom main seam rivets carry the Heiser "Triple-H" monogram, while the maker's cartouche is stamped on the skirt beneath the toe of the

pouch. The holster is patterned for a Colt Single Action Army revolver with 5 1/2 inch barrel. (Courtesy Lacey and Virginia Gaddis Collection)

Certainly, by the time this statement was published, the H. H. Heiser company already was firmly established as the nation's leading fabricator of custom gunleather.

Hermann H. Heiser evidently was among the earliest — if not the first — gunleather craftsmen to utilize a variety of standard pistol patterns (made first of wood and later of cast metal) to fashion fitted holsters for the most common handgun makes and models. This practice ultimately enabled the firm to mold each holster to a specific weapon — a decided advantage in conducting an expanding mail order trade.[91] The firm's literature lauded the merit of this fabrication technique for large scale commercial production:

> Our goods should not be classed with the ordinary gun store merchandise, which being made from a universal pattern, is intended to fit most any gun in an indifferent manner, while all of OUR holsters are "Made to Order" to fit perfectly only one kind and size of gun....[92]

For those holsters made of heavier skirting material, it was suggested that, for "... the much-desired 'pull,' or quick-draw fit...," further shaping to the intended weapon was required. Directions for perspective buyers were provided:

(above) "Mexican Loop" Pattern Holster. H. H. Heiser Saddlery, Denver, Colorado, 1915-1925. Heiser's No. 713 Mexican Loop Belt Holster here features an atypical throat profile without recurve, and also lacks the standard safety strap. Constructed of "selected Oak-Tanned saddle leather," the holster is "Box Fit" to accommodate a variety of large-frame revolvers. This right-hand example has a full, hand-carved body in floral motif with a rawhide-laced main seam running through the closed toe. The plain skirt has two tapered, integral loops and is contoured at the top to create the canted, "Fast Draw" belt loop. The piece retailed at $5.50 in Heiser's 1925 mail order catalog. (Courtesy Private Collection)

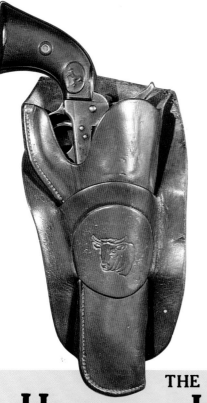

"Mexican Loop" Pattern Holster for Colt Single Action Army Revolver. H. H. Heiser Saddlery, Denver, Colorado, 1920-1930. Heiser's No. 907 Round Loop Belt Holster of medium-weight russet skirting leather retailed for $2.25 during the 1920s. This pattern, with its large circular loop and bovine emboss, actually was a continuation of the earlier, No. 200 Bull's-Head Design. Compact and wide-skirted, the style probably dated back to the mid-1890s. This right-hand specimen houses a .45 caliber Colt Single Action with 4 3/4-inch barrel. (Courtesy Arizona West Galleries)

THE
Hermann H. Heiser
MFG. & SELLING CO.
DENVER, COLORADO

ESTABLISHED 1856   INCORPORATED 1906

"Pioneer Saddlers of the Great West"

SPECIALISTS
In the Manufacture of Custom Quality

Gun Scabbards, Pistol Holsters, Belts and Novelty Leather Goods
SEND US YOUR IDEAS AND SPECIFICATIONS

Anything you may desire will be made up for you at a price as reasonable as consistent with the best of workmanship and finest material.
We solicit correspondence and will be glad at all times to make suggestions.

PERSONAL ATTENTION TO ALL DETAIL

To get the Genuine, INSIST upon seeing either this

 OR

Heiser quality leather goods should not be compared or confused with the similar appearing goods carried in stock by most sporting goods or hardware stores in all parts of the country, since our goods are made to order especially TO PLEASE YOU and to give perfect satisfaction when used in connection with THE ONE PARTICULAR WEAPON that they were intended for, while the "hand me down" goods are made in large quantities from all kinds of material by machine, and as such, one type of holster is supposed to fit in a slipshod manner as many different kinds of guns as possible.

All descriptions are made brief to save you time, since the illustrations are all photogravures and consequently true to the article represented.

IT PAYS TO HITCH TO THE HOUSE OF HEISER Page 3

This title page from Heiser's Catalog No. 20 of circa 1928 reflects the firm's ongoing specialization in the gunleather trade. Note the maker's cartouches then in use on their retail product line (wholesaled goods usually were marked by the secondary outfitting house).

Moisten the holster evenly and thoroughly enough to soften the leather, but do not wet the leather to the extent of saturation; then slip the gun into the holster into just the position you want it, after which press and rub the leather into shape around the cylinder, trigger guard, etc., with the fingers, then withdraw the gun carefully and lay the holster away to dry. After it has become dry, it is ready for use, and if it has become too hard to suit you give the holster a coating of absolutely pure neatsfoot oil....[93]

Today, this form-fitting technique, utilizing machine pressing and hand "boning," has become a standard manufacturing practice among contemporary gunleather producers such as Bianchi International.[94]

By the 1890s, the Heiser firm commanded a solid reputation throughout the West for a diversified line of superior gunleather. By then located in the Paulson Building at 15th and Wynkoop Streets in Denver, the business was catering to the growing mail order market while still perfecting individually designed gunleather elements. A notable development during this period was the founder's creation of the "Heiser Quick-Draw Holster," a popular pattern later patented in 1906 by one of his sons. And, around the turn of the century, the company embarked on a widespread wholesale business, supplying gunleather to a variety of mercantile and sporting goods houses across the country. Among these were Abercrombie & Fitch of New York City and its Chicago competitor, Von Lengerke & Antoine. Other, more regionally oriented houses included Browning Brothers of Ogden, Utah; White & Davis of Pueblo, Colorado; and Greyhound Specialty Company and The Denver Dry Goods Company, both of Denver. Most of this wholesaled gunleather carried the name of the secondary retailing house rather than that of the original manufacturer.[95]

Prior to the First World War, the Heiser company, then under the direction of son Ewald Heiser, continued to expand its gunleather line. Mail order catalogs from this period offered a selection of around 25 distinct holster designs available in more than 100 custom variations based on pistol type and size, leather weight, and gradations of embellishment. By 1930, over 60 different holster patterns were offered in some 300 gradations, many of them for automatic pistols. "Mexican Loop" pattern holsters still accounted for about one-third of this selection, while hip pocket and shoulder holsters were available in 11 individual designs. In addition, seven cartridge belt patterns and five styles of saddle scabbard were offered in 13 and 25 gradations, respectively. Beyond this broad selection, a number of special order features were available at a minimal extra cost. These included chamois holster linings, sewn-in toe plugs, thong-wrapped seams and edges for holsters and saddle scabbards, holster safety straps with snap closures, holster tie-down strings, extra cartridge loops for belts, sewn-on leather spacing strips for belts taking rimless cartridges, and black-dyed finish.[96]

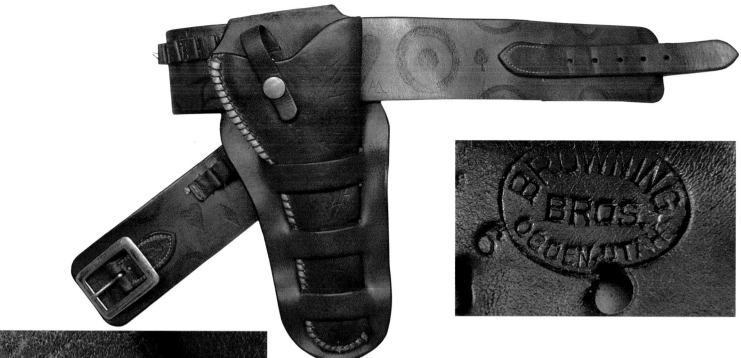

"Mexican Loop" Pattern Holster with Plain Cartridge Belt. Browning Brothers Armory, Ogden, Utah, 1905-1915. Manufactured and wholesaled by the H. H. Heiser Saddlery of Denver, this plain rig was stamped and retailed by the Browning Brothers sporting goods emporium in Ogden, Utah. It combines the Heiser No. 212 holster with the Heiser No. 38 Pattern Cartridge Belt, both constructed of medium-weight russet skirting leather. The right-hand holster features a deep body with shallow throat recurve and rawhide-laced main seam extending through the closed toe. It is secured to the contoured skirt by three integral loops and has an added safety strap with snap closure. The single thickness belt has sewn cartridge loops and billets, a rectangular "California" style buckle, and folk art decoration applied by the owner. Such an outfit would have retailed for $5.00 to $6.00 around 1910. (Courtesy Bill Mackin Collection)

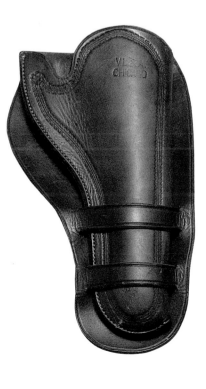

"Mexican Loop" Pattern Holster. H. H. Heiser Saddlery, Denver, Colorado, 1920-1930. The Heiser No. 413 Safety Strap Belt Holster was adapted to "The Box Fit," to accommodate different makes of like-sized revolvers. Constructed of "selected Oak Tanned Saddle leather," the right-hand piece features a deeply-recurved throat, rawhide wrapped main seam and toe, two integral skirt loops of tapered pattern, and a safety strap with snap closure. This large, plain finish grade sold for $4.25 retail in 1925.

"Mexican Loop" Pattern Holster for Colt New Service Revolver. Von Lengerke & Antoine, Chicago, Illinois, 1900-1910. This right-hand holster was probably made in fact by the H. H. Heiser firm of Denver, Colorado. Constructed of medium-weight russet skirting leather, it has an ample skirt with two integral loops securing the body. Typical of the era, the holster's main seam is sewn through the toe and reinforced with a top staple. The body has a rather abruptly-recurved throat profile and rolled border ornamentation with a rosette at the corner. (Courtesy Private Collection)

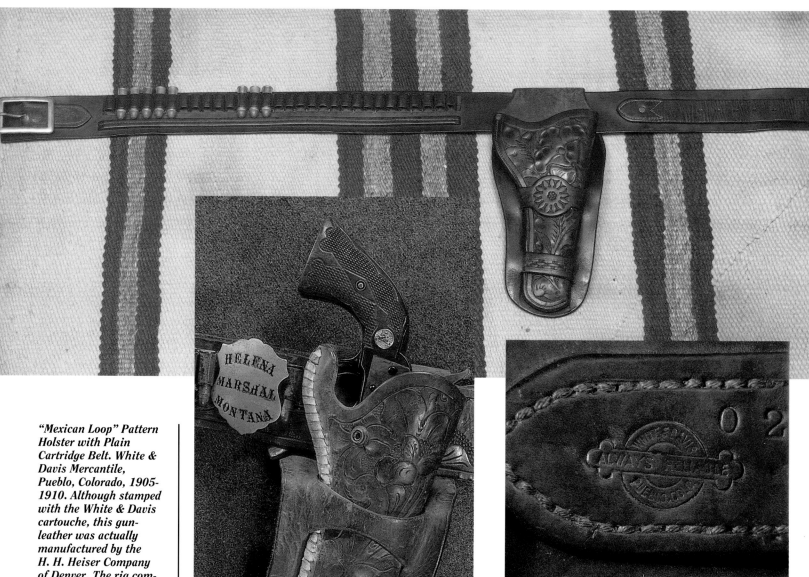

"Mexican Loop" Pattern Holster with Plain Cartridge Belt. White & Davis Mercantile, Pueblo, Colorado, 1905-1910. Although stamped with the White & Davis cartouche, this gunleather was actually manufactured by the H. H. Heiser Company of Denver. The rig combines the Heiser No. 124 Mexican Hand-Carved Revolver Holster and the No. 38 Pattern Cartridge Belt, both constructed of heavy russet skirting leather. The right-hand holster has a full floral-carved body, shallow recurve throat, and main seam sewn through the toe and secured with a top rivet. The contoured skirt features two integral loops; the upper loop of circular design with a stamped rosette, the lower loop stamped with basket-weave ornament. The single thickness belt has sewn cartridge loops with a stitched welt beneath to evenly seat the cartridges. Separate tongue and buckle billets, with a nickeled "California" buckle, complete the outfit. (Courtesy Bill Mackin Collection)

"Mexican Loop" Pattern Holster for Colt Single Action Army Revolver. H. H. Heiser, Denver, Colorado, 1925-1935. Although unmarked, this floral-carved rig appears to incorporate Heiser's No. 713 Mexican Loop Safety Strap holster and No. 72 cartridge belt. Constructed of heavy russet skirting leather, the right-hand holster features tapered skirt loops, thong-wrapped main seam and snap closure for the safety strap (now missing). The outfit originally was owned by Deputy Marshal Ned Goza of Helena, Montana. It is accompanied by a .38 caliber, Colt Single Action Army revolver with checkered walnut stocks and 7 1/2-inch barrel. (Courtesy John E. Fox Collection)

Over the years the Heiser firm promoted the innovative design and superior quality of its diverse gunleather line with a number of marketing slogans. Holsters were proffered in trade literature with the observation that "Life Is Too Short to Take Chances," suggesting that custom-fit gunleather might extend one's longevity. Touting the use of heavy, oak-tanned California skirting leather in its products, the company also boasted that "No Man Ever Lived Long Enough to Wear Out a Heiser Holster."

Some claims, however, were more than a little extravagant. *Catalog No. 20* proclaimed: "It may interest you to know that Heiser originated the Safety Spring [Shoulder] Holster, Snap Button Safety Straps, Combination Belt and Hip Pocket Holster...."[97] With the possible exception of the second item, these claims certainly were dubious if not plainly in error. Still, when the venerable business sold out to The Denver Dry Goods Company in 1945 after 87 years as a family enterprise, there no doubt were many throughout the West who readily subscribed to the firm's long-lived motto: "It Pays to Hitch to the House of Heiser."

"Mexican Loop" Pattern Holster with Matching Cartridge Belt. H. H. Heiser Saddlery, Denver, Colorado, 1925-1935. Combining the firm's No. 512 Heavy Mexican Loop Wrap Edge Holster with the No. 81 Car-

tridge Belt, this matched rig retailed for $12.75 during the late 1920s. The right-hand holster, made of "Extra Heavy selected California saddle leather," features a full-profile skirt with three integral loops, each

"hand basket stamped" like the holster body. The pouch is "hand thong wrap stitched" along the main seam and has a shallow throat recurve trimmed with brass "spots." Also made of "heavy oak

tanned California skirting leather," the unlined, single-thickness belt is 4 1/2 inches wide and faced with two rows of loops to carry necked rifle cartridges. Fixed with a double-frame "California" buckle, the

belt is also fully "hand basket stamped." A .45 caliber, Colt Single Action revolver with ivory stocks and 7 1/2-inch barrel accompanies the outfit. (Courtesy Joe Gish Collection. Image courtesy Bill Manns)

Catalog No. 30 of the H. H. Heiser Saddlery Company, circa 1938, was devoted almost entirely to gunleather. (Author's Collection)

"Buscadero" Gun Belt and Holsters for Colt Single Action Revolvers. H. H. Heiser Saddlery, Denver, Colorado, 1930-1940. This handsome rig joins a pair of No. 752, "full Mexican hand carved" holsters with a No. 48 "Buscadero" pattern cartridge belt of identical finish. Fabricated of "heavy Oak Tanned California skirting leather," the "Mexican Loop" pattern holsters incorporate full-contoured skirts with two integral loops of oval pattern, recurved throats, full leather linings, and "hand thong wrap stitched" main seams that extend through the rounded toes. (The belt loops utilize double snap closures for easy mounting and removal). Constructed of the same material, the belt features 30 cartridge loops, an integral, tapered tongue billet, and a square, double-frame buckle of solid brass. The outfit sold for $21.50 in Heiser's No. 30 catalog of circa 1938. (Courtesy Arizona West Galleries. William Manns, photo)

"Mexican Loop" Pattern Holster. H. H. Heiser Saddlery, Denver, Colorado, 1925-1935. Designed for a "Buscadero" belt rig, the Heiser No. 753 Extra Fine Belt Holster features a narrow belt loop with snap closures. Constructed of "the very best selected heavy Oak Tanned California skirting leather," this right-hand example is "full Mexican hand carved" in floral motif on both body and skirt.

Both elements are also fully "hand thong wrap stitched" with contrasting rawhide lacing. The body has a deep recurve throat profile and open toe, and is secured to the skirt by two integral loops of tapered pattern. The skirt back and pouch interior are lined with smooth leather. The holster retailed in Heiser's 1935 mail order catalog for $10.00. (Courtesy Bill Mackin Collection)

(opposite)
The Heiser firm offered Fancy Spotted Belt Holsters throughout the 1920s in a number of sizes and ornamental variations. They claimed to use solid nickel "spots" in lieu of nickel-plated brass. This cut is from Catalog No. 20 of circa 1928.

No. 415—Large
For Revolvers
With 5½ to 7½" barrels

No. 2710—Medium
For Revolvers
With 4 to 5" barrels

No. 2408—Small
For Revolvers
Under 4" barrels

Fancy Spotted Belt Holsters

No. 415—FANCY DESIGN SPOTTED HOLSTERS

This very ornamental holster is made of heavy California skirting leather, has heavy waxed thread sewed edge, closed end, made of one solid piece of leather and trimmed with solid nickel ornaments. Lined pouch.

	Large	Medium	Small
No. 415—	$6.00	$5.50	$5.00

The following holsters are made of the finest Oak Tanned California skirting leather, and have what is known as the "Quick Draw" belt loop. Waxed thread sewed, open end, riveted at end of stitches, not lined. Design originated by one of the most expert gun men in the West. Ornamented with solid nickel ornaments.

	Large	Medium	Small
No. 2410—Plain smooth finish, fancy spotted	$4.25	$4.00	$3.75
No. 2510—Hand basket stamped, fancy spotted	$5.00	$4.50	$4.25
No. 2710—Mexican hand carved, fancy spotted	$5.75	$5.25	$4.50

The following holsters are same as above three numbers except that they are **thong wrapped stitched edge.**

	Large	Medium	Small
No. 2408—Plain smooth finish, fancy spotted	$4.75	$4.50	$4.25
No. 2508—Hand basket stamped, fancy spotted	$5.50	$5.00	$4.75
No. 2708—Mexican hand carved, fancy spotted	$6.25	$5.75	$5.00

Holsters on this page are not made for automatics.

Page 14 IT PAYS TO HITCH TO THE HOUSE OF HEISER

Illustrated in Heiser's Catalog No. 20 of circa 1928, the No. 2710 Fancy Spotted Belt Holster actually was a richly embellished version of the No. 708 Knapp Pattern with "Quick Draw" belt loop. Constructed of "finest Oak Tanned California skirting leather," this right-hand piece incorporates a deeply recurved throat profile, semi-contoured main seam with top and bottom rivets, and "Mexican hand carved" pouch. The contoured back skirt secures with two integral loops and features a border ornament of 92 nickel silver "spots." Accompanying this specimen, which retailed for $5.75 in the late 1920s, is a .45 caliber, Colt Single Action with 7 1/2-inch barrel. (Courtesy Ron Soodalter. Image courtesy Bill Manns)

Posed in a Montana studio around 1890, these youthful cowboys personified a dying breed of westerner for whom guns and gunleather remained symbolic of a unique lifestyle. (Image courtesy Montana Historical Society, Helena)

TWENTIETH CENTURY WESTERN GUNLEATHER

Although historian Frederick Jackson Turner declared the frontier closed in 1893, firearms and their attendant gunleather continued to be worn fairly widely in more remote areas of the West where social restraints were few. Latter-day cowboys, in particular, consciously perpetuated the mystique of the armed and independent westerner.[98] "Teddy Blue" Abbott perhaps best captured the attitude of his cowboy companions during this period of transition:

> Along about the nineties a lot of people out here began to quiet down and start leaving off their guns....But I wouldn't give mine up....You wouldn't have any of this calling names and brawling and fighting, where every man was wearing a deadly weapon in plain sight. And as for that expression about a son of a bitch, I never heard it said with a smile, as they say, before the nineties.[99]

Ultimately, however, the guns and gunleather that once had been fundamental to survival and settlement were put aside, to remain little more than a tangible reminder of the western epic. What followed — the "Buscadero" and "Fast Draw" rigs portrayed in Hollywood westerns — was but a pale and misleading imitation of the genuine article.

There are probably few Americans who have not seen the Hollywood hero strap on his fancy "Buscadero" gunbelt or low-slung "Fast Draw" rig in preparation for the fictional showdown in some dusty cowtown street. But such semi-formal duels actually were few, and gunleather worn by historical shootists, as described heretofore, bore little resemblance to that seen in the film industry's epics and oaters. Indeed, the gunleather of the Hollywood western was largely a creation of the twentieth century, a marriage of modern functionalism and unbridled romanticism.

The characters and equipage of the Old West graduated into national (ultimately international) folklore through the "Wild West" shows and burgeoning western films that appeared prior to 1920. These early mediums frequently were quasi-documentary and often featured real cowboys sporting traditional gunleather and other gear. But during the late 1920s, the western movie took on more flamboyance and romance, creating myths around heroes like Tom Mix, Jack Hoxie, Ken Maynard and Hoot Gibson. It was here that the "Buscadero" belt and holster rig was introduced to set the star apart from lesser characters wearing more pedestrian (i.e. historic) gunleather. This style of Hollywood harness predominated in western film from 1930 to roughly 1950.[100]

Early "Buscadero" Gun Belt with "Mexican Loop" Pattern Holster. Makers Unknown, 1920-1930. Probably made up for a latter-day "Wild West" performer, this precursor of the true "Buscadero" rig combines a modified cartridge belt of heavy russet skirting material with a typical, commercially manufactured "Mexican Loop" holster of medium-weight russet bridle leather. The belt, originally designed with a tapered tougue and buckle chape, is mounted with two additional, metal-tipped tongue billets which join corresponding bridle buckles. A long rectangular slot has been cut in the body of the belt for suspending the right-hand holster, while the face has been overlayed at top and bottom with thin, machine-ornamented leather strips secured with large nickeled "spots." This showy, "home-made" affair carries a .44 caliber, Merwin Hulbert revolver with thermal plastic grips and a 7-inch barrel. (Courtesy Private Collection)

Posed in 1905, Captain Seth Bullock's "Wild West" cowboys introduced American audiences to basically authentic western costume and gunleather in their frontier extravaganzas. Tom Mix is in the front row, third from right; like most of his cohorts, he carries a Colt Single Action revolver in a "Mexican Loop" pattern holster. (Image courtesy National Cowboy Hall of Fame and Western Heritage Center)

In this circa 1928 image, cowboy-actor Tom Mix carries his Colt Single Action Army revolver in a machine-stamped, "Mexican Loop" pattern holster with a wide, three-quarter-circle skirt loop and an open, rounded toe.

The holster is suspended from the slotted tab of a border-tooled, "Buscadero" pattern cartridge belt unknown in the historic West. (Image courtesy National Cowboy Hall of Fame and Western Heritage Center)

"Buscadero" Gun Belt and Holsters for Colt Single Action Revolvers. The George Lawrence Co., Portland, Oregon, 1935-1940. Combining a pair of No. 212, "hand basket stamped" holsters with a matching, No. 50 "Buscadero" cartridge belt, this rig retailed for $22.25 in Lawrence's

1937 catalog. Constructed of "heavy steer hide," the holsters are of "Mexican Loop" pattern with gracefully recurved throats, thong-laced main seams and separate, sewn-on skirt loops. Of similar material, the belt is "cut on a curve" with lowered slots, 30 sewn cartridge loops, and

sewn tongue and buckle billets. The piece is mounted with a custom, "Ranger" style buckle set of sterling silver. A pair of .45 caliber, Colt Single Action Army revolvers with 5 1/2-inch barrels accompanies the outfit. (Courtesy Arizona West Galleries)

Evidently the joint inspiration of Texas Ranger John R. Hughes and master saddler S. D. Myres of El Paso, Texas, the "Buscadero" gunbelt was developed during the early 1920s. Hughes employed a short strap, fixed diagonally on the face of a wide cartridge belt, that slipped through the holster's belt loop and secured with a buckle, canting the holster and pistol grip slightly forward for a faster draw. Myres simplified the design, introducing a slotted tab that extended along the lower edge of the cartridge belt at the hip. A modified "drop loop" holster, with a belt loop designed to cant the pouch forward as in the Hughes' prototype, was suspended from the integral belt tab by passing the back skirt/panel through the slot and securing it to pouch through the skirt loops or, more commonly, by means of an attached strap and buckle. Unlike historic western holsters, which rode high on the hip for comfort in the saddle, the "Buscadero" holster rode lower on the thigh and nearer the gun hand.[101]

Popular for a time among southwestern peace officers, the "Buscadero" pattern gunbelt found its real market with the celluloid buckaroos of Hollywood. Wide, hip-hugging belts, in either single or double holster form, appeared with "Ranger" pattern buckle sets of engraved silver. (The holsters, too, usually were secured to their back panels with cross straps having "Ranger" buckles and keepers in lieu of integral or riveted loops.) Hollywood leather artisan Edward H. Bohlin brought the "Buscadero" pattern to

its stylistic apex with hand-tooled, edge-laced and silver-mounted outfits custom-made for the most prominent "B" western serial stars. Among them were Tim McCoy, Tex Ritter, Duncan Renaldo (The Cisco Kid), William Boyd (Hopalong Cassidy), Roy Rogers, Gene Autry and Clayton Moore (The Lone Ranger). Meanwhile, out in the western hinterlands, other quality saddlers, like Al. Furstnow, H. H. Heiser, George Lawrence and S. D. Myres, produced less ostentatious "Buscadero" rigs for the general public. The form ultimately commenced a decline from favor following the Second World War, as serial theater westerns were supplanted by the television genre.[102]

"Buscadero" Pattern Holster for Colt Single Action Army Revolver. Edward H. Bohlin, Hollywood, California, 1935-1945. The product of meticulous craftsmanship, this right-hand specimen typifies the work of the Bohlin shop during the heyday of "B" western films. Constructed of medium-weight russet leather, the deep, semi-contoured pouch is fully suede-lined and incorporates a pleasing throat recurve and tightly thong-laced main seam. The pouch and back skirt are finely carved in floral and foliate motif over a stippled black background; they are secured with two riveted straps fixed with "Ranger" pattern buckle sets of engraved silver. Typical of the style, hammer and leg thongs are attached. Accompanying the holster is a .45 caliber, Colt Single Action Army revolver with ivory grips and 7 1/2-inch barrel. (Courtesy Arizona West Galleries)

"Buscadero" Pattern Gunbelt for Colt Single Action Revolver. H. H. Heiser Saddlery, Denver, Colorado, 1935-1945. Fabricated of the usual, "Heavy Oak Tanned Skirting Leather" and "full Mexican Hand Carved" throughout, this outfit combines a variant of the No. 714 Loop Style Holster with the No. 49 Belt with integral slotted panel. Retaining excellent condition, the rig carries a .32-20 caliber, Colt Single Action with 5 1/2 inch barrel. (Courtesy A. P. Hayes Collection)

"Buscadero" Pattern Gunbelt for Colt Single Action Army Revolvers. N. Porter Saddlery, Phoenix, Arizona, 1930-1940. This well-made outfit incorporates semi-modern, "Mexican Loop" pattern holsters having extended and canted belt loops; deep throat recurves at the trigger areas; snap-fastened safety straps; single, riveted skirt loops; and rounded, sewn-through toes. The calfskin-lined belt utilizes separate, contoured and slotted panels that are stitched on rather than integral, and carries twelve loops for .45 caliber cartridges. All major elements are finished in a carved oak leaf motif. A brace of .45 caliber, Colt Single Actions with 4 3/4-inch barrels accompanies the rig. (Courtesy Arizona West Galleries)

"Buscadero" Pattern Holster for Colt Single Action Army Revolver. H. H. Heiser Saddlery, Denver, Colorado, 1935-1945. Reflecting changes in design and use, Heiser's No. 754 New Style Belt Holster was particularly adapted for use on slotted, "Buscadero" cartridge belts. Fabricated of heavy russet skirting leather, the pouch of this right-hand specimen is virtually uncontoured and features a low-cut throat profile, sewn main seam running through the toe, and "full Mexican hand carved" embellishment. The full-contoured back skirt secures the pouch with two riveted loops, here fixed with custom silver buckles in lieu of the standard snaps. The belt loop fold is angled at 30 degrees to cant the pistol grip forward. The holster retailed for $4.50 in Heiser's Catalog No. 30 of circa 1938. With this example is a .45 caliber, Colt Single Action Army revolver with 7 1/2-inch barrel. (Courtesy Arizona West Galleries)

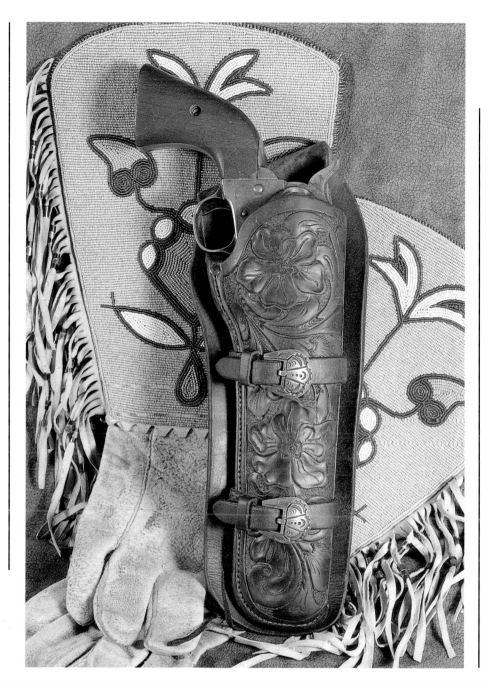

"Buscadero" Gun Belt and Holsters for Colt Single Action Revolvers. S. D. Myres, El Paso, Texas, 1940-1950. A superb example of gunleather craftsmanship, this double "Buscadero" rig combines a pair of No. 545 "Jockstrap" pattern holsters with a No. 50X belt (the outfit retailed for $75.00 when manufactured). All elements are fully lined with smooth elkskin and finely embellished in a hand-carved, floral and oak leaf motif. The holsters, constructed of medium weight russet skirting leather, feature the separate, elongated skirt loops peculiar to S. D. Myres and are entirely "Mexican edge laced" in contrasting color. The belt of heavy skirting leather utilizes low-profile, slotted tabs to suspend the holsters, and incorporates sewn-on billets for the tongue and "California" pattern buckle. A pair of .32 caliber, Colt Single Action Army revolvers with nickel finish and pearl grips completes the outfit. (Courtesy Bill Mackin Collection)

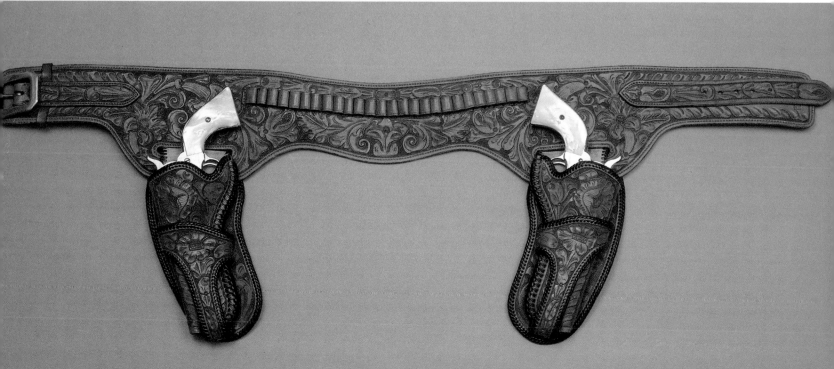

In this circa 1940 movie still, "B" western star Tex Ritter displays the showy, "Buscadero" pattern rig popularized in Hollywood serials. Note the floral tooling, laced border trim, and "Ranger" pattern buckle on the low profile holster. (Image courtesy National Cowboy Hall of Fame and Western Heritage Center)

"Buscadero" Pattern Gun Rig for Colt Single Action Revolvers. Edward H. Bohlin, Hollywood, California, 1948-1952. Incorporating typical Bohlin craftsmanship, this "Dick Dickson" style outfit joins a finely tooled and silver-ornamented gunbelt with matching gauntlet gloves. The holsters feature shallow throat recurves, sewn-through toes, and broad back skirts secured with single riveted straps and "Ranger" pattern buckles. The double-layered, matching cartridge belt utilizes integral, slotted panels for holster suspension, and a nicely engraved, "Ranger" pattern buckle set for closure. A pair of .45 caliber, Colt Single Actions with stag grips, nickel-plated finish, and 5 1/2-inch barrels compliment the rig. (Courtesy George Pitman Collection. Image courtesy Bill Manns)

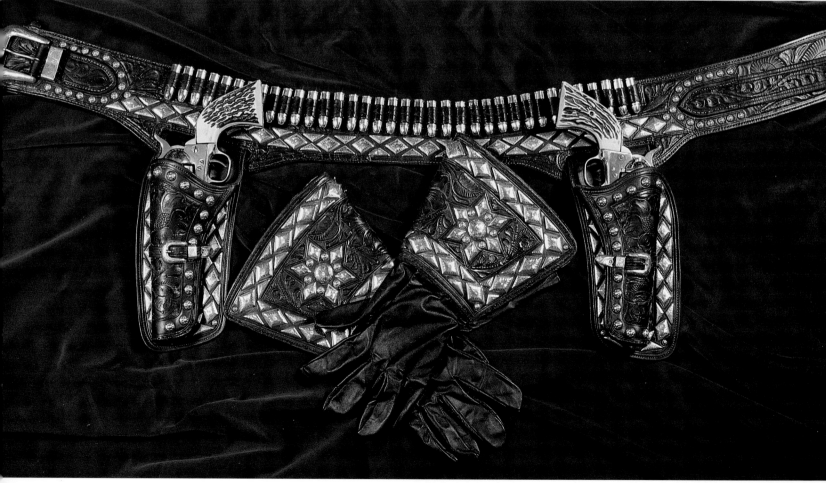

The prevalence of the Hollywood, "Fast Draw" pattern gunbelt is illustrated in this publicity still of Warner Brothers' stable of television stars from the 1960s. Note the "drop loop" holster design (placing the abbreviated pouch at mid-thigh) and the consistent use of tie-down thongs. (Image courtesy National Cowboy Hall of Fame and Western Heritage Center)

"Buscadero" Gun Belt with "Fast Draw" Pattern Holster. Arvo Ojala, Hollywood, California, 1960-1965. A classic example of the Hollywood "Fast Draw" rig, this presentation outfit was made by noted gunleather artisan Arvo Ojala for western actress Barbara Stanwyck. The "Buscadero" pattern belt is constructed of double-layered, medium-weight skirting leather and is contoured in a descending arc that places the slotted tab in an extremely low-slung position. Separate tongue and buckle billets are sewn on and secure with a square, "California" pattern buckle. The right-hand, "Fast Draw" holster also is constructed of double skirting leather and is sewn over a rigid, sheet metal body with an arched throat profile, heavily welted main seam, and open toe. The integral, contoured back skirt is of extended, drop-loop pattern and secures to the holster at the toe by means of the tie-down thong. The holster accommodates a .45 caliber, Colt Single Action Army revolver with full nickel finish and pearl grips. (National Cowboy Hall of Fame Collection)

Through the influence of Hollywood fast draw coach and gunleather artisan Arvo Ojala, a new gunbelt pattern was adopted by the stars of television and western movies during the mid-1950s. The "Fast Draw" rig utilized a specially contoured, "Buscadero" pattern cartridge belt that placed the slotted tab still lower on the hip. A low-cut, "drop loop" holster with a slim, nearly tubular body was suspended from the belt tab, placing the pistol grip at hand level with the arm extended.

This new holster body design was reinforced with a rigid, sheet metal or steel liner that allowed hammer cocking and cylinder rotation before the revolver actually began to clear leather. Hammer and leg thongs were employed to secure both the revolver and the holster. Some versions extended the shaped metal liner upward within the face of the "drop loop" or shank portion of the holster, canting the pistol slightly outward for faster acquisition and adding stability during the draw. The holster body typically was finished with a strap that buckled over the mid-section, giving an appearance vaguely reminiscent of the traditional "Mexican Loop" pattern.[103]

"Buscadero" Gun Belt and Holster for Colt Single Action Revolver. Edward H. Bohlin, Hollywood, California, circa 1935. Custom-crafted for western star Buck Jones, this handsome outfit epitomizes the showy artisanry of the Bohlin shop. Constructed throughout of best quality skirting material, the major elements are tightly edge-laced and hand-carved in a foliate and floral motif over a black, stippled ground. The slotted cartridge belt secures with a finely engraved and gold-overlayed "Ranger" pattern buckle set of sterling silver with inset rubies. The relatively uncontoured, right-hand holster body is mounted with a scalloped concho of engraved silver and secures to the back skirt with a riveted strap fixed with a buckle of silver. (Laced-through tie-down thongs also secure holster and skirt at the toe.) Accompanying the rig is a .45 caliber, Colt Single Action revolver silver-inlaid and engraved in Bohlin's unique style. The carved and silver-mounted grips of ivory are enameled in red and green and mounted with gold name plaques. (Courtesy Gene Autry Western Heritage Museum, Los Angeles)

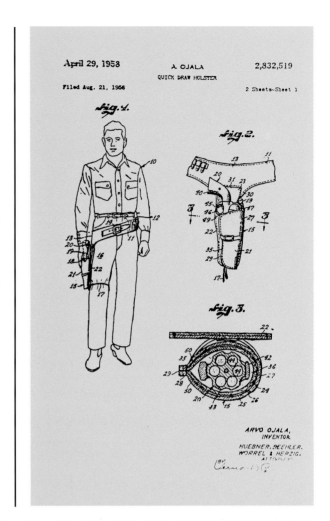

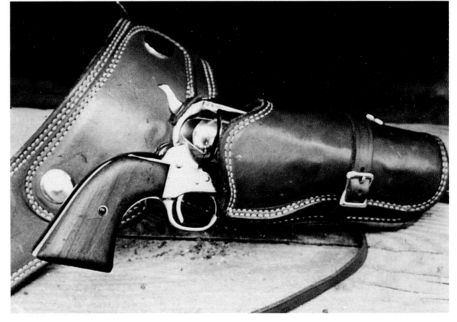

Public participation in recreational fast draw competitions, which arose in the late 1950s, inspired further developments in this form of quasi-western gunleather. Andy Anderson, an associate of Ojala, designed the so-called "Walk and Draw" pattern, which incorporated a leather-covered, metal hip plate over or behind the cartridge belt to further anchor the rig, and also introduced a muzzle-forward rake to the holster for increased speed and safety. This type of outfit was popularized by Clint Eastwood in his several "Spaghetti Westerns," and it became the mainstay of movie and television western stars well into the 1970s. Other specialists, like Ernie Hill and Alfonso, crafted similar "Fast Draw" gunleather. Such rigging did much to perpetuate the myth of the "Old West" shootist wearing a low-slung holster tied to his leg, his pistol secured with a hammer thong in its low-cut pouch. But, as seen heretofore, such sophisticated "Fast Draw" rigs were unknown in the historic frontier West.[104]

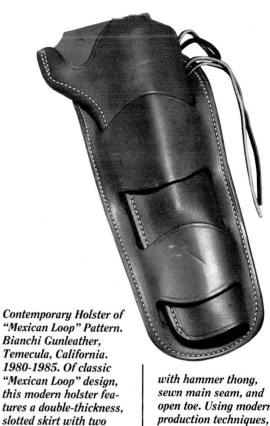

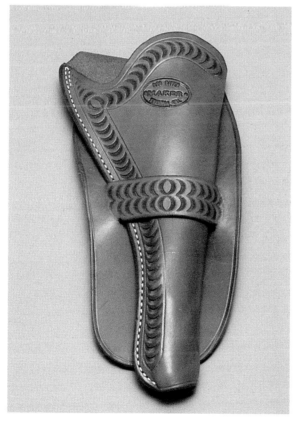

During the 1970s increasing interest in western material culture, particularly within the collecting fraternity, generated an upward spiral in the cost of original frontier gunleather. At much the same time, "Old West" reenactment groups and some fast draw afficionados, such as those in today's Single Action Shooting Society, began to create a demand for authentically patterned gunleather that could be worn and used without fear of damaging a valuable historic piece.

The first commercial firm to respond to this new-found market was Red River Frontier Outfitters of Tujunga, California, which introduced a line of reproduction gunleather in 1973 that copied historic, nineteenth century designs. The reborn El Paso Saddlery of El Paso, Texas, followed suit around 1975 with a selection of both military and civilian reproductions that also captured the look and flavor of original rigging. Only a few of the larger commercial manufacturers, like Bianchi Gunleather of Temecula, California, and the Lawrence Leather Company of Portland, Oregon, responded to the burgeoning trend. They created reproduction holsters and gunbelts in pseudo-historic patterns, but these anachronistic offerings did not incorporate the true architecture or detail of century-old gunleather. Most of Bianchi's western line, for example, consisted of combination "Buscadero" and "Fast Draw" rigs; only their "Model 1873 Old West" holster incorporated "Mexican Loop" design and it was equipped with atypical hammer and leg thongs.[105]

As the price of historic gunleather skyrocketed throughout the 1980s, interest in accurate reproduction and reenactment material grew apace. Over the decade several speciality shops, like Old West Reproductions of Kalispell (now Florence), Montana, and Stewart Saddlery of Show Low, Arizona, also commenced crafting holsters and belts patterned on original designs. Today, these and other houses offer a diversified selection of classic, reproduction gunleather that duplicates historic elements ranging from "California" and "Mexican Loop" pattern holsters to combination cartridge/money belts, saddle scabbards and even pommel bag-holsters! And, for the enthusiast desiring the look and feel of history, a few artisans, like Bill Cleaver of Vashon Island, Washington, custom-make meticulously crafted pieces with age stressing and antique patination reminiscent of century-old specimens.[106]

In the main, reproduction western gunleather is of substantial quality. The best of it, in fact, often equals and occasionally surpasses its nineteenth century forerunner in materials and craftsmanship. Over the past dozen years, such contemporary gunleather has been utilized increasingly in western films — a hopeful sign of Hollywood's tardy, but welcome recognition of a rich frontier legacy.

Contemporary Holster of "California" Pattern. El Paso Saddlery Co., El Paso, Texas, 1990. Patterned on a Main & Winchester original, this "Californian" model incorporates a right-hand, contour-fit design for the Colt Model 1851 Navy revolver. Constructed of russet skirting leather with full lining, the holster has a triple-recurved throat profile, stamped vine and floral ornamentation, and the classic, sewn-in toe plug. (National Cowboy Hall of Fame Collection)

(below)
Contemporary Holster of "California" Pattern. Stewart Saddlery, Show Low, Arizona, 1980-1985. Retailing for $110.00 in Stewart's Catalog No. 3, this right-hand specimen is a faithful reproduction of the classic West Coast form. Fashioned of medium-weight skirting leather, the contour-fit holster is full flower-tooled and dyed black. The body incorporates a triple throat recurve, sewn belt loop and sewn-in muzzle plug. With the holster is a .44 caliber, Richards conversion of the Colt Model 1860 Army revolver with 8-inch barrel. (Courtesy J. C. Stewart)

Contemporary "Mexican Loop" Pattern Holster with Cartridge/Money Belt. Stewart Saddlery, Show Low, Arizona, 1980-1985. Incorporating a fine reproduction of the "Cheyenne" variant holster, this matched rig retails for $260.00 in Stewart's No. 3 catalog. Constructed of medium-weight russet skirting material, the right-hand holster is floral-tooled and features a recurved throat profile, a welted and contoured main seam, and a sewn-in toe plug of "tear drop" configuration. The truncated back skirt secures the pouch with two integral loops above and below the main seam swell. The combination belt is fashioned of supple cowhide with cartridge loops and billets of skirting stock; it secures with a brass roller buckle. A .45 caliber, Colt Single Action with pearl grips and 7 1/2-inch barrel accompanies the outfit. (Courtesy J. C. Stewart)

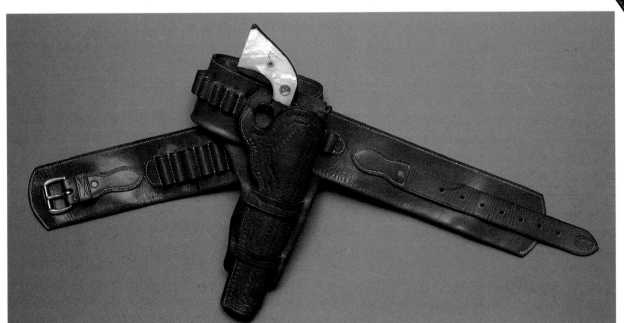

Contemporary "Mexican Loop" Pattern Holster with Cartridge/Money Belt. R. M. Bachman, Kalispell, Montana, 1990. This fine reproduction of classic western gunleather combines a "Cheyenne" pattern, "Mexican Loop" holster with a well-proportioned cartridge/ money belt. Constructed of russet skirting leather, the right-hand holster features the swollen main seam contour and sewn-in toe plug typical of the northern plains variation. The throat is pleasingly recurved, while the body and skirt loops are ornamented with rolled border patterns and rosettes. The belt of soft cowhide is made in the usual fashion with riveted and sewn billets for the nickeled, double-frame buckle. The rig houses a .45 caliber, Colt Single Action Army revolver with 7 1/2-inch barrel and carved ivory grips. (National Cowboy Hall of Fame Collection)

Contemporary "Mexican Loop" Pattern Holster with Matching Cartridge Belt. Wild Bill's Originals, Vashon Island, Washington, 1990. Hand crafted by leather artisan Bill Cleaver, this rig was custom-made and "antiqued" to replicate the look and feel of an original northern plains outfit, c. 1880. Constructed of dark russet skirting leather, the holster incorporates a relatively shallow throat recurve, a contour-fit main seam, a sewn-in toe plug of "tear drop" configuration, and a slight "swell" between the integral skirt loops to retain the pouch when the revolver is drawn — all attributes of the classic Cheyenne pattern popularized by saddlers E. L. Gallatin, J. S. Collins and F. A. Meanea. The single-thickness belt features the early, tapered end pattern with plain, double-frame buckle and cartridge loops that are woven through the body and secured with end rivets — a sturdier method atypical of the usual sewn technique. Both elements are ornamented with precisely-rolled border patterns and the holster has a typical, single floral rosette stamped on the upper pouch. Accompanying the rig is a .45 caliber, Colt Single Action Army revolver with 7 1/2-inch barrel. (Courtesy "Wild Bill" Cleaver)

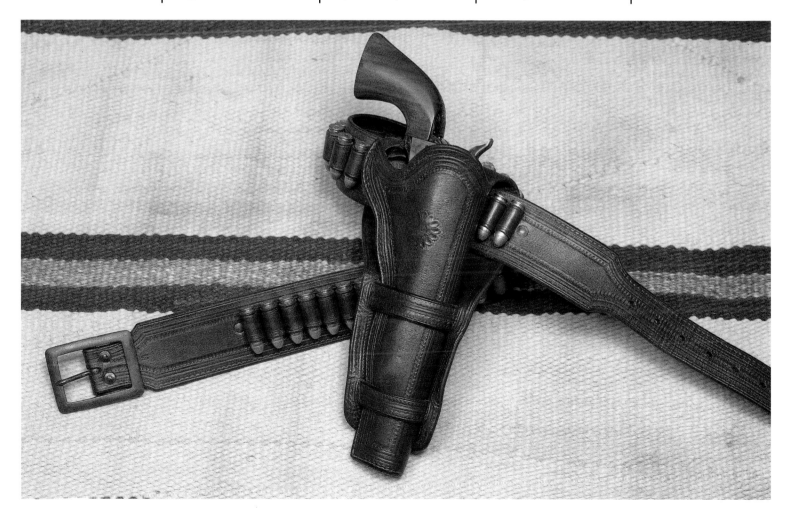

END NOTES

PART ONE

1. For historical treatments of the military in the West, see Francis Paul Prucha, *The Sword of the Republic: The United States Army on the Frontier, 1783-1846*; and Robert M. Utley, *Frontiersmen in Blue: The United States Army and the Indian, 1848-1865*, and *Frontier Regulars: The United States Army and the Indian, 1866-1891*.
2. Prucha, pp. 245-247; Utley, *Frontiersmen in Blue*, pp. 20-22.
3. Edward Scott Meadows, *U. S. Military Holsters and Pistol Cartridge Boxes*, p. 24.
4. Quoted in Meadows, p. 22.
5. Randy Steffen, *The Horse Soldier, 1776-1943*, Vol. 1, pp. 84, 156; Vol. 2, pp. 51, 53.
6. Meadows, pp. 47-48, 79-80.
7. Charles King, *Starlight Ranch and Other Stories of Army Life on the Frontier*, p. 205.
8. Quoted in Steffen, Vol. 1, p. 143.
9. Quoted in Steffen, Vol. 1, p. 107; and Meadows, p. 21. Also see Lt. Col. R. T. Huntington, "Dragoon Accouterments and Equipments, 1834-1839: An Identification Guide," *Plains Anthropologist*, Vol. 12, No. 38 (1967), pp. 347-348.
10. Quoted in Steffen, Vol. 1, p. 152.
11. Steffen, Vol. 1, pp. 168, 173.
12. Quoted in Meadows, p. 22.
13. Steffen, Vol. 1, p. 140.
14. Meadows, pp. 35-39; Col. B. R. Lewis, "Colt Walker-DragoonHolsters," *Gun Digest*, Vol. 12 (1958), pp. 43-45; Craig G. Caba, *Historic Southern Saddles, 1840-1865*, p. 40.
15. *Ibid.*
16. Quoted in Steffen, Vol. 1, p. 173.
17. Steffen, Vol. 1, p. 173; Caba, p. 40.

18. *Ibid.*, Vol. 2, pp. 50-51.
19. U. S. Patent No. 13,864 of 4 December 1855.
20. Quoted in Meadows, p. 47.
21. Quoted in Steffen, Vol. 2, p. 53.
22. Meadows, pp. 47-48.
23. Rod Casteel, "History and Evolution of the Revolver Holster of the Nineteenth Century," *Muzzle-loader*, Vol. 10, No. 3 (1983), pp. 60-61; John Bianchi, *Blue Steel & Gunleather: A Practical Guide to Holsters*, p. 3.
24. Meadows, pp. 47-55.
25. Colonel Berkeley R. Lewis, *Notes on Cavalry Weapons of the American Civil War, 1861-1865*, pp. 21-26; Meadows, pp. 62-74.
26. Quoted in Steffen, Vol. 2, p. 35.
27. Quoted in Meadows, p. 47.
28. Meadows, p. 48.
29. *Ibid.*, pp. 88-90.
30. Quoted in Steffen, Vol. 2, pp. 176-177.
31. Meadows, p. 95.
32. Quoted in Meadows, p. 96.
33. *Ibid.*, p. 97.
34. Quoted in Steffen, Vol. 2, p. 195.
35. Meadows, pp. 101-103.
36. *Ibid.*, pp. 104-105.
37. *Ibid.*, pp. 106-109.
38. Quoted in Steffen, Vol. 3, p. 42.
39. Meadows, pp. 110-111.
40. *Ibid*, pp. 112-113.
41. Quoted in Meadows, p. 146.
42. Meadows, pp. 124-147.
43. U. S. Patent No. 252,448 of 17 January 1882; Meadows, pp. 133-134.
44. Huntington, pp. 346, 348.
45. Quoted in Steffen, Vol. 1, p. 139.
46. Steffen, Vol. 2, p. 35.
47. Quoted in Steffen, Vol. 2, p. 159.
48. *Ibid.*, Vol. 3, p. 42.
49. Huntington, pp. 346, 348-349.
50. Quoted in Steffen, Vol. 1, p. 152.
51. Steffen, Vol. 1, pp. 168-169; Vol. 2, pp. 13, 59.
52. Quoted in Steffen, Vol. 2, pp. 61-62.
53. *Ibid.*, p. 164.
54. *Ibid.*, p. 193.

55. *Ibid.*
56. Steffen, Vol. 2, pp. 193, 195.
57. James S. Hutchins, ed., *Horse Equipments and Cavalry Accoutrements*, pp. 15-17.
58. *Ibid.*, pp. 17, 38-39.
59. Quoted in Steffen, Vol. 3, p. 40.
60. Hayes Otoupalik, III, "Discovered: U. S. Model 1778 Dragoon Waist Cartridge Belt," *The Gun Report*, Vol. 13, No. 5 (October 1977), p. 66-67.
61. Bill Mackin, "Frontier Cartridge Belts," *Arms Gazette*, Vol. 5, No. 12 (August 1978), pp. 22-23; R. Stephen Dorsey, *American Military Belts and Related Equipments*, p. 66.
62. Tom Horn, *Life of Tom Horn...Written by Himself*, p. 183.
63. Mackin, *op. cit.*, p. 22.
64. Dorsey, pp. 66-67.
65. Huntington, pp. 347-348; Steffen, Vol. 1, p. 137.
66. Quoted in Meadows, p. 386.
67. Quoted in Steffen, Vol. 1, p. 139.
68. Meadows, pp. 387, 391-393; Ernest Lisle Reedstrom, *Bugles, Banners and War Bonnets*, p. 238.
69. Meadows, pp. 389, 392-393; Dorsey, pp. 33, 57-58; Steffen, Vol. 2, pp. 164, 176-177.
70. Quoted in Steffen, Vol. 3, pp. 42-43.
71. Dorsey, pp. 61-65; Reedstrom, pp. 241-242.
72. Dorsey, pp. 66, 68-69; Reedstrom, p. 242.
73. Anson Mills, *My Story*, p. 111.
74. King, p. 204.
75. Quoted in Steffen, Vol. 2, pp. 177, 180.
76. Dorsey, pp. 34-35.
77. Quoted in Douglas C. McChristian, "The Model 1876 CartridgeBelt," *The Military Collector and Historian*, Vol. 34 (Fall 1982), p. 111.
78. Quoted in James S. Hutchins, "Captain Michaelis Reports on

Army Weapons and Equipments on the Northern Plains, 1876-1879," *Guns at the Little Bighorn: The Weapons of Custer's Last Stand/A Man at Arms Special Publication*, p. 28.
79. Dorsey, pp. 69-70; McChristian, pp. 111-112.
80. McChristian, pp. 112-115; Dorsey, pp. 71-74; Steffen, Vol. 2, pp. 198, 200.
81. McChristian, p. 115; Dorsey, pp. 68, 77. Also see, Albert A. Lethern and William P. Wise, *The Development of The Mills Woven Cartridge Belt*, pp. 1-7.
82. Quoted in McChristian, p. 115.
83. Dorsey, p. 68.
84. *Ibid.*, pp. 79, 81, 83.
85. *Ibid.*, pp. 77-79; Sidney B. Brinckerhoff, *Metal Uniform Insignia of the U. S. Army in the Southwest, 1846-1902*, Museum Monograph No. 3., 1965, pp. 17-19; J. Edward Green, Presidio Army Museum, to author, 23 July 1991, author's files.
86. Dorsey, pp. 77, 85-91; Steffen, Vol. 3., pp. 83-84.
87. Dorsey, pp. 77, 80, 83-84.
88. Quoted in Steffen, Vol. 3, p. 42.

PART TWO

1. For an historical overview of civilian settlement in the West, see Ray Allen Billington, *Westward Expansion: A History of the American Frontier*, section III. The central role of firearms in the West, which provides a valuable context in understanding the place of associated gunleather, is thoroughly treated in Louis A. Garavaglia's and Charles G. Worman's two-volume work, *Firearms of the American West, 1803-1865*, and *Firearms of the American West, 1866-1894*.
2. Cursory treatments of the

genesis of western gunleather can be found in Phil Spangenberger, "Frontier Gun Leather," in *Guns & Ammo Guide To Guns Of The Gunfighters*, ed. Garry James (1975), pp. 106-111, 208-209; Berkley McCollum, "Frontier Holsters," *American Rifleman*, Vol. 129, No. 11 (November 1981), pp. 22-25, 73; and in Rod Casteel, "History and Evolution of the Revolver Holster of the Nineteenth Century," *Muzzle-loader*, Vol. 10, No. 3 (1983), pp. 58-61.
3. Historical and biographical profiles of the more prominent western saddlers, virtually all of whom produced quality gunleather, appear in Lee M. Rice and Glenn R. Vernam, *They Saddled the West*. An interesting, localized sketch of the saddlery/gunleather trade is presented in Robert E. McNellis, "Ninety Years of El Paso Holsters," *Arms Gazette*, Vol. 4, No. 4 (December 1976), pp. 22-25. For an extensive, but still incomplete compilation of known, gunleather-producing saddlers in the West, see John A. Kopec, "Frontier Holsters and Belts," in *Old West Antiques and Collectables*, ed. Joe Goodson (1979), pp. 16-51, *passim*.
4. Garavaglia and Worman, *Firearms of the American West, 1803-1865*, pp. 81-82; Casteel, pp. 58-59.
5. Francis Parkman, *The Oregon Trail*, p. 11.
6. William Kelly, Jr., *An Excursion to California*, Vol. 1, p. 44.
7. Edward Scott Meadows, *U. S. Military Holsters and Pistol Cartridge Boxes*, p. 24; Col. B. R. Lewis, "Colt Walker - Dragoon Holsters," *Gun Digest*, Vol. 12 (1958), pp. 44-45; Rice and Vernam, pp. 6-9, 28; Richard H. Ahlborn, ed., *Man Made*

Mobile: Early Saddles of Western North America, pp. 59, 65-68; James Wilson Nichols, *Now You Hear My Horn,* pp. 62-64.

8. Ahlborn, pp. 59, 70, 113-117.

9. John C. Cremony, *Life Among the Apaches, 1850-1868,* p. 23.

10. Richard Rattenbury, "Packing Iron: A Survey of Western Gunleather," *Persimmon Hill,* Vol. 19, No. 1 (1991) p. 28; Spangenberger, "Pistol Packin' in the Old West," *Guns & Ammo,* Vol. 33, No. 1 (January 1989), p. 103; Kopec, "Frontier Holsters and Belts," p. 32; Noel M. Loomis, *Wells Fargo,* pp. 19, 34-35.

11. Main & Winchester, *Illustrated Catalog No. 11,* circa 1898, p. 71. This appellation evidently derives from the Mexican, *cantina,* when specifying a saddlebag. Other variations common to today's collecting fraternity include *cantana* and *cantenna* (Bill Mackin, *Cowboy and Gunfighter Collectibles,* p. 75; and R. M. Bachman, *Old West Reproductions...Catalog No. 9,* p. 15), neither of which appear in Spanish usage. See for example, Colin Smith, *Collins Spanish-English/English-Spanish Dictionary,* p. 100.

12. Collections of R. M. Bachman, Florence, MT; and Bill Mackin, Meeker, CO. Also see, Main & Winchester, p. 71.

13. Mackin, *Cowboy and Gunfighter Collectibles,* pp. vi, 75; The Denver Manufacturing Company, *Illustrated Catalogue of the Denver Manufacturing Company....,* 1883, p. 90; S. C. Gallup & Frazier, *Illustrated Catalogue and Price List....,* 1896, pp. 78, 85.

14. Rattenbury, "Packing Iron," p. 28; Main & Winchester, p. 71; R. T. Frazier, *1900 Illustrated Catalogue and Price List,* p. 113.

15. Garavaglia and Worman, *Firearms of the American West, 1803-1865,* pp. 88-104, 275-300; Spangenberger, "Frontier Gun Leather," pp. 106, 109.

16. Meadows, p. 61.

17. Kopec, "The Western Holster," *Arms Gazette,* Vol. 4, No. 10 (June 1977), p. 33.

18. Casteel, p. 60; Spangenberger, "Frontier Gun Leather," p. 109; Kopec,

"Frontier Holsters and Belts," pp. 8-9.

19. Casteel, p. 60.

20. Quoted in Garavaglia and Worman, *Firearms of the American West, 1803-1865,* p. 204.

21. Kopec, "The Western Holster," p. 33; Spangenberger, "Frontier Gun Leather," p. 109. The appearance of holsters altered by removal of their protective cover flaps generally was concurrent with the transition in firearms technology from percussion to metallic cartridge ignition, which required less protection from moisture. Such modified, or "transitional," holsters typically incorporated straight or somewhat arched throat profiles.

22. See Manufacturers' Trade Catalogs in the bibliography.

23. Kopec, "Frontier Holsters and Belts," pp. 51-53.

24. Casteel, p. 59; Kopec, "Frontier Holsters and Belts," pp. 8-9.

25. The "California" appellation for this holster pattern derives from its evident place of origin. The contemporary collecting fraternity often uses the term "Slim Jim" to denote the style. While descriptive, this bit of jargon has no historical basis and is avoided in this treatment. See, for example, Casteel, p. 59.

26. Rattenbury, "Packing Iron," p. 24; Kopec, "Frontier Holsters and Belts," p. 9.

27. Rattenbury, "Packing Iron," pp. 29-30; Casteel, pp. 59-60.

28. Garavaglia and Worman, *Firearms of the American West, 1803-1865,* pp. 275-292, 312-319, 337-338; Rattenbury, "Packing Iron," p. 29.

29. Casteel, p. 60; Kopec, "The Western Holster," pp. 33-34; Joseph G. Rosa, *Guns of the American West,* p. 175; Rattenbury, "Packing Iron," p. 30.

30. Rattenbury, "Packing Iron," p. 30; Kopec, "Frontier Holsters and Belts," pp. 9, 29, 34-36; Spangenberger, "Barbary Coast '49ers," *Guns & Ammo,* Vol. 32, No. 10 (October 1988), pp. 86-88, and "Frontier Gun Leather," p. 109; Casteel, p. 60.

31. See, for example, Ralph Waldo Emerson's essay "Beauty" in *The Complete Works of Ralph Waldo*

Emerson, ed. Edward Waldo Emerson, Vol. 6, pp. 289-290; and Horatio Greenough, *The Travels, Observations, and Experiences of a Yankee Stonecutter,* ed. Nathalia Wright, pp. 162-190, passim. For a general overview of "vernacular" form and design, see John A. Kouwenhoven, *The Arts in Modern American Civilization,* pp. 13-33, 82-91.

32. For example, E. Dixon Larson, "The Heritage of the American Western Holster," *American Rifleman,* Vol. 124, No. 4 (April 1976), p. 33; Kopec, "Frontier Holsters and Belts," p. 8, and "The Western Holster," p. 33; Rosa, *Guns of the American West,* pp. 174-175; and John Bianchi, *Blue Steel & Gunleather,* p. 5.

33. Meadows, p. 47.

34. Casteel, p. 59; Kopec, "Frontier Holsters and Belts," p. 9; Garavaglia and Worman, *Firearms of the American West, 1866-1894,* p. 335; The Denver Manufacturing Company, p. 100.

35. Rattenbury, "Packing Iron," p. 30; Casteel, p. 61.

36. The term "Mexican Loop" for this holster pattern derives from its supposed area of origin and from terminology used in early twentieth century trade literature (for example, H. H. Heiser, Catalog Nos. 14 and 19). Other appellations (such as "Border Loop," "Denver Loop," "Frontier Loop" and "Kansas Loop"), which attempt to identify regional or stylistic variation, represent terminology introduced by the contemporary collecting fraternity. Ambiguously defined and inconsistently applied in previous writings, these names are eschewed in this treatment.

37. Casteel, p. 61; Spangenberger, "Frontier Gun Leather," p. 110; Kopec, "Frontier Holsters and Belts," pp. 9-10; Rattenbury, "Packing Iron," p. 31.

38. *Ibid.*

39. Edgar Beecher Bronson, *Reminiscences of a Ranchman,* pp. 24-25.

40. Evan G. Barnard, *A Rider of the Cherokee Strip,* p. 15.

41. Rattenbury, "Packing Iron," pp. 32, 42-45; Mackin, *Cowboy and Gunfighter Collectibles,* pp. 73, 76-81; Kopec,

"Frontier Holsters and Belts," pp. 10, 17-31, 36-48.

42. Rattenbury, "Packing Iron," pp. 32, 42; Spangenberger, "Frontier Gun Leather," p. 110; Kopec, "Frontier Holsters and Belts," pp. 10, 17, 22; Bianchi, pp. 9-10.

43. Kopec, "Frontier Holsters and Belts," pp. 10-11, 44-45; Bill Cleaver to author, 16 October 1990, author's files; Rick Bachman, Old West Reproductions, telephone consultation with author, 16 November, 1990; Rattenbury, "Packing Iron," pp. 32, 44. It is the author's opinion that E. L. Gallatin probably developed this contoured, toe-plugged design from his earlier experience in fabricating "California" pattern holsters. His nephew and understudy, F. A. Meanea, certainly popularized the style, while J. S. Collins and others interpreted it regionally.

44. Kopec, "Frontier Holsters and Belts," pp. 11, 19 21; Rattenbury, "Packing Iron," pp. 32, 46; R. T. Frazier, *Illustrated Catalogue and Price List [No. 8],* circa 1907, unpaged; Main & Winchester, p. 86; S. D. Myres, *S. D. Myres Saddlery...,* Sweetwater, 1916, p. 109; S. D. Myres, *S. D. Myres Saddle Co.,* El Paso, circa 1927, p. 103; S. D. Myres, *S. D. Myres Holsters-Belts-Art Leather,* El Paso, circa 1944, pp. 11, 13, 15, 17, 22-23.

45. Rattenbury, "Packing Iron," p. 32; Spangenberger, "Frontier Gun Leather," pp. 108, 110.

46. Spangenberger, "Frontier Gun Leather," pp. 108-109; Kopec, "Frontier Holsters and Belts," pp. 26, 30-31, 51, 54, 56. Also see, for example, H. H. Heiser, *The Hermann H. Heiser Saddlery Co., Catalogue No. 14,* p. 12; H. H. Heiser, *The Hermann H. Heiser Manufacturing & Selling Co., Catalog No. 19,* pp. 15, 18; R. T. Frazier, *R. T. Frazier Saddlery, Catalog No. 17,* pp. 83, 96; and F. P. Alonso, *La Palestina, Catalogo Ilustrado No. 4,* pp. 18-21.

47. Kopec, "Frontier Holsters and Belts," pp. 41, 51-53; Mackin, *Cowboy and Gunfighter Collectibles,* pp. 76-80. Also see, Smith-Worthington, *The Smith-Worthington Company...Manufacturers,*

Importers and Exporters [of] Harness and Saddlery, circa 1905, pp. 150, 167; Montgomery Ward & Co., *Catalogue & Buyers' Guide No. 57, Spring and Summer 1895,* p. 481; and Sears, Roebuck & Co., *Sears, Roebuck & Co....Catalogue No. 111,* 1902, p. 333.

48. U. S. Patent No. 252,448 of 17 January 1882. The name "Bridgeport Rig" for this device is derived from its sole commercial manufacturer, the Bridgeport Gun Implement Company of Bridgeport, Connecticut.

49. Specifications, U. S. Patent No. 252,448 of 17 January 1882; Bianchi, p. 9; Spangenberger, "Pistol Packin' in the Old West," p. 74, and "Frontier Gun Leather," pp. 111, 208.

50. U. S. Patent No. 252,448 of 17 January 1882; Meadows, pp. 133-134; Bill Mackin, telephone consultation with author, 28 May 1991.

51. As quoted in Eugene Cunningham, *Triggernometry: A Gallery of Gunfighters,* pp. 427-428.

52. Garavaglia and Worman, *Firearms of the American West, 1866-1894,* pp. 294-295; Cunningham, p. 427.

53. *Tascosa Pioneer* (Tascosa, Texas), July 16, 1887.

54. Spangenberger, "Frontier Gun Leather," p. 110; Mackin, *Cowboy and Gunfighter Collectibles,* pp. 73, 82.

55. U. S. Patent No. 309,292 of 16 December 1884.

56. U. S. Patent Nos. 309,292 of 16 December 1884; 317,128 of 5 May 1885; 468,556 of 9 February 1892; 653,779 of 17 July 1900; and 837,156 of 27 November 1906.

57. H. H. Heiser, *The Hermann H. Heiser Saddlery Co., Catalogue No. 14,* pp. 7-8; Victor Marden, *The Marden Saddles,* circa 1914, p. 81; Padgitt Brothers, *Padgitt Bros. Co., Catalog No. 89,* p. 30; and S. D. Myres, *S. D. Myres Saddlery, Catalogue No. 4,* Sweetwater, p. 61.

58. Spangenberger, "Pistol Packin' in the Old West," p. 75; Rattenbury, "Packing Iron," pp. 32-33; Mackin, "Frontier Shoulder Holsters," *Arms Gazette,* Vol. 5, No. 8 (April 1978), p. 19; N. Flayderman & Co., *N. Flayderman & Co., Purveyors of Military & Nautical Antiquities, Catalog No. 86,* New Milford,

1970, item 1450; Cunningham, pp. 426, 431.

59. Mackin, "Frontier Shoulder Holsters," p. 19; Rattenbury, "Packing Iron," p. 33; S. C. Gallup, *The S. C. Gallup Saddlery Co., Catalogue No. 7*, p. 107.

60. Spangenberger, "Frontier Gun Leather," p. 111; William Foster-Harris, *The Look of the Old West*, p. 145; Mackin, "Frontier Shoulder Holsters," p. 19.

61. Rattenbury, "Packing Iron," p. 33; Mackın, "Frontier Shoulder Holsters," pp. 19-20; Foster-Harris, p. 145; H. H. Heiser, *The Hermann H. Heiser Saddlery Co., Catalogue No. 14*, p.11.

62. U. S. Patent No. 609,317 of 16 August 1898.

63. Mackin, "Frontier Shoulder Holsters," pp. 19-20; Al. Furstnow, *Illustrated Catalogue and Price List No. 21, Al Furstnow Wholesale and Retail Saddlery*, p. 146.

64. See Manufacturers' Trade Catalogs in the bibliography.

65. Mackin, "Frontier Shoulder Holsters," p. 20; Rattenbury, "Packing Iron," p. 33; U. S. Patent No. 981,292 of 10 January 1911.

66. The place of longarms among civilians in the West is thoroughly treated in Garavaglia and Worman, *Firearms of the American West, 1803-1865*, pp. 33-52, 225-264, and *Firearms of the American West, 1866-1894*, pp. 103-222.

67. Richard Conn, *Circles of the World: Traditional Art of the Plains Indians*, pp. 82, 128, 147-148; Gary Galante, Museum of the American Indian, telephone consultation with author, 22 May 1991; Spangenberger, "Frontier Gun Leather," p. 209.

68. Conn, *Native American Art in the Denver Art Museum*, p. 78; Glenn E. Markoe, ed., *Vestiges of a Proud Nation: The Ogden B. Read Northern Plains Indian Collection*, pp. 132-133; Richard A. Pohrt, *The American Indian - The American Flag*, p. 141.

69. Spangenberger, "Frontier Gun Leather," p. 209; Rattenbury, "Packing Iron," p. 28; Spangenberger to author, 11 July 1991, author's files.

70. Randy Steffen, *The Horse Soldier, 1776-1943*, Vol. 2, p. 195.

71. Nichols, p. 62. Also see,

J. Evetts Haley, *Charles Goodnight: Cowman & Plainsman*, p. 37.

72. Spangenberger, "Frontier Gun Leather," p. 209; Rattenbury, "Packing Iron," p. 28; Mackin, "Winchesters Wore Leather Too!," *Arms Gazette*, Vol. 5, No. 4 (December 1977), p. 12.

73. Baylis Fletcher, *Up the Trail in '79*, p. 32.

74. Reginald Aldridge, *Life on a Ranch*, pp. 223-224.

75. Mackin, "Winchesters Wore Leather Too!," pp. 12, 16; H. H. Heiser, *The Hermann H. Heiser Saddlery Co., Catalogue No. 14*, pp. 29-31.

76. Rattenbury, "Packing Iron," pp. 28, 36; Mackin, *Cowboy and Gunfighter Collectibles*, pp. 118-120, and "Winchesters Wore Leather Too!," pp. 12-16.

77. Rattenbury, "Packing Iron," p. 28; Mackin, *Cowboy and Gunfighter Collectibles*, pp. 118-120; R. T. Frazier, *1900 Illustrated Catalogue and Price List....*, p. 113; Frank Olzer, *Arizona Saddlery Company...Catalogue No. 5*, p. 54.

78. Mackin, *Cowboy and Gunfighter Collectibles*, p. 118; S. C. Gallup, *Catalogue No. 14 and Price List of the S. C. Gallup Saddlery Co.*, p. 112.

79. Spangenberger, "Frontier Gun Leather," p. 208.

80. Mackin, "Frontier Cartridge Belts," *Arms Gazette*, Vol. 5, No. 12 (August 1978), pp. 23-24.

81. Curry & Bro., *Price List [of] 1884*, p. 38.

82. Rattenbury, "Packing Iron," pp. 31, 40; Montgomery Ward & Co., *Catalogue and Buyers' Guide No. 57, Spring and Summer 1895*, p. 481; U. S. Patent No. 237,673 of 15 February 1881; Francis Bannerman, *Military Goods Catalogue*, 1915, p. 276; N. Curry & Bro., p. 38; Mackin, "Frontier Cartridge Belts," (August 1978), p. 29. Also see, J. Duncan Campbell, *New Belt Buckles of the Old West*, pp. iii-xiv, 85, 87-90.

83. Spangenberger, "Frontier Gun Leather," p. 208; Kopec, "Frontier Holsters and Belts," p. 13.

84. Rattenbury, "Packing Iron," pp. 31, 41; Mackin, "Frontier Cartridge Belts," *Arms Gazette*, Vol. 6, No. 1 (September 1978), p. 23; Kopec, "Frontier Holsters and Belts," pp. 42, 45; The Denver Manufacturing

Company, p. 99; Victor Marden, *The Marden Saddles*, circa 1914, p. 81; H. H. Heiser, *The Hermann H. Heiser Manufacturing & Selling Co., Catalog No. 19*, p. 47; S. D. Myres, *S. D. Myres Saddle Co.*, El Paso, circa 1927, p. 105.

85. Rattenbury, "Packing Iron," p. 31; E. C. Abbott and Helena Huntington Smith, *We Pointed Them North: Recollections of a Cowpuncher*, p. 80.

86. Rattenbury, "Packing Iron," p. 31, 41; Mackin, "Frontier Cartridge Belts," (September 1978), pp. 21-22; Kopec, "Frontier Holsters and Belts," p. 13; H. H. Heiser, *The Hermann H. Heiser Saddlery Co., Catalogue No. 14*, p. 28; R. T. Frazier, *Illustrated Catalogue and Price List [No. 8]*, circa 1907, unpaged.

87. Mackin, "Frontier Cartridge Belts," (September 1978), p. 21; L. Frank, *Catalogue No. 1...*, 1891, p. 266; Main & Winchester, p. 88; S.C. Gallup & Frazier, pp. 83, 85; R. T. Frazier, *R. T. Frazier Saddlery, Catalog No. 17*, pp. 83, 96; H. H. Heiser, *The Hermann H. Heiser Saddlery Co., Catalogue No. 14*, p. 28.

88. Kopec, "Frontier Holsters and Belts," p. 13; Mackin, "Frontier Cartridge Belts," (September 1978), p. 48. Also see, Manufacturers' Trade Catalogs in the bibliography.

89. Walt King, "Ninety-Six Years of the Triple H Brand," *The Western Horseman*, Vol. 19, No. 11 (November 1954), pp. 18, 44; Rice and Vernam, pp. 29-30; Bill Mackin, telephone consultation with author, 23 July 1991; Jim Laird, telephone consultation with author, 24 July 1991.

90. H. H. Heiser, *The Hermann H. Heiser Manufacturing & Selling Co., Catalog No. 19*, p. 4.

91. King, p. 44; Rice and Vernam, p. 30.

92. H. H. Heiser, *The Hermann H. Heiser Saddlery Co., Catalogue No. 14*, p. 4.

93. *Ibid.*, p. 6.

94. Bianchi, p. 233.

95. King, p. 19; Rice and Vernam, pp. 30-31; Kopec, "Frontier Holsters and Belts," pp. 51-52; Mackin, *Cowboy and Gunfighter Collectibles*, pp. 79-80; White & Davis, *White & Davis "Always*

Reliable" Catalog No. 19, p. 125; The Denver Dry Goods Company, *The Denver Dry Goods Co., Stockmens Supplies*, circa 1921, p. 28.

96. H. H. Heiser, *The Hermann H. Heiser Saddlery Co., Catalogue No. 14*, pp. 7-21, 24-32; H. H. Heiser, *The Hermann H. Heiser Manufacturing & Selling Co., Catalog No. 20*, pp. 4-43, 47-50; H. H. Heiser, *The Hermann H. Heiser Saddlery Company, Catalog No. 30*, p. 3. Heiser's only near competitor during the 1930s and 1940s was the S. D. Myres Saddlery of El Paso, Texas, which presented a selection of only about a dozen "Mexican Loop" and law enforcement pattern holsters in four gradations of embellishment. (For which see, S. D. Myres, *S. D. Myres Holsters-Belts-Art Leather*, El Paso, circa 1944, pp. 8-20.)

97. H. H. Heiser, *The Hermann H. Heiser Manufacturing & Selling Co., Catalog No. 20*, p. 1.

98. Laurel E. Wilson, "'I was a pretty proud kid:' An Interpretation of Differences in Posed and Unposed Photographs of Montana Cowboys," unpublished MS, 1990, author's files, pp. 3, 15, 17-20, 23.

99. Abbott and Smith, p. 210.

100. Bianchi, p. 11; William K. Everson, *A Pictorial History of the Western Film*, pp. 39-43, 57-69, 80-97, 124-200.

101. Cunningham, pp. 428-429; Sandra L. Myres, *S. D. Myres: Saddlemaker*, p. 92; Haldeen Braddy, "The Birth of the Buscadero," *Guns*, Vol. 8, No. 1 (January 1962), pp. 38-39.

102. Spangenberger, "Bohlin Made: Hollywood's Stamp of Quality," in *1989 Annual Guns & Ammo*, ed. Garry James (1989), pp. 77-79; Edward H. Bohlin, *Catalog of "The World's Finest" Riding Equipment...and Silver & Leather Goods from The Bohlin Shop*, circa 1930, p. 71; Al. Furstnow, *Illustrated Catalogue No. 31....*, p. 118; H. H . Heiser, *The Her-*

mann H. Heiser Saddlery Company, Catalog No. 30, pp. 32-33; The George Lawrence Company, *Lawrence Catalog of Saddles and Cowboy Equipment*, circa 1937, p. 56; S. D. Myres, *S. D. Myres Holsters-Belts-Art Leather*, El Paso, circa 1944, pp. 22-23; George N. Fenin and William K. Everson, *The Western: From Silents to the Seventies*, pp. 255-262, 300-317.

103. James A. Dunham, untitled and unpublished MS, circa 1989, author's files, pp. 2-3; Bob Arganbright, "The Funny Guns and Gear of the Western Fast Draw Game," *Gun Digest*, Vol. 39 (1985), p. 39; U. S. Patent No. 2,832,519 of 29 April 1958.

104. Arganbright, pp. 39-40, 45; Dunham, pp. 2-5.

105. Phil Spangenberger, Red River Frontier Outfitters, telephone consultation with author, 1 July 1991; Bianchi, *Bianchi Gunleather 1979*, pp. 10-13.

106. See, for example, Red River Frontier Outfitters, *Red River Frontier Outfitters: Frontier Clothing, Western Americana [and] Military Americana*, 1990, pp. 2-7; El Paso Saddlery, *El Paso Saddlery Co., Finest Quality Holsters and Belts, Catalogue No. 94*, pp. 18-24; R. M. Bachman, *Old West Reproductions, Frontier Leather and Accessories from 1860 to 1900, Catalog No. 10*, pp. 1-11, 15, 17, 20-23; J. C. Stewart, *Stewart Saddlery...Catalog No. 3*, pp. 13-15; Old West Dry Goods, *Catalog No. 1, Old West Outfitters*, pp. 18-20; Bill Cleaver, *Wild Bill's Originals and Authentic Reproduction Holsters, Gunbelts and Accessories*, 1989, unpaged; Mike Nesbitt, "The Ultimate in Reproduction Leather: New Holsters Aged To Look 100 Years Old," *Guns*, Vol. 33, No. 11 (November 1987), pp. 28-29, 62.

GLOSSARY

BELT HOLSTER: a shaped leather receptacle designed to carry a pistol suspended from a waist belt.

BELT LOOP: integral or attached leather opening or sleeve on the upper back of the holster body for belt mounting (also called a belt slot).

BILLET: a strip of leather sewn to a wider belt panel to engage and secure the buckle (also see Chape).

BODY: the principal element of a holster or scabbard within which the weapon is retained (also called the pouch or well).

BONING: the process of rubbing the contours of a pistol into the surface of a holster as part of the wet-molding procedure.

BOOT: a short, flared and open-ended leather receptacle fixed to the saddle rigging for the carriage of carbines in the military.

BRIDGEPORT RIG: a pronged fixture for mounting a pistol on a cartridge belt without the use of a holster.

BUCKET: a saddle-mounted leather receptacle, consisting of a muzzle fixture and elongated straps, for the carriage of carbines and short rifles in the military. Used in association with a carbine strap.

BUSCADERO: a style of gunbelt consisting of a curved belt with a slotted panel, and a holster with an extended drop loop that is suspended from the slot.

CALIFORNIA BUCKLE: a usually rectangular or square, double-frame buckle having clipped corners and nickel-plated finish used on cartridge and cartridge/money belts.

CALIFORNIA HOLSTER: a regional form typified by a recurved throat and contour-fit main seam, common during the percussion era.

CANTENA: an anglo bastardization of the Mexican *cantina;* here referring to pommel bag-holsters (also *cantana* and *cantenna*).

CARTOUCHE: a stamped maker's mark usually with name and location surrounded by an oval or rectangular borderline, applied to gunleather elements in various locations.

CARTRIDGE BELT: a leather or fabric waist belt fixed with a series of attached or integral loops for the carriage of self-contained fixed ammunition (also termed a Thimble Belt in early usage).

CARTRIDGE BOX: a usually rectangular leather receptacle with a cover flap and belt loop for carrying ammunition on a waist belt.

CARTRIDGE LOOP: one of a series of small, open-ended receptacles fixed to the face of a waist belt for retaining cartridges (also called a thimble).

CARTRIDGE/MONEY BELT: a folded cartridge belt having a hollow interior for safekeeping money or documents.

CARTUCHERA: (Mexican) cartridge belt.

CARVING: the cutting away of surface leather with hand tools to create a decorative motif.

CHAPE: a short leather strip securing the edge or center-bar of a buckle and sewn to a wider belt panel (billet often is substituted for this term in modern usage).

CHEYENNE HOLSTER: a regional variation of the Mexican Loop pattern popular on the northern plains.

CLOSURE: the means by which cover flaps are secured over the holster. These may include metal finials or strap leathers fixed on the face of the holster body which retain either the flap proper or an attached tab leather.

CONCHO: a metal disk of silver, German silver or nickeled brass sometimes used to ornament gunleather elements (also concha).

CONNECTING LEATHER: the segment joining the bodies, or body and pouch, of a pommel holster outfit (also strap or panel).

COVER FLAPS: the integral or attached leather panels that close over the top of a holster body to protect and secure the weapon. Basic variations are the "full" and "half-flap" patterns.

CREASING: an ornamental border line formed along the edge of a leather element with hand tools or dies (also crimping)

CROSSDRAW: a holster worn on the opposite side of its intended configuration with the gun butt forward.

DECORATIVE MOTIFS: any of several ornamental patterns carved or embossed on gunleather elements to enhance appearance; these typically include floral, foliate, basket—weave, and waffle designs, usually accompanied by various border elements.

DROP LOOP: a Buscadero or Fast Draw pattern holster having an extended belt loop, or shank leather, above the pouch which lowers the holster body to thigh level when suspended form the belt slot.

EDGING: removing the square edges from leather elements and seams with a cutting tool (bevelling).

EMBOSSING: the hand or machine stamping of a pattern on leather surfaces.

END CAP: the shaped brass receptables fixed over the lower extremity of pommel holsters.

FACE: the outermost surface or section of a holster, scabbard or belt, usually the grain side of tanned leather.

FAST DRAW: a style of gunbelt consisting of a deeply curved belt, usually with a slotted panel, and a low-cut, metal-lined holster that is suspended from the slot.

FINIAL: a knobbed post or stud, usually of brass, utilized for flap closure on holsters and cartridge boxes.

FUNDA DE PISTOLA: (Mexican) pistol holster.

GUSSET: an elongated leather strip sewn between two panels to create an expandable compartment.

HAMMER THONG: a narrow-diameter strip of latigo leather designed to secure the pistol in the holster by looping over the hammer spur.

HIP POCKET HOLSTER: a relatively small, shaped leather receptacle utilizing a contoured panel for pistol carriage in the hip pocket.

HORN LOOP: an open-ended leather receptacle fixed at the saddle pommel for the carriage of longarms on horseback.

JOCKSTRAP HOLSTER: a regional variation of the Mexican Loop pattern briefly popular in Texas and the Southwest.

JUEGO DE FUNDA: (Mexican) holster rig or gunbelt.

LEFT-HAND: a holster that carries the pistol butt-to-the-rear when worn on the left side of the body.

LEG THONG: a narrow-diameter strip of latigo leather fixed at the toe of the holster and tied around the leg to secure the holster during the draw.

LINING: a thin, inner layer of chamois, glove leather or fabric glued and sewn on the inside of the holster body.

MAIN SEAM: the longitudinal, contoured edge joint that is sewn, or sometimes thong-wrapped, to close the folded leather panel forming a holster or scabbard.

MEXICAN LOOP HOLSTER: an indigenous western form typified by one-piece construction utilizing an integral belt loop/back skirt, common during the metallic cartridge era.

MILLS CARTRIDGE BELT: a military and commercial design utilizing woven cotton webbing with integral cartridge loops.

PIPE: the lower, narrowed, sometimes cylindrical segment of the holster body.

PISTOL CASE: an early term for a belt holster, common in the military.

POMMEL BAG-HOLSTER: a saddlebag-like outfit incorporating a pistol holster beneath one of the pouch cover flaps and mounting on the saddle pommel.

POMMEL HOLSTER: a shaped leather receptacle designed to carry a pistol or pistols at the front of the saddle (also referred to as a saddle holster).

PRAIRIE CARTRIDGE BELT: a military (or civilian) design utilizing a canvas body cover and loops to reduce verdigris formation.

RANGER BUCKLE: a usually fancy, horseshoe-shaped buckle with separate metal keepers commonly used on Buscadero gunbelts.

RIFLE CASE: a soft leather sheath of Indian origin designed for the protection of longarms.

RIGHT-HAND: a holster that carries the pistol butt-to-the-rear when worn on the right side of the body.

ROSETTE: a circular, often floral design commonly embossed on gunleather elements during the late nineteenth century.

SADDLE SCABBARD: an elongated leather receptacle designed for the carriage of rifles or carbines on horseback.

SCABBARD: usually an enlongated leather receptacle designed to carry a carbine or rifle on horseback; the term also was applied to pistol holsters during the period 1850-1880 and was so used in Texas well into the twentieth century.

SCABBARD LEATHERS: the long, relatively narrow strips of leather fixed with adjustable buckles for mounting carbine and rifle scabbards on saddles.

SHANK: the leather belt loop element extending above the pouch on a fast draw holster; often reinforced with a metal lining (also see Drop Loop).

SHOULDER HOLSTER: a shaped leather receptacle designed to carry a pistol suspended beneath the arm from a shoulder harness. Basic variants were the Texas (full pouch) and Skeleton (clip spring) patterns.

SKIRT: a contoured leather element or panel usually integral with the holster body that is folded down behind the body to form the belt loop in a Mexican Loop pattern holster.

SKIRT LOOP: the integral or attached leather band(s) or collar secured to the back skirt to retain the body in Mexican Loop pattern holsters.

SLING: a belt-like leather strap worn over the shoulder and fixed with a swiveled hook for the carriage of shoulder arms by mounted troops.

SOCKET: a leather receptacle of circular pattern fixed to the saddle rigging for the carriage of carbines in the military. Sometimes referred to as "thimble" in army nomenclature.

STAMPING: the embossing of leather surfaces with hand-held tools or machine plates.

THROAT: the upper opening of a holster or scabbard body (also the mouth). Usually straight, arched or recurved in profile.

TOE: the lower, muzzle end of a holster or scabbard body.

TOE PLUG: a thick, circular or ovoid-shaped leather piece sewn into the bottom of pommel and belt holsters (and early saddle scabbards) to close the muzzle (also referred to as a "bottom" or muzzle plug).

UTILITY POUCH: the leather bag with cover flap forming half of a pommel holster outfit as typically issued to enlisted dragoons.

VAINA DE CARABINA/DE FUSIL: (Mexican) carbine or rifle scabbard.

VERDIGRIS: a waxy, green residue formed by copper or brass cartridge cases (or rivets) in contact with leather.

WELT: a narrow, often tapered leather spacer sewn into a seam to add interior space and strength.

WET-MOLDING: the process of shaping a holster to a model of its intended weapon.

BIBLIOGRAPHY

BOOKS

Abbott, E. C., and Helena Huntington Smith. *We Pointed Them North: Recollections of a Cowpuncher.* Norman, OK: University of Oklahoma Press, 1955.

Ahlborn, Richard E., ed. *Man Made Mobile: Early Saddles of Western North America.* Washington, D.C.: Smithsonian Institution Press, 1980.

Aldridge, Reginald. *Life On A Ranch.* New York: Argonaut Press, Ltd., 1966.

Arganbright, Bob. *The Fastest Guns Alive.* Saint Louis: the author, 1978.

Ball, Robert W.D., and Ed Vebell. *Cowboy Collectibles and Western Memorabilia.* West Chester, PA: Schiffer Publishing, Ltd., 1991.

Barnard, Evan G. *A Rider of the Cherokee Strip.* Boston: Houghton Mifflin Company, 1936.

Bianchi, John. *Blue Steel & Gunleather: A Practical Guide to Holsters.* Temecula, CA: Bianchi International, 1986.

Billington, Ray Allen. *Westward Expansion: A History of the American Frontier.* 4th ed. New York: Macmillan Publishing Co., Inc., 1974.

Brinkerhoff, Sidney B. *Metal Uniform Insignia of the U. S. Army in the Southwest.* Museum Monograph No. 3. Tucson, AZ: Arizona Pioneers' Historical Society, 1965.

Bronson, Edgar Beecher. *Reminiscences of a Ranchman.* Chicago: A.C. McClurg & Co., 1911.

Caba, G. Craig. *Historic Southern Saddles, 1840-1865.* Enola, PA: Civil War Antiquities, 1982.

Campbell, J. Duncan. *New Belt Buckles of the Old West.* n.p.: the author, 1973.

Conn, Richard. *Circles of the World: Traditional Art of the Plains Indians.* Denver: Denver Art Museum, 1982.

_____. *Native American Art in the Denver Art Museum.* Denver: Denver Art Museum, 1979.

Cremony, John C. *Life Among the Apaches, 1850-1868.* Reprint ed., Glorieta, NM: Rio Grande Press, 1969.

Cunningham, Eugene. *Triggernometry: A Gallery of Gunfighters.* Caldwell, ID: The Caxton Printers, Ltd., 1941.

Dorsey, R. Stephen. *American Military Belts and Related Equipments.* Union City, TN: Pioneer Press, 1984.

Emerson, Ralph Waldo. *The Complete Works of Ralph Waldo Emerson.* Edited by Edward Waldo Emerson. 12 vols. Boston: Houghton Mifflin & Company, 1903.

Everson, William K. *A Pictorial History of the Western Film.* Secaucus, NJ: The Citadel Press, 1969.

Fenin, George N. and William K. Everson. *The Western: From Silents to the Seventies.* New York: Grossman Publishers, 1973.

Flayderman, Norm. *Flayderman's Guide to Antique American Firearms...and Their Values.* 3rd ed., Northfield, IL: DBI Books, 1983.

Fletcher, Baylis. *Up the Trail in '79.* Norman, OK: University of Oklahoma Press, 1968.

Forbis, William H., et. al. *The Cowboys.* New York: Time-Life Books, 1973.

Foster-Harris, William. *The Look of the Old West.* New York: The Viking Press, 1955.

Friedman, Michael. *Cowboy Culture: The Last Frontier of American Antiques.* West Chester, PA: Schiffer Publishing, Ltd., 1992.

Gallatin, E. L. *What Life Has Taught Me.* n.p.: John Frederic, Printer, 1900.

Garavaglia, Louis A., and Charles G. Worman. *Firearms of the American West, 1803-1865.* Albuquerque, NM: University of New Mexico Press, 1984.

_____. *Firearms of the American West, 1866-1894.* Albuquerque, NM: University of New Mexico Press, 1985.

Goodson, Joe, ed. *Old West Antiques & Collectables.* Austin, TX: Great American Publishing Company, 1979.

Greenough, Horatio. *The Travels, Observations and Experiences of a Yankee Stonecutter.* Edited by Nathalia Wright. Gainesville, FL: Scholars' Facsimiles & Reprints, 1958.

Haley, J. Evetts. *Charles Goodnight: Cowman & Plainsman.* Boston: Houghton Mifflin Company, 1936.

Horn, Tom. *Life of Tom Horn, Government Scout and Interpreter, Written by Himself.* Reprint ed., Norman, OK: University of Oklahoma Press, 1964.

Hutchins, Dan and Sebie. *Old Cowboy Saddles & Spurs: Identifying the Craftsmen Who Made Them.* Santa Fe, NM: the authors, 1992.

Hutchins, James S., ed. *Horse Equipments and Cavalry Accoutrements.* Pasadena, CA: Socio-Technical Publications, 1970.

James, Garry, ed. *Guns & Ammo Guide To Guns of the Gunfighters.* Los Angeles: Petersen Publishing Company, 1975.

Kelly, William, Jr. *An Excursion to California.* 2 vols. London: Chapman and Hall, 1851.

King, Charles. *Starlight Ranch and Other Stories of Army Life on the Frontier.* Philadelphia: Lippincott Publishers, 1890.

Knight, Oliver. *Life and Manners in the Frontier Army.* Norman, OK: University of Oklahoma Press, 1978.

Kouwenhoven, John A. *The Arts in Modern American Civilization.* New York: The Norton Library, 1967.

Laird, James R. *The Cheyenne Saddle: A Study of Stock Saddles of E. L. Gallatin, Frank A. Meanea and the Collins Brothers.* Cheyenne, WY: Cheyenne Corral of Westerners International, 1982.

Lethern, Albert A. and William P. Wise. *The Development of the Mills Woven Cartridge Belt.* London: The Mills Equipment Company, 1956. Reprint ed., Madison, CT: The Ordnance Chest, n.d.

Lewis, Colonel Berkeley R. *Notes on Cavalry Weapons of the American Civil War, 1861-1865.* Washington D.C.: The American Ordnance Association, 1961.

Loomis, Noel M. *Wells Fargo.* New York: Clarkson N. Potter, Inc., Publishers, 1968.

Mackin, Bill. *Cowboy and Gunfighter Collectibles: A Photographic Encyclopedia with Price Guide and Makers Index.* Missoula, MT: Mountain Press Publishing Company, 1989.

Maddox, William A. *Historical Carving in Leather.* San Antonio, TX: The Naylor Company, 1940.

Markoe, Glenn E., ed. *Vestiges of a Proud Nation: The Ogden B. Read Northern Plains Indian Collection.* Burlington, VT: Robert Hull Fleming Museum, 1986.

Meadows, Edward Scott. *U.S. Military Holsters and Pistol Cartridge Boxes.* Dallas, TX: Taylor Publishing Company, 1987.

Mills, Anson. *My Story.* Edited by C. H. Clandy. Washington, D.C.: the author, 1918.

Mowbray, Andrew, ed. *Guns at the Little Bighorn: The Weapons of Custer's Last Stand / A Man at Arms Special Publication.* Lincoln, RI: Andrew Mowbray Inc. 1988.

Myres, Sandra L. *S.D. Myres: Saddlemaker.* Kerrville, TX: the author, 1961.

Nichols, James Wilson. *Now You Hear My Horn.* Edited by Catherine W. McDowell. Austin, TX: University of Texas Press, 1967.

Parkman, Francis. *The Oregon Trail.* Philadelphia: The John C. Winston Company, 1931.

Phillips, William G. and John P. Vervloet. *U.S. Single Action Cartridge Handgun Holsters, 1870-1910.* Bloomfield, Ontario: Museum Restoration Service, 1987.

Pohrt, Richard A. *The American Indian – The American Flag.* Flint, MI: Flint Institute of Arts, 1975.

Prucha, Francis Paul. *The Sword of the Republic: The United States Army on the Frontier, 1783-1846.* Lincoln, NE:University of Nebraska Press, Bison Books, 1986.

Reedstrom, Ernest Lisle. *Bugles, Banners and War Bonnets.* Caldwell, ID: The Caxton Printers, Ltd., 1977.

Rice, Lee M. and Glenn R. Vernam. *They Saddled the West.* Cambridge, MD: Cornell Maritime Press, Inc., 1975.

Rickey, Don. *$10 Horse, $40 Saddle: Cowboy Clothing, Arms, Tools and Horse Gear of the 1880's.* Fort Collins, CO: The Old Army Press, 1976.

Rosa, Joseph G. *The Gunfighter: Man or Myth?* Norman, OK:University of Oklahoma Press, 1969.

_____. *Guns of the American West.* New York: Crown Publishers, Inc., 1985.

Smith, Colin, et.al. *Collins Spanish-English/English-Spanish Dictionary.* London & Glasgow: William Collins & Co. Ltd., 1981.

Steffen, Randy. *The Horse*

Soldier, 1776-1943. 4 vols. Norman, OK: University of Oklahoma Press, 1977-1979.

Trachtman, Paul, et. al. *The Gunfighters*. New York: Time-Life Books, 1974.

U.S. Army. *A History of Watervliet Arsenal, 1813-1982*. Watervliet, NY: Watervliet Arsenal, 1982.

Utley, Robert M. *Frontiersmen in Blue: The United States Army and the Indian, 1846-1865*. New York: Macmillan Publishing Co., Inc. 1967.

_____. *Frontier Regulars: The United States Army and the Indian, 1866-1891*. New York: Macmillan Publishing Co., Inc., 1973.

Watts, Peter. *A Dictionary of the Old West, 1850-1900*. New York: Alfred A. Knopf, 1977.

Westermeier, Clifford P., ed. *Trailing the Cowboy: His Life and Lore as Told by Frontier Journalists*. Caldwell, ID: The Caxton Printers, Ltd., 1955.

Wilson, R.L., *The Peacemakers: Arms and Adventure in the American West*. New York: Random House, 1992.

ARTICLES

Arganbright, Bob. "The Funny Guns and Gear of the Western Fast Draw Game," *Gun Digest*, Vol. 39 (1985): 39-45.

Braddy, Haldeen. "The Birth of the Buscadero," *Guns*, Vol. 8, No. 1 (January 1962): 38-39, 60.

Casteel, Rod. "History and Evolution of the Revolver Holster of the Nineteenth Century," *Muzzleloader*, Vol. 10, No. 3 (July/August 1983): 58-61.

Dunn, Nora H., et.al., "Frank A. Meanea, Pioneer Saddler," *Annals of Wyoming*, Vol. 26 (January 1954): 25-32.

Franklin, Dwight. "Gun Toting in the Old West," in Paul W. Galleher, ed., *The Westerners Brand Book*, pp. 49-55. Los Angeles, CA: Los Angeles Corral, 1948.

Griffin, Bert. "Miles City Saddlery," *Persimmon Hill*, Vol. 6, No. 2 (Spring 1976): 30-35.

Hacker, Rick. "Sixgun Leather," *American Rifleman*, Vol. 138, No. 4 (April 1990): 19-21, 60.

Huntington, Lt. Col. R.T. "Dragoon Accouterments and Equipments, 1834-1849: An Identification Guide," *Plains Anthropologist*, Vol. 12, No. 38 (November 1967): 345-355.

Hutchins, James S. "Captain Michaelis Reports on Army Weapons and Equipments on the Northern Plains, 1876-1879," in Andrew Mowbray, ed., *Guns at the Little Bighorn: The Weapons of Custer's Last Stand*, pp. 27-37. Lincoln, RI: Andrew Mowbray Inc., 1988.

Jordan, Philip D. "The Pistol Packin' Cowboy," *Red River Valley Historical Review*, Vol. 11, No. 1 (Spring 1975): 65-91.

King, Walt. "Ninety-six Years of The Triple H Brand," *The Western Horseman*, Vol. 19, No. 11 (November 1954): 18-19, 44-45.

Knight, Oliver. "Western Saddlemakers, 1865-1920," *Montana Magazine*, (Spring 1983): 17-19.

Kopec, John A. "Frontier Holsters And Belts," in Joe Goodson, ed., *Old West Antiques and Collectibles*, pp. 7-61. Austin, TX: Great American Publishing Company, 1979.

_____. "Frontier Revolvers," *American Rifleman*, Vol. 124, No.9 (September 1976): 32-33.

_____. "The Western Holster," *Arms Gazette*, Vol. 4, No. 10 (June 1977): 32-36.

Larson, E. Dixon. "The Heritage Of The American Western Holster," *American Rifleman*, Vol. 124, No. 4 (April 1976): 32-34.

Lewis, Col. B. R. "Colt Walker-Dragoon Holsters," *Gun Digest*, Vol. 12 (1958): 43-45.

McChristian, Douglas C. "The Model 1876 Cartridge Belt," *The Military Collector and Historian*, Vol. 34, No. 3 (Fall 1982): 109-116.

McCollum, Berkley. "Frontier Holsters," *American Rifleman*, Vol. 129, No. 11 (November 1981): 22-25, 73.

McNellis, Robert E. "Ninety Years of El Paso Holsters," *Arms Gazette*, Vol. 4, No. 4 (December 1976): 22-25.

Mackin, Bill. "Frontier Cartridge Belts," *Arms Gazette*, Vol. 5, No. 12 (August 1978): 22-25, 29; and Vol. 6, No. 1 (September 1978): 20-23, 48.

_____. "Frontier Shoulder Holsters," *Arms Gazette*, Vol. 5, No. 8 (April 1978): 18-20.

_____. "Winchesters Wore Leather Too!", *Arms Gazette*, Vol. 5, No. 4 (December 1977): 12-16, 49.

Myres, Sandra L. "S.D. Myres and the Myres Saddle Company of Sweetwater," *West Texas Historical Association Yearbook*, Vol. 26 (October 1960): 116-136.

Nesbitt, Mike. "Wild Bill's Originals: Leather With Character," *The New Gun Week*, Vol. 23, No. 1104 (May 1988): 1, 8.

_____. "The Ultimate In Reproduction Leather: New Holsters Aged To Look 100 Years Old," *Guns*, Vol. 33, No. 11 (November 1987): 28-29, 62.

Otoupalik, Hayes. "Discovered: U.S. Model 1778 Dragoon Waist Cartridge Belt," *The Gun Report*, Vol. 13, No. 5 (October 1977): 66-67.

Parker, Watson. "Armed And Ready: Guns On The Western Frontier," in Ronald Lora, ed., *The American West: Essays in Honor of W. Eugene Hollon*, pp. 155-170. Toledo, OH: The University of Toledo Press, 1980.

Rattenbury, Richard C. "Packing Iron: A Survey of Western Gunleather," *Persimmon Hill*, Vol. 19, No. 1 (Spring 1991):26-47.

_____. "Going Heeled: A Look at Frontier Belt Holsters," *Man at Arms*, Vol. 15, No. 1 (January/February 1993): 8-18.

Rice, Lee M. "Porters," *The Western Horseman*, Vol. 19, No. 5(May 1954): 36-37, 71-75.

_____. "T. Flynn Saddlery of Pueblo," *The Western Horseman*, Vol. 13, No. 10 (October 1948): 57 ff.

_____. "The Visalia Stock Saddle Company," *The Western Horseman*, Vol. 34, No. 12 (December 1969): 116-117, 186.

Rossi, Paul. "Makers of the Forty Dollar Saddle," *Persimmon Hill*, Vol. 4, No. 2 (Spring 1974): 50-65.

Spangenberger, Phil. "Barbary Coast '49ers," *Guns & Ammo*, Vol. 32, No. 10 (October 1988): 86-88.

_____. "Bohlin Made: Hollywood's Stamp of Quality," in Garry James, ed., *1989 Annual Guns & Ammo*, pp. 76-81. Los Angeles: Petersen Publishing Co., 1989.

_____. "Frontier Gun Leather," in Garry James, ed., *Guns & Ammo Guide To Guns Of The Gunfighters*, pp. 106-111, 208-209. Los Angeles: Petersen Publishing Co., 1975.

_____. "Pistol Packin' In The Old West," *Guns & Ammo*, Vol. 33, No. 1 (January 1989): 70-75, 102-103.

Stevens, S. P. "The Old Collector," *The Texas Gun Collector*, (Spring 1990): 34-43.

MANUFACTURERS' TRADE CATALOGS

*The best primary source of information on civilian gunleather in the West is located in the trade catalogs published and distributed by the more successful, or prominent, saddle and leather goods manufacturers. While the great bulk of this material postdates the focus of this study, it nevertheless is valuable in identifying the stylistic attributes of different artisans. Because surviving examples of this literature are quite scarce and difficult to locate, an access code is appended to each entry indicating the source repository. Contemporary manufacturers of historic pattern gunleather are indicated by ** preceding the entry. This is only a selected listing of available catalogs encountered.*

AC	Author's Collection, Edmond, OK
DPL	Denver Public Library, Western History Collection, Denver, CO
MHS	Montana Historical Society, Helena, MT
NCHF	National Cowboy Hall of Fame, Oklahoma City, OK
NSHML	Nita Stewart Haley Memorial Library, Midland, TX
PC	Private Collection(s)
PPHM	Panhandle-Plains Historical Museum, Canyon, TX
PPL	Pueblo Public Library, Pueblo, CO
PUL	Princeton University Library, Philip Ashton Rollins Collection, Princeton, NJ
UTL	University of Texas Library, Barker Texas History Center, Austin, TX
UWL	University of Wyoming Library, American Heritage Center, Laramie, WY

Fernando Perez ALONSO, Mexico, D.F. *"La Palestina"/Catalogo Ilustrado No. 40*. Mexico City: F. P. Alonso, [c. 1932]. (PPHM, UWL)

E. T. AMONETT Saddlery, El Paso, TX, and Roswell, NM. *E. T. Amonett Saddlery/ Illustrated [sic] and Descriptive Catalogue and Price List*. El Paso, TX: E. T. Amonett, [c. 1928]. (PPHM)

E. T. AMONETT, Roswell, NM. *No. 37 Catalog of E.T. Amonett/ Roswell, New Mexico/Hand Made Boots/ Hand Made Saddles*. Roswell, NM: E. T. Amonett, [c. 1935]. (NSHML)

R. J. ANDREW & Son, San Angelo, TX. *Catalogue/R. J. Andrew & Son/Manufacturers and Dealers in Saddles and Harness.../and Everything Carried in Stock by a Live, Up-to-Date Saddle House*. San Angelo, TX: Holcombe-Blanton Printery, [c. 1928]. (PPHM)

ARIZONA Saddlery Company, Prescott, AZ. *Arizona Saddlery/Company/Prescott, Arizona/Makers of/Saddles that Suit/CatalogueNo. 5*. Prescott, AZ: Frank Olzer, [c. 1910]. (PC, UWL)

ASKEW Saddlery Co., Kansas City, Mo. *Askew/Saddlery/ Co./Kansas City, Mo.* Kansas City: The Askew Saddlery Co., [c. 1910]. (PC)

** R.M. BACHMAN, Florence, MT. *Old West Reproductions/FrontierLeather and Accessories from/1860 to 1900/Catalog No. 10*. Kalispell, MT: Thomas Printing, 1991. (AC)

** BIANCHI, Temecula, CA. *Bianchi Gunleather 1979*. Temecula, CA: Bianchi, 1979. (NCHF)

**_____ . *Bianchi Gunleather 1982*. Temecula, CA: Bianchi, 1982. (NCHF)

** BIANCHI INTERNATIONAL, Temecula, Ca. *Bianchi/ Share the Adventure/1989 Catalog*. Temecula, CA: Bianchi International, 1989. (NCHF)

Edward H. BOHLIN, Hollywood, CA. *Catalog/of/"The World's Finest"/ Riding Equipment/Riding Accessories/and/Silver & Leather Goods/from/The Bohlin Shop*. Hollywood, CA: Edward H. Bohlin, [c. 1930]. (PPHM)

**Wild Bill CLEAVER, Vashon Island, WA. *Wild Bill's/ Originals and/ Authentic Reproduction Holsters/ Gunbelts and Accessories*. n.p.: n.p., 1989. (AC)

Alfred CORNISH & Co., Omaha, NE. *Catalogue/ Alfred Cornish & Co./Successors to Collins & Morrison/Manufacturers of the/ FamousCollins Saddles....* South Omaha, NE: Magic City Printing Co., 1907. (PC)

N. CURRY & BRO., San Francisco, CA. *Price List [of] 1884 [for]N. Curry & Bro*. Facsimile edition. Berkeley, CA: Paradox Press, 1965. (AC)

The DENVER DRY GOODS Company, Denver, CO. *The Denver Dry Goods Co./ Stockmens Supplies*. Denver, CO: The Denver

Dry Goods Company, [c. 1921]. (DPL, PPHM)

The DENVER MANUFAC-TURING COMPANY, Denver, CO. *Illustrated Catalogue/of the/Denver Manufacturing Company/Tanners,/Manufacturers and Wholesale Dealers/in/Leather, Leather Goods/...and Saddlery Hardware.* Denver, CO: Daily Times Steam Printing House, 1883. (DPL)

DODSON Saddlery Company, Dallas, TX. *Ranch King Saddles/Wild West Show Outfits And Riding Equipments/Catalog No. 23/Dodson Saddlery Company/Dallas, Texas.* Dallas, TX: J. M. Coville & Son, [c. 1917]. (PC)

DUHAMEL Company, Rapid City, SD. *Duhamel Company Catalog No.3/Manufacturers of Saddles and Harness.* Rapid City, SD: Duhamel Company, [c. 1927]. (PPHM)

** EL PASO Saddlery Company, El Paso, TX. *El Paso Saddlery Co./Finest Quality Holsters and Belts.* El Paso, TX: El Paso Saddlery Company, [c. 1983]. (AC)

**_____. *El Paso Saddlery Co./Finest Quality Holsters and Belts/Catalogue No. 94.* El Paso, TX: El Paso Saddlery Company, 1990. (NCHF)

Otto F. ERNST, Inc., Sheridan, WY. *Otto F. Ernst, Inc./Sheridan, Wyoming/Makers of Fine Saddles/Catalogue No.13.* Sheridan, WY: The Mills Company, [c. 1930]. (PPHM)

The T. FLYNN Saddlery Co., Pueblo, CO. *The T. Flynn Saddlery Co./Catalog No. 26/Makers of the Best/Saddles and Harness/In the West.* Pueblo, CO: O'Brien Printing Co., [c. 1925]. (DPL, MHS)

L. FRANK Saddles & Harness, San Antonio, TX. *Catalogue No. 1/L. Frank/Manufacturer of/Saddlery, Harness/and Jobber of/Saddlery Hardware....* San Antonio, TX: Guessaz & Ferlet, Expert Printers, 1891. (UTL)

R. T. FRAZIER'S Saddlery, Pueblo, CO. *1900/Illustrated Catalogue/and Price List/of/R. T. Frazier's/Saddlery/High Grade/Stock Saddles, Bridles, Bits,/Spurs, Cow Men's Equipments, &c./Pueblo, Colorado, U.S.A. [Catalog No. 3].* Pueblo, CO: R. T. Frazier, 1900. (PC)

_____. *1903/Illustrated Catalogue and Price List/of/R. T. Frazier's/Saddlery/High Grade/Stock Saddles, Bridles, Bits, Spurs,/Cowmen's Equipments, &c./Pueblo, Colorado, U.S.A. [Catalog No. 6].* Pueblo, CO: R.T.Frazier, 1903. (PC)

_____. *R. T./Frazier/Saddlery/Pueblo,/Colorado./Catalogue No. 8.* Pueblo, CO: R. T. Frazier, [c. 1907]. (PC)

_____. *Illustrated and Descriptive/Catalogue and Price List/of/R. T. Frazier's/Saddlery/Pueblo, Colorado, U.S.A. [Catalog No. 17].* Pueblo, CO: R. T. Frazier, [c. 1916]. (UWL)

FURSTNOW & COGGSHALL Saddlery, Miles City, MT. *Illustrated Catalogue and Price List/of/Furstnow & Coggshall/Wholesale/Saddlery/.../Montana Art Leather Work.* Miles City, MT: Furstnow & Coggshall, [c. 1895]. (PC)

Al. FURSTNOW Saddlery, Miles City, MT. *Illustrated Catalogue and Price List/No. 21/Al. Furstnow/Wholesale and Retail/Saddlery.* Miles City, MT: Al. Furstnow, [c. 1920]. (PPHM)

Al. FURSTNOW Saddlery Company, Miles City, MT. *Illustrated Catalogue No. 31/Al. Furstnow/Saddlery Company/Wholesale and Retail/Saddlery.* Miles City, MT: Al. Furstnow Saddlery Company [c. 1930]. (AC)

S. C. GALLUP & FRAZIER, Pueblo, CO. *Illustrated Catalogue/and Price List/of/S. C. Gallup & Frazier/Saddlery/.../Pueblo, Colorado, U.S.A.* Chicago: The Blakely Printing Co., 1896. (PPL)

The S. C. GALLUP Saddlery Company, Pueblo, CO. *Illustrated Catalogue and Price List/No. 7/The S. C. Gallup Saddlery Co./Pueblo, Colorado, U.S.A.* Chicago: The Blakely Printing [c. 1905-1907]. (PUL)

_____. *Catalogue No. 10/and Price List/of/The S. C. Gallup/Saddlery Co./.../Pueblo, Colorado, U.S.A.* Pueblo, CO: Chieftan Press, [c. 1909]. (PC)

_____. *Catalogue No. 14/and Price List/of/The S. C. Gallup Saddlery Co./... /Pueblo, Colorado, U.S.A.* Chicago: The Blakely Printing Co., [c. 1912]. (UWL)

G. S. GARCIA, Elko, NV. *G.S. Garcia's/Illustrated Catalogue,1903/Manufacturer and Dealer in/Saddles, Harness, SaddleTrees, Silver-Mounted Bits and Spurs, Reatas,/Chapareras, Etc., Etc.* Elko, NV: Elko Free Press Print, [1903]. Reprint ed., San Gabriel, CA: Pitman's Treasures &

Co., 1990. (AC)

_____. *Everything For The Vaquero/G. S. Garcia's/Illustrated Catalogue/Number 19...Season of 1918/Elko, Nevada.* Elko, NV: G. S. Garcia, 1918. (PUL)

HAMLEY & Company, Pendleton, OR. *Hamley Saddles/For Men Who Care/1919. [Catalog No. 14].* Pendleton, OR: Hamley & Co., 1919. (PPHM)

_____. *Hamley Cowboy Catalog 32.* Pendleton, OR: Hamley & Co., [c. 1931]. (PPHM)

Hermann H. HEISER, Denver, CO. *The/Hermann H. Heiser/Saddlery Company/Exponents of Quality. [Catalog No. 14].* Denver, CO: Hermann H. Heiser, [c. 1910]. (DPL)

_____. *The/Hermann H. Heiser/Manufacturing & Selling Co./Gun Scabbards, Pistol Holsters, Belts/and Novelty Leather Goods. [Catalog No. 19].* Denver, CO: H. H. Heiser Mfg. & Selling Co., [c. 1924]. (PPHM)

_____. *The/Hermann H. Heiser/Manufacturing & Selling Co. [Catalog No. 20].* Denver, CO: Peerless Ptg. & Staty. Co., [c. 1928]. (PPHM, UWL)

_____. *The/Hermann H. Heiser/Saddlery Company/Denver Colorado/"Pioneer Saddlers of the Great West"/Specialists/In the Manufacture of Custom Quality/GunScabbards, Pistol Holsters, Belts and/ Novelty LeatherGoods. [Catalog No. 30].* Denver, CO: Hermann H. HeiserSaddlery Co., [c. 1940]. (PC)

The KINGSVILLE Lumber Company, Kingsville, TX. *Illustrated Catalogue and Price List Number 23/of the/Famous Running W Brand Saddles/Manufactured and Guaranteed by/The Kingsville Lumber Company.* Kingsville, TX: Kingsville Lumber Co., [c. 1925]. (PPHM)

The GEORGE LAWRENCE Company, Portland, OR. *Lawrence Catalog of Saddles/and Cowboy Equipment.* Portland, OR: The GeorgeLawrence Company, [c. 1937]. (UWL, PC)

** LAWRENCE Leather Company, Portland, OR. *One Hundred and Thirty Years of Excellence Since 1857/Catalog No. 130.* Portland, OR: Lawrence Leather Company, [1987]. (AC)

MAIN & WINCHESTER, San Francisco, CA. *Illustrated*

Catalog No. 11/Main & Winchester/214, 216, 218 and 220 Battery Street/San Francisco, California U.S.A. San Francisco: Main & Winchester, [c. 1898]. (PPHM)

Victor MARDEN, The Dalles, OR. *The Marden Saddles/Manufactured in the Largest Saddle Factory in the World.* The Dalles, OR:Victor Marden and The Dalles Chronicle Printers, [c. 1914]. (PC)

MARKS BROTHERS Saddlery Company, Omaha, NE. *Marks Bros. Saddlery Co./Catalogue No.6/Manufacturers of the Celebrated Marks Bros./Saddles, Harness & Collars.* Omaha, NE: Marks Bros. Saddlery Co., 1897. (UTL)

F. A. MEANEA, Cheyenne, WY. *Catalogue and Price List/No. 4/F. A. Meanea/Manufacturer of and Dealer in/Saddles...Chaps, Etc.* Cheyenne, WY: S. A. Bristol Company, [c. 1905]. (PUL)

_____. *Meanea Saddles/Light and Heavy Harness/Bits, Spurs, Ropes, Chaps/.../Catalogue No. Twelve/F. A. Meanea.* Cheyenne, WY: The S. A. Bristol Company, [c. 1914]. (PC)

_____. *Meanea Saddles/.../Catalogue No. 20.* Cheyenne, WY: S. A. Bristol Company [?], 1923 and reissued 1927. (PPHM)

MILES CITY Saddlery, Miles City, MT. *Illustrated Catalogue and Price List/Miles City Saddlery Co./Manufacturers of the Original/Coggshall Saddles....* Miles City, MT: Miles City Saddlery, [c. 1900]. (PUL)

_____. *Illustrated Catalogue and Price List/MilesCity Saddlery Co./Manufacturers of the Original/CoggshallSaddles....* Saint Paul, MN: Allied Printing, [c. 1912]. (UWL)

_____. *Illustrated Catalogue and Price List/No.26/Miles City Saddlery Co./Manufacturers of the Original/ Coggshall Saddles....* Saint Paul, MN: McGill-Warner Co.,[c. 1925]. (NCHF)

MILLS Woven Cartridge Belt Company, Worcester, MA. *Mills Woven Military Equipments [c. 1915].* Facsimile edition. Eugene, OR: R. Stephen Dorsey Antique Militaria, [c. 1985]. (NCHF)

MONTGOMERY WARD and Company, Chicago, IL. *Montgomery Ward & Co./Spring & Summer 1895/Catalogue & Buyers' Guide No. 57.* Chicago: Mont-

gomery Ward and Company, [1895]. (PC)

S. D. MYRES, Sweetwater, TX. *Catalogue No. 4/S. D. Myres/Saddlery/Sweetwater, Texas/Makers of The/Celebrated/Sweetwater Saddles.* Sweetwater, TX: S. D. Myres, [1911]. (PC)

_____. *S. D. Myres/Saddlery/Sweetwater, Texas/Manufacturer of Fine Stock Saddles/Ranch Supplies and/Art Leather Goods.* Sweetwater, TX: S. D. Myres, 1916. (DPL)

S. D. MYRES, El Paso, TX. *S. D. Myres Saddle Co./Manufacturers of/Fine Stock Saddles/Ranch Supplies and/Art Leather Goods.* El Paso, TX: S. D. Myres, [c. 1927]. (PPHM)

_____. *S. D. Myres/Holsters-Belts/Art Leather.* El Paso, TX: S. D. Myres, [c. 1944]. (DPL, PPHM)

** OLD WEST DRY GOODS Corporation, Scottsdale, AZ. *Catalog No.1/Old West/Outfitters.* Scottsdale, AZ: Old West Dry Goods Corporation, 1989. (AC).

Frank OLZER Saddlery, Gillette, WY. See Arizona Saddlery Company.

PADGITT BROTHERS, Dallas, TX. *Padgitt Bros. Co./Catalog No. 89/Manufacturers and Jobbers/Dallas, Texas/The Oldest/Saddlery and Harness Manufacturers/in the State.* Dallas, TX: Padgitt Brothers, [c. 1915-1920]. (PPHM)

N. PORTER Saddle & Harness Co., Phoenix, AZ. *N. Porter Saddle & Harness Co./Phoenix, Arizona/ Catalog No. 17/for the Summer-Fall 1929/and Spring 1930.* Phoenix, AZ: N. Porter Co., 1929. (PPHM)

_____. *N. Porter/Saddle & Harness/Company/Catalog Number 26.* Phoenix, AZ: N. Porter Co., [c. 1937]. (NSHML)

* * RED RIVER Frontier Outfitters, Tujunga, CA. *Red River/Frontier Outfitters/Frontier Clothing/Western Americana/ Military Americana.* Tujunga, CA: Red River, 1990. (AC)

The SCHOELLKOPF Company, Dallas, TX. *Illustrated and Descriptive/Catalogue Number 25/The Schoellkopf/Company/Manufacturers and Jobbers of/Saddlery ...and Accessories/Dallas, Texas, U.S.A.* Dallas, TX: Johnston Printing and Advertising Company, [c. 1925]. (PPHM)

SEARS, ROEBUCK & Co., Chicago, IL. *Sears, Roebuck and Co./Cheapest Supply House on Earth/The Great Price Maker/*

Catalogue No. 111. Reprint of the 1902 ed., New York: Bounty Books, 1969. (PC)

Charles P. SHIPLEY Saddlery and Mercantile Co., Kansas City, MO. *Catalog No. 19/Chas. P. Shipley Saddlery and/Mercantile Co./Exclusive Manufacturers of/Chas. P. Shipley's Celebrated Saddles.../and Leather Novelties.* Kansas City, MO: Chas. E. Brown Printing Co., 1923. (NCHF)

The SMITH-WORTHINGTON Company, New York, NY. *The Smith- Worthington Company/New York/Manufacturers, Importers and Exporters/Harness and Saddlery.* Cincinnati, OH: Cohen & Co., Printers and Engravers, [c. 1905]. (NCHF)

** J. C. STEWART, Show Low, AZ. *Stewart Saddlery/Maker of Fine Saddles,/Riding Bridles, Saddlebags,/Gun Leather & Personal Accessories... Catalog No. 3.* Show Low, AZ: Commercial Graphics, 1991. (AC)

STOCKMAN-FARMER Supply Co., Denver, Co. *Stockman/Farmer Supply Co./Catalog/No. 34/Spring/1929.* Denver, CO: Stockman-Farmer, 1929. (PPHM)

VISALIA Stock Saddle Co., San Francisco, CA. *Catalogue for 1896/Visalia Stock Saddle Co./H. A.*

Wegener/Successor to/Walker & Wegener/and D. E. Walker. [Catalog No. 10], San Francisco: Visalia Stock Saddle Co., 1896. (PUL)

_____. *Catalog No. 31/Visalia Stock Saddle Co./Copyright 1935/San Francisco, Cal.* San Francisco: Visalia Stock Saddle Co., 1935. (PPHM)

VISALIA Stock Saddle Co., Sacramento, CA. *Catalog No.35/Visalia Stock Saddle Company/Since 1870.* Sacramento, CA: Visalia Stock Saddle Company, 1952. (PPHM)

WESTERN Saddle Manufacturing Co., Denver, CO. *The Western Saddle Mfg. Company/Price List No. 30-1926.* Denver, CO: Western Saddle Mfg. Co., 1926. (PPHM)

WHITE & DAVIS, Pueblo, CO. *White & Davis/"Always Reliable"/Spring & Summer 1922/Catalog No. 19.* Pueblo, CO: Rocky Mountain Bank Note Co., 1922. (DPL, PPHM)

AUCTION & SALES CATALOGS

Francis BANNERMAN. *Military Goods Catalogue.* New York: Francis Bannerman, 1915. (AC)

Richard A. BOURNE Co., Inc. *Antique Firearms & Related Items/ March 17 & 18, 1982.* Hyannis, MA: Bourne Co., 1982. (AC)

BUTTERFIELD & BUTTERFIELD. *The Gaines de Graffenried Estate: A Texas Legacy.* San Francisco: Butterfield & Butterfield, 1991. (AC)

CHRISTIE, MANSON & WOODS International. *The Collection of Albert J. Weatherhead III/American Firearms/Wednesday, November 16, 1983.* New York: Christie's East, 1983. (AC)

_____. *Fine American Firearms from the Collection of Bernard and Edna L. Braverman/Wednesday, November 14, 1984.* New York: Christie's East, 1984. (AC)

N. FLAYDERMAN & Co., Inc. *N. Flayderman & Co., Inc./Purveyors of Military & Nautical Antiquities/Catalog No. 86.* New Milford, CT: N. Flayderman & Co., 1970. (AC)

_____. *N. Flayderman & Co., Inc./Purveyors of Military & Nautical Antiquities/Catalog No. 112.* Fort Lauderdale, FL: N. Flayderman & Co., 1987. (AC)

John GANGEL and Richard ELLIS. *An Auction Featuring The Robert Settani Collection.* Moline, IL: Richard Ellis Publications, 1992. (AC)

Tom KEILMAN and Son Auctioneers. *Tom Keilman's Eighth Antique and Modern Firearms, Art, Western and Indian Relic Auction.* Round Rock, TX: Tom Keilman and Son Auctioneers, 1985. (AC)

_____. *The Raymond Brown Collection.* Round Rock, TX: Tom Keilman and Son Auctioneers, 1986. (AC)

MANUSCRIPTS

Dunham, James A. Untitled script on gunleather and fast draw techniques, [c. 1989]. Unpublished, photocopy in author's files.

Wilson, Laurel E. " 'I was a pretty proud kid:' An Interpretation of Differences in Posed and Unposed Photographs of Montana Cowboys," [1990]. Unpublished, photocopy in author's files.

U. S. GOVERNMENT DOCUMENTS

U. S. Department of the Interior, Patent Office. Patents for holsters and other items of gunleather are filed according to patent number by the U. S. Patent and Trademark Office, Washington, D. C. Modern Patent Office classification system places holsters under the generic heading, "Handgun Holder Formed of Leather, Fabric or Other Flexible Material." Fugitive entries in the old *Official Gazette* may be found under sub-categories of HOLDER, as well as under HOLSTER, SCABBARD, PISTOL and REVOLVER. Individual patent documents can be located through the following published resources:

Leggert, M. D., comp. *Subject-Matter Index of Patents for Inventions Issued by the United State Patent Office from 1790 to 1873, Inclusive.* 3 vols. Washington, D. C.: Government Printing Office, 1874.

U. S. Department of the Interior, Patent Office. *General Index of the Official Gazette and Monthly Volumes of Patents of the United State Patent Office.* 54 vols. Washington, D.C.: Government Printing Office, 1872-1925.

*"A Fight in the Street"
by Frederic Remington*

213

A System of Tactics, 12
Abbott, E.C., 177, 192
Abercrombie & Fitch, 132, 171, 186
Aldridge, Reginald, 166
Alfonso, 202
Allegheny Arsenal, 40
Allen & Wheelock revolver, 22
Allison, Lt. James, 23
Anderson, Andy, 202
Anderson, J. A. E., 152
Arizona Rangers, 174
Arizona Saddlery Co., 141, 169
Aten, Ira, 167
Audubon, John Woodhouse, 52
Autry, Gene, 195

Bachman, R. M., 205
Bandoleers, 48, 177, 179
Bannerman's, 173
Barrea, Jose, 146
Belgian "Boxer" revolver, 151
Belt plates, civilian:
    Bear's head, 170, 173
    Dog's head, 170, 176
    spurious, 173
Belt plates, military:
    1851 pattern, 44-45
    "Mills" pattern, 46, 48-49, 170
Benecia Arsenal, 44, 46
Bianchi Gunleather, 203
Blackfeet Indians, 160
Bohlin, Edward H., 194-195, 198, 200-201
Bools & Butler, 184
Boyd, William, 195
Bradbury, Lon, 157
Brauer Brothers, 132, 135
Bridgeport Gun Implement Co., 147-149
Bridgeport Rig, 31, 146-149
Bronson, Edgar, 97
Browere, A. D. O., 74
Brown, Peter, 199, 202
Browne, G. W., 151-152
Browning Brothers, 186-187
Buckles, civilian:
    "California" pattern, 101, 108-112, 114, 118, 126, 128-129, 134, 136-138, 140-141, 171, 173, 176-178, 187-189, 197, 199
    double frame, 135, 171, 174-175, 205
    "Ranger" pattern, 194-195, 198, 200-201
    rectangular, 99, 104, 171, 174-176, 182
    roller, 128, 172, 176, 184
    round, 96, 113, 142-143
    single frame, 172
Buffalo Bill Wild West Show, 115, 131
Buffalo hunters, 90, 170-171
Bullock, Capt. Seth, 193

"California" Holsters: *see Holsters, civilian*
California Horn Loop, 162

California oak tanned leather, 173, 184-185, 189-191, 196
Cantenas, 56
Cap Pouch, military, 41, 42
    as pistol cartridge box, 42, 47
Carbines, military:
    Burnside, 35
    Joslyn, 35
    Krag, 28, 32, 39
    Merrill, 35
    Model 1843 Hall-North, 32, 34
    Model 1855 Springfield, 35
    Model 1877 Springfield, 37
    Model 1884 Springfield, 37, 39
    Sharps, 35
    Spencer, 33, 35
    "Trapdoor" Springfield, 37, 38, 49
Carbine Boots, military, 32, 37-39
Carbine Buckets, military, 32, 34-35
Carbine Loops, military, 32, 36-37
Carbine Slings, military, 32-34
Carbine Sockets, military, 21, 32, 35, 37
Cartridge Belts, civilian, 170-179, 186
    "Buscadero" pattern, 190, 193-194, 196-197, 199-202
    combination/Money pattern, 97, 101, 104, 108-112, 114-123, 126, 128-129, 134, 136-138, 141-143, 147, 174-179, 184, 204-205
    design of, 171, 177-178
    embellishment of, 178
    hunter's, 172
    "Mills" pattern, 100, 170-171, 173, 176
    origin of, 170-171
    plain pattern, 89, 92-93, 99, 102, 104, 111, 124, 135, 137, 140-141, 171, 173-174, 176-178, 182, 184, 187-189, 205
    "Prairie" pattern, 90, 170
    two-piece pattern, 130
    use of, 97, 104, 170
Cartridge Belts, military, 40-41, 43-49
    compared with boxes, 40-41
    evolution of, 44-46, 48
    "Mills" pattern, 27-29, 31, 45-49, 170
        alterations of, 29, 32, 38, 48-49
    origin of, 43-44
    "Prairie" pattern (Model 1876), 27, 43-47, 170-171
        modifications of,

45, 47
    Unger pattern, 45
Cartridge Boxes, military, 40-43
    ante-bellum patterns, 40
    Civil War patterns, 41-42
    compared with belts, 40-41
    Dyer pattern (pouch), 42-43, 46
    Hagner patterns, 42
    McKeever pattern, 43
Cartridge Loop attchment (Hazen), 43-44, 46
Chicago Firearms Co. palm pistol, 158
Civil War, 11, 16, 19-22, 33, 35, 40-43, 48, 51-52, 66, 94, 165
Clay, W. H., 169
Cleaver, Bill, 204-205
Coggshall, Charles, 157
Cohen & Brother, 83
Collins, G. H. & J. S., 99
Collins, J. S., 108, 147, 174-175, 205
Collins, J. S. & Co., 119, 174-175, 179
Colt firearms, 104, 106-107
    Bisley Model, 129, 135
    Dragoon Models, 15-17, 20, 54, 56, 63, 66, 75-78, 81
    Model 1849 Pocket, 57, 60, 66-68, 76, 83-84
    Model 1851 Navy, 15, 17-18, 21, 55, 57-61, 65-67, 69, 73-80, 82, 84, 86-89, 94, 204
    Model 1860 Army, 17, 19, 21, 56, 69-70, 87-88, 203
    Model 1860 Army conversion, 23, 42, 45, 87, 90, 204
    Model 1861 Navy, 96
    Model 1861 Navy conversion, 98-99, 104
    Model 1862 Pocket Navy conversion, 69, 71
    Model 1862 Police, 60, 82
    Model 1873 Single Action Army, 23-32, 42, 60-61, 89, 91-95, 97-115, 117-133, 138-146, 148, 151, 155-156, 159, 171, 179, 181-186, 188-190, 193-205
    Model 1877 Lightning, 127, 154-156
    Model 1878 Frontier, 102, 116-117, 158
    Model 1911 Automatic, 132
    New Pocket, 152
    New Service, 187
    Paterson (Texas model), 64
    Root Model, 66
    Walker Model, 15, 63-64, 66
    Whitneyville-Hartford

Dragoon, 66, 70
Condict, J. E., 41
Cooper, Tex, 168
Craig, Col. H. K., 11, 21
Cremony, John, 55
Crow Indians, 160
Curry, N. & Brother, 171-172

Delgado, Felipe, 87
Denver Dry Goods Co., 186, 188
Denver Manufacturing Co., 60
Dickson, Dick, 198
Donaldson, Capt. James, 53
Duhamel Saddlery, 157

Earnshields, Victor, 58
Eastwood, Clint, 202
Eighth Cavalry, 30, 147
El Paso Saddlery, 13;
    (New), 203-204
Elder, Jim, 70
Emerson, Ralph Waldo, 84

"Fair Weather Christian Belt," 43-44
"Fast Draw" competitions, 202-203
Fifth Infantry, 44
First Cavalry, 11, 16, 18
First Dragoons, 11
Flatau, Louis S., 146-147
Flatau Pistol and Carbine Holder, 31, 146-149
Fletcher, Baylis, 166
Flynn, Thomas, 127, 157
Frank, L., 102, 168
Frazier, R. T., 60, 113, 116, 126, 128, 132, 137, 157-158
Freeman, Lt. Col. W. G., 16
French, M. E., 129
Freund, F. W. & Brother, 88
Ford, John S., 77
Forehand & Wadsworth revolver, 72
Fort Abraham Lincoln, Dakota Territory, 45
Fort Bridger, Wyoming Territory, 43
Fort Laramie, Wyoming Territory, 44
Fort Ringgold, Texas, 30
Fort Union, New Mexico, 31
Furstnow, Al., 113, 121, 141, 150-151, 156-158, 195
Furstnow & Coggshall, 114

Gallatin & Gallup, 88
Gallatin, E. L. 55-56, 84, 87, 94, 108, 205
Gallatin, E. L. & Co., 84, 88, 115
Gallup & Gallatin, 181
Gallup, S. C., 60, 128, 139, 157
Gallup, S. C. & Co., 89
Gambler's Vest, 153-154
Garcia, G. S., 157
Gardner, George, 142
Gaylord, E., 20
George Lawrence Co., 124, 194-195
Gibson, Hoot, 192

Gilbert Loom Co., 46, 170-171
Gillett, James B., 148
Goettlich, E., 107, 109, 140
Greenough, Horatio, 84
Greyhound Specialty Co., 186
Grimsley, Thorton & Co., 14-15, 55
Gunleather, development of western, 51, 55-56, 60, 63, 66, 68, 75, 78-79, 94-95, 97, 146-148, 151-154, 157, 160, 162, 170, 178
Gunleather, reproduction, 203-205
Gunleather, twentieth century, 192-205
Gun Rigs (modern):
    "Buscadero," 192, 194-198, 200-201, 203
    "Fast Draw," 192, 199, 202-203
    "Speed Rig," 202
    "Walk and Draw," 202

Hamley & Co., 68, 157
Hammer Thong, 132, 202
Hanscom, O. M., 151-152
Hardin, John Wesley, 203
Harper's Weekly, 160
Hartley & Graham, 148
Hartman Split-spring Socket, 35, 37
Hatch, L. H., 145
Hawken rifle, 160
Hazen, Col. William B., 44
Heilig, H. C., 104-105
Heiser, Ewald, 186
Heiser, Hermann H., 51, 181-183
Heiser Saddlery, 60-61, 68, 152, 154, 156-158, 178, 180-191, 195-197
Henry rifle, 163, 165
Hibbard, Spencer, Bartlett & Co., 132, 136
Hickok, James B., 88
Hill, Ernie, 202
Hip Pocket Holsters: *see Holsters, civilian*
Hoffman Swivel (belt loop), 23-25
Hollywood, California, 132, 192, 194, 199, 202, 204
Holsters, civilian, 63, 66-68, 75-76, 78-79, 84, 94-95, 97, 104, 108, 110, 116, 127, 132, 146-149, 151-154, 157-158
    "Buscadero" pattern, 190, 194-197, 200-201
    "California" pattern, 31, 51, 74-95, 164, 203-204
        design of, 76, 78
        embellishment of, 79, 83-84
        flap-top variants, 76-78
        open-top variants, 74-76, 78, 80-95, 203-204
        origin of, 75, 84

"Drop Loop" pattern, 194, 199, 202
eastern commercial, 62-73
   evolution of, 63, 66-67
   flap-top variants, 63-70, 72-73
   half-pouch variant, 71
"Fast Draw" pattern, 199
Hip Pocket patterns, 151-154, 186, 188
"Mexican Loop" pattern, 30-31, 51, 70, 96-146, 165-166, 168, 171-175, 178, 182-190, 193-194, 196, 203-205
   "Cheyenne" variant, 102, 108-110, 115-117, 119-122, 174-175, 204-205
   commericial variants, 127, 132, 134-137
   design of, 97, 104, 108, 110
   embellishment of, 116, 127, 131
   flap-top hybrid, 121
   Olive patent variant, 132-133
   origin of, 97
   "Texas Jockstrap" variant, 110, 116, 123-125, 197
open-top variants, 62-64, 66, 73
prototype variants, 63-64
Shoulder patterns, 150-151, 153-159, 186, 188
   "Half-Breed" pattern, 158-159
   "Skeleton" pattern, 150-151, 154, 156-158, 186, 188
   "Texas" pattern, 153-155, 157
transitional types, 67, 69-71, 73
Holsters, military, 18-31, 70, 84, 94
   design of, 18, 20
   early patterns, 18-21
   1872 Pattern, 23
   1874 Pattern, 23-25
   1875 Pattern, 23, 25
   1878/79 Pattern, 24-26
   1881 Pattern, 25-29, 31, 47
   experimental variants, 29-31
      Fechet, 31
      Forsyth, 29, 31-32, 38
      Gaston, 31
      Ropes, 30-31
   modification of, 20-21, 23-25, 29, 31-32, 38
   origin of, 18
Holtzer, H. A., 110, 123-124
Horn Loop, civilian, 161-163, 165

Horn Loop, military, 32, 36-37
Horn, Tom, 41
Horstman Brothers, 44
Hoxie, Jack, 192
Hughes, John R., 194
Hunting knife, military, 47-48

Indian Wars, 25, 33, 35, 39, 42, 46

Johnson, Ira N., 13-14
Jones, Buck, 201
Jones, John Thomson, 90

Kall, Lt., 24
Keller, H., 98
Kelly, E. J., 102
Kelly, William, 52
Kentucky rifle, 51
King, Charles, 11, 44
Kingsville Lumber Co., 145
Kipper, L. & Sons, 106
Kittridge & Co., 67
Knapp & Spencer Co., 136

Lawrence Leather Co., 203
Leavenworth, Col. Jesse, 55-56, 84
Lewis, F. R., 158

Main & Winchester, 55, 57-60, 68, 75, 79, 83, 87, 116, 204
Marden, Victor, 68, 152, 157
Marfa Saddlery, 111
Marlin rifles, 164
Mason, J. P., 60
Mayer, Frank, 14, 34
Maynard, Ken, 192
McClellan, Capt. George B., 18
McCoy, Tim, 195
McGinnis, Maj. John, 24
McGowan, Alice, 115
Meanea, F. A., 108, 115, 118, 120-121, 138, 157, 164, 205
Meldrum, Bob, 145
Merwin & Bray Co., 137
Merwin Hulbert & Co. revolvers, 73, 92, 136, 159, 193
Metallic cartridges, influence of, 40, 170
"Mexican Loop" Holsters: see Holsters, civilian
Mexican War, 15, 53
Michaelis, Capt. O. E., 44
Miles City Saddlery, 157
Miles, Col. Nelson A., 44
Mills, Anson, 43, 45-46, 49, 170
Mills-Orndorff Co., 28, 46, 48-49, 171
Mix, Tom, 192-194
Montgomery Ward & Co., 95, 132, 135-136
Moore, Clayton, 195
Moran Brothers, 112, 117, 179
Morrison, Ben, 110
Mueller, Fred, 111
Myres, S. D., 51, 110, 116, 124-125, 152, 157-159, 194-195, 197

Newton & Andrews, 177
Nichols, James Wilson, 165
North American Gutta Percha Co., 18
Northwest Mounted Police, 165

Ojala, Arvo, 199, 202
Old West Reproductions, 204-205
Olzer, Frank, 142-143, 169
O'Malley, D. J., 97
Ordnance Manual...of the United States, 13-15, 33-35, 41
Orndorff, T. C., 46, 48-49, 170

Padgitt Brothers, 152, 157, 165
Palmer Brace System, 43
Parkman, Francis, 52
Patton & Co., 111
Pettengill Army revolver, 22
Phillips, R.M.G., 152
Pickard, W. L. & Son, 60
Pistol Cases: see Holsters
Pistols, civilian:
   deringer, 114
   horse, 52-53, 63
   Kentucky, 62
   pepperbox, 63, 66
   single-shot, 12, 23, 52, 63, 66
   underhammer, 154
Pistols, military:
   Model 1819, 13
   Model 1842, 13-14
   Model 1855, 16
   Remington single shot, 23
Plains rifle, 51
Polk, J. K., 166
Pommel Bag-Holsters, 56-61, 204
   design of, 60
   evolution of, 60
   origin of, 56
Pommel Holsters, civilian, 52-56, 63
   design of, 55
   embellishment of, 54, 56
   use of, 52-53, 56
Pommel Holsters, military, 12-17
   Campbell patent, 16
   design of, 12-15
   origin of, 12
   use of, 15-16
Pommel Holsters, para-military, 52-54, 56
Porter, N., 104, 196

Quantrill's guerillas, 83

Red River Frontier Outfitters, 203
Re-enactment groups, 203-204
Regulations for the Government of the Ordnance Department, 12, 41
Remington firearms, 42, 104
   Double Deringer, 153, 159
   Model 1875 Single Action Army, 90, 107, 134
   No. 1 Sporting rifle, 165
Remington, Frederic, 33, 160-162, 165
Renaldo, Duncan, 195
Rice & Childress, 55
Rice, R. E., 101
Rifle Cases, 160-162
Ritter, Tex, 195, 198
Rock Island Arsenal, 24-29, 31, 33, 37, 39, 43, 47-48, 147-148

Rogers, Roy, 195
Roosevelt, Theodore, 173
Ropes, Capt. James, 30-31

Saddle Scabbards, civilian, 162-169, 204
   design of, 168
   embellishment of, 168
   origin of, 166
Saddle Scabbards, military, 32, 39
Saddlers, role of, 51, 75, 97, 157-158, 173, 181
Saddles, military:
   Campbell, 16
   Grimsley, 15, 34-35
   McClellan, 21, 35-37
   Ringgold, 12
   Whitman, 36-37
San Antonio Arsenal, 16, 30, 147
Schiefelin, Ed, 95
Sears, Roebuck & Co., 95, 132
Second Cavalry, 11, 16, 18
Second Dragoons, 11
Seventh Cavalry, 33, 42, 44
Shaffer, Emma May, 131
Shapleigh Hardware Co., 132, 151
Sharps rifles:
   Military conversion, 90
   Model 1874 Sporting, 95, 163, 171
   Model 1878 Borchardt, 166
Shelton-Payne Arms Co., 177
Shipley, C. P., 144, 158
Shotshell Belts, civilian:
   "Mills" pattern, 170, 172
   plain pattern, 172
Shoulder Holsters: see Holsters, civilian
Single Action Shooting Society, 203
Sioux Indians, 131, 160
Sixth Cavalry, 31
Slaughter, John, 172
Smith, W. I., 149
Smith & Wesson firearms, 95, 104
   American Model, 72, 91, 94, 108, 134, 136
   Double Action Frontier, 126
   Model 1903 Hand Ejector, 149
   No. 2 Army Model, 68, 71
   Russian Model, 91
   Schofield Models, 23, 25-27, 29-31, 130, 137
Smith-Worthington Co., 132
Spangenberg, G. F., 106
Spangenberger, Phil, 148, 158
Spanish-American War, 28
Springfield Arsenal, 49
Stanwyck, Barbara, 199
Starr Model 1858 D. A. revolver, 22
Steubing, Theodore, 126
Stewart Saddlery, 204
Stone, L. D. Co., 75
"Suicide Specials," 151
Sullivan, Jos. & Co., 102-103
Swope, Charles, 127

Tackabar, E., 102
Tascosa Pioneer, 151
Taylor, Buck, 100

Ten Eyck, W. B., 110
Tenth Cavalry, 147
Texas Rangers, 31, 55, 148, 194
"Thimble" Belt, military, 43-45, 171
Thompson, Ben, 153
Tie-down strap or thong, 132, 145, 186, 202
Tileston sleeve, 23
Tilghman, Bill, 70
Townsend, J.W., 152-153
Truitt Brothers, 62
Turner, Frederick Jackson, 192

U.S. Commissary General of Purchases, 11
U.S. Dragoons, 13-16, 33-35
U.S. Mounted Riflemen, 11
U.S. Ordnance Department, 11-12
U.S. Quartermaster Department, 11

Varga, Ben, 90
Verdigris, 41, 44-45, 171, 173
Von Lengerke & Antoine, 186-187

Waist Belts, civilian, 62, 96
Waist Belts, military:
   Model 1851, 21
   Model 1874, 26, 147
   Whittemore pattern, 27-28
Waist Belts, para-military, 72, 83
Warner Brothers, 199
Washington, George, 84
Watervliet Arsenal, 23-26, 33-35, 42-47, 170
Watkinds, W. H. & Co., 82
Wells Fargo & Co., 56, 58
Wesson rifle, 174
Western films, influence of, 132, 192, 194, 198
White & Davis, 186, 188
Whitney revolvers, 20
Whitney rifles, 164
Wild Bill's Originals, 205
Wild West Shows, influence of, 132, 192-193
Winchester firearms, 160, 164, 167
   Model 1866, 164
   Model 1873, 161, 164, 166-167
   Model 1876, 165
   Model 1885, 160, 167
   Model 1887, 172
   Model 1892, 166
   Model 1894, 169
   Model 1895, 166
Winchester Repeating Arms Co., 170, 173
Wrist Holster (clip spring), 159

Yellow Coyote (Apache scout), 49

Zimmerman, E. D., 156-157

Tom Mix was a 101 Ranch Wild West Show performer and early Hollywood western film hero. This 1914 photo shows him in one of his silent film roles. (Photo courtesy Brian Lebel)

End paper photo by William Manns. (Courtesy Dominick Cervone Collection)